OXFORD MEDIEVAL TEXTS

General Editors

J. W. BINNS   W. J. BLAIR

M. LAPIDGE   T. REUTER

THE MIRACLES OF SAINT ÆBBE OF COLDINGHAM AND SAINT MARGARET OF SCOTLAND

THE MIRACLES OF SAINT ÆBBE OF COLDINGHAM AND SAINT MARGARET OF SCOTLAND

EDITED AND TRANSLATED BY
ROBERT BARTLETT

CLARENDON PRESS · OXFORD

OXFORD

UNIVERSITY PRESS

Great Clarendon Street, Oxford OX2 6DP

Oxford University Press is a department of the University of Oxford.
It furthers the University's aim of excellence in research, scholarship,
and education by publishing worldwide in

Oxford New York

Athens Bangkok Buenos Aires Cape Town Chennai
Dar es Salaam Delhi Hong Kong Istanbul Karachi Kolkata
Kuala Lumpur Madrid Melbourne Mexico City Mumbai Nairobi
São Paulo Shanghai Taipei Tokyo Toronto

Oxford is a registered trade mark of Oxford University Press
in the UK and in certain other countries

Published in the United States
by Oxford University Press Inc., New York

British Library Cataloguing in Publication Data

Data available

Library of Congress Cataloguing in Publication Data
Data available
ISBN 0-19-925922-4

1 3 5 7 9 10 8 6 4 2

Typeset in Ehrhardt
by Joshua Associates Ltd., Oxford
Printed in Great Britain
on acid-free paper by
Biddles Ltd., Guildford and King's Lynn

ACKNOWLEDGEMENTS

Valuable advice has been furnished by Ian Doyle, Judith George, John Higgitt, Richard Sharpe, Norman Shead, Simon Taylor, and Donald Watt. Jim Amelang and Elena Lopez made consultation of the Madrid manuscript easy and pleasant. The general editors have been characteristically acute and helpful. Time for work on these texts was provided by the Mortimer and Raymond Sackler Institute of Advanced Studies, Tel Aviv University. This is much appreciated.

R.B.

CONTENTS

ABBREVIATIONS

AASS	*Acta sanctorum*, ed. Society of Bollandists (68 vols. to date, Antwerp, etc., 1643– , 3rd edn. Paris, 1863–75) (cited by month and vol.)
ASC	*Anglo-Saxon Chronicle* (with letter-symbol indicating version), ed. Charles Plummer, *Two of the Saxon Chronicles Parallel* (2 vols., Oxford, 1892–9)
BHL	*Bibliotheca hagiographica latina*, ed. Society of Bollandists (2 vols. and supplement, Brussels, 1898–1901, 1986) (cited by item number)
BL	British Library
Bower, *Scotichronicon*	Walter Bower, *Scotichronicon*, ed. Donald Watt *et al.* (9 vols., Aberdeen and Edinburgh, 1987–98)
CCSL	*Corpus Christianorum, series latina* (Turnhout, 1954–)
Charters of David I	*The Charters of David I*, ed. G. W. S. Barrow (Woodbridge, 1999)
DB	Domesday Book
Dict. Med. Lat.	*Dictionary of Medieval Latin from British Sources*, ed. R. E. Latham and D. R. Howlett (Oxford, 1975–)
HE	Bede, *Ecclesiastical History of the English People*, ed. Bertram Colgrave and R. A. B. Mynors (OMT, 1969)
JW	John of Worcester, *Chronicle*, ed. R. R. Darlington and P. McGurk (OMT, 1995–)
OMT	Oxford Medieval Texts
PL	*Patrologiae cursus completus, series latina*, ed. J.-P. Migne (221 vols., Paris, 1844–64)
Raine, *North Durham*	James Raine, *The History and Antiquities of North Durham* (London, 1852), appendix
Reginald, *Libellus*	Reginald of Durham, *Libellus de admirandis beati Cuthberti virtutibus*, ed. James Raine (Surtees Soc. i, 1835)
RS	*Rerum Britannicarum Medii Aevi Scriptores* ('Rolls Series') (251 vols., London, 1858–96)

Symeon, ed. Arnold	*Symeonis monachi opera omnia*, ed. Thomas Arnold (2 vols., RS, 1882–5)
Symeon, ed. Hinde	*Symeonis Dunelmensis opera et collectanea*, i, ed. J. Hodgson Hinde (Surtees Society, li, 1868)
Symeon, *Libellus*	Symeon of Durham, *Libellus de Exordio atque Procursu istius hoc est Dunhelmensis Ecclesie*, ed. David Rollason (OMT, 2000)

INTRODUCTION

The two texts edited and translated here are previously unprinted accounts of the miracles of St Æbbe of Coldingham and St Margaret of Scotland. Both saints were royal ladies of Anglo-Saxon descent and both were buried in what was, by the eleventh century, the southern part of the Kingdom of Scots, at Coldingham and Dunfermline respectively. The texts tell of the miracles performed at or in the vicinity of their shrines in the twelfth and thirteenth centuries. Æbbe was a seventh-century abbess, whose cult was taken up by the monks of the Benedictine priory of Coldingham in the twelfth century, while Margaret, much better known, was queen of Scots and wife of Malcolm Canmore. After her death in 1093 her body lay in the church at Dunfermline which she herself had founded for Benedictine monks.

Although there are several Lives of Scottish saints in print (including a famous one of St Margaret),[1] hitherto no collection of accounts of their miracles has been published. Such collections (*libri miraculorum* or *miracula*) survive elsewhere in Europe in their hundreds, if not thousands, from the medieval period and later. Some were produced as part of a canonization process, but most were assembled by clerics or religious attached to the saint's shrine to edify their own ecclesiastical community and to instruct—or warn—the laity of the region. They might be based on eye-witness observation or on written or oral traditions and were sometimes written serially over the course of years, decades, or (as in the case of the *Miracula sancti Benedicti*) centuries.[2] Some substantial examples from high

---

[1] e.g. W. M. Metcalfe (ed.), *Pinkerton's Lives of the Scottish Saints* (2 vols., Paisley, 1889); *Lives of St Ninian and St Kentigern*, ed. A. P. Forbes (*The Historians of Scotland*, v, Edinburgh, 1874). For a survey, see Alan MacQuarrie, *The Saints of Scotland* (Edinburgh, 1997), pp. 1–14, 'The hagiography of medieval Scotland'. The Life of Margaret is Turgot's *Vita sanctae Margaretae Scotorum reginae* (*BHL* 5325), in Symeon, ed. Hinde, pp. 234–54, and in Metcalfe, *Pinkerton's Lives*, ii. 159–82. There are translations by Metcalfe, *Ancient Lives of Scottish Saints* (Paisley, 1895), pp. 295–321, reprinted in *Lives of the Scottish Saints* (Llanerch, 1990), pp. 43–69, and William Forbes-Leith, *The Life of St Margaret* (3rd edn., Edinburgh, 1896), reprinted in Mary-Ann Stouck (ed.), *Medieval Saints: A Reader* (Peterborough, Ontario, 1999), pp. 273–94.

[2] Ed. E. de Certain, *Miracles de S. Benôit* (Société de l'histoire de France, 1858); see David Rollason, 'The miracles of St Benedict: a window on early medieval France', in *Studies in Medieval History presented to R. H. C. Davis*, ed. Henry Mayr-Harting and R. I. Moore (London, 1985), pp. 73–90.

medieval England are Reginald of Durham's *Libellus de admirandis beati Cuthberti uirtutibus*, a collection of Cuthbert's miracles composed over the years 1166–74 and running to almost 300 pages in the printed edition; the collection of Becket's miracles made in the decade or so after his death in 1170 by the monks William of Canterbury and Benedict of Peterborough, containing over 700 miracles; and the canonization process of Thomas de Cantilupe, dating to 1307, which involved depositions by over 200 witnesses.[3] The miracle collections of Æbbe and Margaret are not of that scale, containing accounts of 43 and 45 miracles respectively, but both texts illuminate the religious and social life of southern Scotland in a period for which the narrative sources are not very rich.

Recent work on the miracle accounts of the Middle Ages has transformed our knowledge of the pattern of cult and supernatural power in the period. Thousands of individual cases from France and England have been analysed, as well as those contained in canonization processes.[4] This means that an examination of Æbbe's and Margaret's miracles can immediately distinguish the common from the unusual, and thus give a specific profile to the miraculous activities of the two saints and the clientele of their shrines. Moreover, as is well recognized, such miracle accounts form a wonderful source of incidental information about everyday life. In these texts we find a reference to a Scottish fiddler; mention of what is probably the earliest named Scottish artist; and a great deal on illness, madness, demons, and visions.

THE MIRACLES OF ST ÆBBE OF COLDINGHAM

The historical Æbbe

The historical Æbbe, as described in the pages of Bede, the anonymous *Vita S. Cuthberti*, and Eddius Stephanus' *Vita S. Wilfrithi*, was a member of the Northumbrian royal family and abbess of the double

[3] Reginald, *Libellus*; William of Canterbury, *Miracula sancti Thomae*, ed. J. C. Robertson, *Materials for the History of Thomas Becket* (7 vols., RS, 1875–85), i. 137–546; Benedict of Peterborough, *Miracula sancti Thomae*, ibid., ii. 21–281; the canonization process of Thomas de Cantilupe is contained in MS Vatican City, Biblioteca Apostolica Vaticana, Vat. Lat. 4015. There are excerpts in *AASS*, Octobris, i. 539–705. An edition is under preparation for this series by Professor Susan Ridyard.

[4] R. C. Finucane, *Miracles and Pilgrims: Popular Beliefs in Medieval England* (London, 1977); P.-A. Sigal, *L'Homme et le miracle dans La France médiévale: XIe.–XIIe. siècles* (Paris, 1985); A. Vauchez, *La Sainteté en Occident aux derniers siècles du Moyen Age* (Rome, 1981), Eng. tr. Jean Birrell, *Sainthood in the Late Middle Ages* (Cambridge, 1997).

monastery of *Coludi urbs* (St Abb's Head in Berwickshire) in the later seventh century.[5] Here she was visited by St Cuthbert. Her monastery was destroyed by fire after her death. Excavations by Leslie Alcock and others in 1980 revealed a possible site for the early monastery on St Abb's Head, including a burnt palisade of the seventh century.[6]

Bede terms Æbbe the 'uterine sister' (*soror uterina*) of King Oswiu, which would normally mean his half-sister on his mother's side. Oswiu was king of Bernicia (northern Northumbria) from 642 and added Deira (southern Northumbria) to it *c.*655, thus laying the foundations of the united kingdom of Northumbria. After his death in 670 the kingdom was ruled by his son Ecgfrith (670–85), who was thus Æbbe's nephew, a relationship mentioned by Bede. Oswiu was the son of Æthelfrith, king of Bernicia and Deira (d. 616), but there has been debate over who was his mother. Although she is often stated to have been Acha, daughter of Ælle, king of Deira, who was the mother of Oswiu's predecessor Oswald, arguments have been raised against this. If these are valid, his mother would then be unknown.[7] In any event, Æbbe was the half-sister and aunt of kings. According to the Anonymous *Vita S. Cuthberti*, she was a widow when she served as abbess,[8] but no other source mentions this and in the account of her miracles given here she is consistently referred to as a virgin saint. The *Vita S. Wilfrithi* presents her rebuking her nephew, Ecgfrith, for his imprisonment of the bishop.[9]

---

[5] Bede, *HE* iv. 19, 25, pp. 392, 420–6; *Vita S. Cuthberti auctore anonymo*, ii. 3; Bede, *Vita S. Cuthberti*, c. x, both ed. Bertram Colgrave, *Two Lives of Saint Cuthbert* (Cambridge, 1940), pp. 80, 188; *The Life of Bishop Wilfrid by Eddius Stephanus*, ed. Bertram Colgrave (Cambridge, 1927), p. 78 (c. xxxix).

[6] Leslie Alcock *et al.*, 'Reconnaissance excavations on early historic fortifications and other royal sites in Scotland, 1974–84: 1, excavations near St Abb's Head, Berwickshire, 1980', *Proceedings of the Society of Antiquaries of Scotland*, cxvi (1986), 255–79.

[7] Molly Miller, 'The dates of Deira', *Anglo-Saxon England*, viii (1979), 35–61, at pp. 42–3, argues that, since Oswiu married Edwin's daughter Eanflæd with episcopal approval, they could not have been first cousins and hence Oswiu was not the son of Edwin's sister Acha. Consequently 'Oswiu's mother is unknown'. She then proceeds to make the case that, despite the usual meaning of the phrase *soror uterina*, Æbbe was full sister to Oswiu, hence a daughter of King Æthelfrith and this unknown mother. There seems to be no reason why Oswiu could not be the son of Æthelfrith and the unknown mother, and Æbbe the daughter of the unknown mother by an unknown (previous or later) husband. In this case her parentage would be completely unknown. The complexity of the issue is reflected in the Bollandists' forlorn reference to the 'quaestionem genealogicam, quam operiosius examinare nolumus', *AASS*, Augusti, v. 195.

[8] *Vita S. Cuthberti auctore anonymo*, ii. 3, ed. Colgrave, p. 80.

[9] *Life of Bishop Wilfrid*, ed. Colgrave, p. 78 (c. xxxix).

In the *Historia ecclesiastica* Bede tells the story of the destruction of Æbbe's monastery.[10] The Irishman Adomnán, who was a member of the community, was forewarned by a mysterious night-time visitor that the laxity and misbehaviour of the majority of the nuns and brethren would be punished by fire (but only after Æbbe's death). This eventually came to pass. The survivors were scattered and one of them, Eadgisl, entered Bede's monastery and was his informant for this story. The dating of both Æbbe's death and the destruction of her monastery is uncertain. The story in the *Vita S. Wilfrithi* shows that she was alive in 681. In the *Historia ecclesiastica* Bede places his account of the destruction of the monastery between events dated to 680 and 684 respectively. The Anglo-Saxon Chronicle (E) places the destruction of the monastery in 679, but this is probably merely a much later conjecture. Writing in the very early twelfth century, Symeon of Durham placed the destruction of the monastery early in Cuthbert's pontificate (685–7).[11] The date for Æbbe's death given in the text edited here is 683, although it inconsistently gives 680 for the destruction of the monastery.

The Durham priory

There is a more or less total silence about Æbbe between the time of Bede and the eleventh century, when first hints of a cult begin.[12] In the early part of that century the relic collector Ælfred Westou toured the sites of old monasteries and churches in Northumbria, digging up the bones of the saints he found there and displaying them for veneration, after taking a selection for his own community at Durham.[13] Supposedly Æbbe was one of the saints treated in this way, although, as we shall see, it would be difficult to harmonize this account with the one given in the text edited here. Durham certainly claimed some of Æbbe's bones, as is clear from a relic list of the period 1104 × 1152.[14] Far from Northumbria, the dedication of St Ebbe's church in Oxford is attested from 1091 and shows an

---

[10] *HE* iv. 25, pp. 420–6.   [11] Symeon, *Libellus*, ii. 7, p. 106.

[12] The 'more or less' is necessitated by the inevitable claims of Glastonbury, which asserted that relics of 'Hebba' and other Northumbrian saints had been acquired in the eighth cent.: John Scott, *The Early History of Glastonbury: An Edition, Translation and Study of William of Malmesbury's De antiquitate Glastonie Ecclesie* (Woodbridge, 1981), pp. 68, 194.

[13] Symeon, *Libellus*, iii. 7, p. 164.

[14] C. F. Battiscombe (ed.), *The Relics of Saint Cuthbert* (Oxford, 1956), p. 113.

unexpected, and unexplained, outlier, if indeed the titular saint of this church is to be identified with the Northumbrian saint.[15]

Most important in the further development of Æbbe's cult was the foundation of a priory of Durham monks at Coldingham, not far from St Abb's Head. The impetus to this was a grant by Edgar, king of Scots (d. 1107), of the church and estate of Coldingham to the monks of Durham, a grant recorded in some of the earliest charters issued by a Scottish king.[16] In the wake of King Edgar's grant, a priory was established. 'Edward the monk of Coldingham' is mentioned between 1124 and 1136, although he may simply have been sent by Durham to supervise the estate, but reference to 'monks serving the church of Coldingham' in 1139 makes it certain that the priory was established by that date.[17] The first reference to a prior ('H. prior of Coldingham') is from c.1147.[18] The settlement of the Durham monks at Coldingham is reflected in an apparent change of the dedication of Coldingham church, from Mary alone to Mary and Cuthbert.[19] Cuthbert was Durham's especial patron whose incorrupt body

---

[15] *Eynsham Cartulary*, ed. H. E. Salter (2 vols., Oxford Historical Society, xlix, li, 1907–8), i, nos. v, vii, pp. 34, 36; the former is a charter of Bishop Remigius from 1091, accepted as genuine in *English Episcopal Acta* i: *Lincoln 1067–1185*, ed. David M. Smith (London, 1980), no. 3 (pp. 3–4); the latter is a confirmation of Henry I from 1109, calendared in *Regesta regum anglo-normannorum*, ed. H. W. C. Davis *et al.* (4 vols., Oxford, 1913–69), iii, no. 928, p. 89. Susan Kelly (ed.), *Charters of Abingdon Abbey*, i (Oxford, 2000), p. cxcviii, considers it 'difficult to see a context for the early veneration of a Northumbrian saint in Oxford'. See also John Blair, 'A handlist of Anglo-Saxon saints', in Richard Sharpe and Alan Thacker (eds.), *Local Saints and Local Churches in the Early Medieval West* (Oxford, 2002), pp. 502–3.

[16] *Early Scottish Charters prior to 1153*, ed. Archibald C. Lawrie (Glasgow, 1905), nos. XV–XXII, pp. 12–18. Their authenticity has been debated: see A. A. M. Duncan, 'The earliest Scottish charters', *Scottish Historical Review*, xxxvii (1958), 103–35; J. Donnelly, 'The earliest Scottish charters?', ibid. lxviii (1989), 1–22; A. A. M. Duncan, 'Yes, the earliest Scottish charters', ibid. lxxviii (1999), 1–38. The existence of a genuine writ of William II of England confirming Edgar's grant of Coldingham makes the fact of the grant, as distinct from the genuineness of the charters, certain: T. A. M. Bishop and P. Chaplais (ed.), *Facsimiles of English Royal Writs to A.D. 1100* (Oxford, 1957), plate VIII, no. 9.

[17] *Charters of David I*, nos. 43, 51, 68–9, pp. 75, 77–8, 85–6; see also Geoffrey Barrow, *The Kingdom of the Scots* (London, 1973), pp. 167–9.

[18] *Early Scottish Charters*, ed. Lawrie, no. CLXXXII, pp. 146–7.

[19] One of Edgar's charters refers to the 'the dedication of the church of St Mary at Coldingham': *Early Scottish Charters*, ed. Lawrie, no. XX, p. 17; the original charters of David I and his son, earl Henry, refer consistently to 'the church of St Mary and St Cuthbert of Coldingham': *Charters of David I*, nos. 68–9, 102, 158, 160, pp. 85–6, 102–3, 128–30; there is one reference in an original charter of David I simply to 'the church of Coldingham', but this dates to 1127 and therefore probably before the priory was created (ibid., no. 30, pp. 68–9); and one cartulary copy of a charter from 'probably 1147 × 1153' mentions 'the church of St Mary of Coldingham' (ibid., no. 162, p. 131).

rested in Durham cathedral. Original charters of Kings Malcolm IV and William I record grants 'to God and St Cuthbert of Coldingham and the monks serving God there'.[20] Coldingham was a large priory, comparable indeed to many abbeys in numbers. Documents of the 1230s show that a total community of 30 monks was envisaged there at a time when the complement of the mother house was only 70.[21]

The priory church of Coldingham was located about two miles from St Abb's Head, the site of Æbbe's monastery of *Coludi urbs*. Although there was no institutional continuity whatever between the two monasteries and although the later house was a slight distance away from the earlier one, twelfth-century monks read Bede and would thus be familiar with the names and saints of the locality in early Anglo-Saxon times. In this respect Coldingham can be compared with Melrose, another twelfth-century foundation close to, but not on, the site of an early monastery whose traditions were preserved in the pages of Bede. Although there had been an abortive attempt to revive monasticism at the site of Old Melrose in the 1070s, the Cistercian monastery of Melrose, founded in 1136, was located just over two miles from the spot where, famously, Cuthbert had entered the religious life. Just as the monks of Melrose could read about the seventh-century monastic house that had stood nearby, so too the monks of Coldingham read of Æbbe's monastery, of Cuthbert's visit to it, and the prophetic warnings of Adomnán. Given a group of monks at Coldingham who knew that a royal abbess named Æbbe, with a reputation as a saint, had lived and died in the vicinity, it is not entirely surprising that eventually her body was discovered. It is not the only example of the remarkable rediscovery ('invention' is the usual and appropriate medieval term for such an event) of the body of an early saint by the members of the new monasteries during the monastic boom of 1050–1200 (Mildburg of Much Wenlock, discovered in 1102, provides a good parallel).[22]

---

[20] *Acts of Malcolm IV, King of Scots, 1153–65*, ed. Geoffrey Barrow (*Regesta regum Scottorum*, i, Edinburgh, 1960), no. 200, p. 236; *Acts of William I, King of Scots, 1165–1214*, ed. Geoffrey Barrow (*Regesta regum Scottorum*, ii, Edinburgh, 1971), no. 101A, p. 191.

[21] *Historiae Dunelmensis scriptores tres*, ed. J. Raine (Surtees Soc. ix, 1839), xliii.

[22] Odo of Ostia, *Translation of St Milburga*, ed. A. J. M. Edwards, 'An early twelfth century account of the translation of St Milburga of Much Wenlock', *Transactions of the Shropshire Archaeological Society*, lvii (1961–4), 134–51.

The text

The discovery of the saint's body and the consequent revival of Æbbe's cult in the twelfth century are described in detail in the text edited here, which survives only in the fourteenth-century Durham compilation MS Oxford, Bodleian Library, Fairfax 6, where it occupies fos. 164–173ᵛ. The manuscript contains around twenty hagiographic and historical items of Durham interest, including Bede's Lives of Cuthbert, Symeon of Durham's *Libellus de exordio atque procursu istius hoc est Dunhelmensis Ecclesie*, and Reginald of Durham's *Libellus de admirandis beati Cuthberti uirtutibus* and *Vita S. Oswaldi*. It is a large and carefully executed manuscript with standard rubrication and decoration throughout. The scribe gives his name on the first folio: 'Nomen scriptoris est Petrus Plenus Amoris'. Peter Fullalove was clearly working at or for Durham priory. Several good and detailed descriptions of the manuscript exist.[23]

The explicit of the text on fo. 173ᵛ reads 'Explicit sermo de uita et miraculis sancte Ebbe uirginis ex compilatione Reginaldi Dunolm' monachi' ('Here ends the sermon on the life and miracles of St Æbbe the virgin from the compilation of Reginald, monk of Durham'). It has been demonstrated by Ian Doyle that this ascription to Reginald of Durham is not medieval but the work of the sixteenth-century Durham antiquary William Claxton.[24] Whether Claxton's guess was a good one can only be resolved by comparing the *Vita et miracula S. Ebbe* with other acknowledged works of Reginald's and with the sparse details known of his life.

Reginald was a fairly prolific author of hagiographical works. His largest production is his compendium of Cuthbert's miracles, but he also produced Lives of the hermit Godric of Finchale (d. 1170) and of the seventh-century royal saint Oswald, the latter drawn mainly from Bede.[25] A case has been made for regarding him as the author also of

[23] *A Summary Catalogue of Western Manuscripts in the Bodleian Library at Oxford*, ii, pt. 2, ed. F. Madan, H. H. E. Craster, and N. Denholm-Young (Oxford, 1937), pp. 773–5 (no. 3886); *Two Lives of Cuthbert*, ed. Colgrave, pp. 23–4; Symeon, *Libellus*, pp. xxxvii–xxxix.

[24] A. I. Doyle, 'William Claxton and the Durham chroniclers', *Books and Collectors 1200–1700: Essays presented to Andrew Watson*, ed. James P. Carley and C. G. C. Tite (London, 1997), pp. 335–55, esp. 343.

[25] *Libellus de vita et miraculis sancti Godrici heremitae de Finchale*, ed. Joseph Stevenson (Surtees Soc. xx, 1845); *Vita sancti Oswaldi regis et martyris*, Symeon, ed. Arnold, i. 326–85. In general, see Victoria Tudor, 'Reginald of Durham and Godric of Finchale', Ph.D. thesis (Reading, 1979).

the *De ortu sancti Cuthberti*, a short tract describing Cuthbert's supposed Irish boyhood.[26] Reginald was witnessing Cuthbert's miracles in Durham as early as 1153, for in his collection of the saint's miracles he describes an event set during the vacancy of the bishopric of Durham after the death of William of Sainte-Barbe (1152–3) 'which we saw with our own eyes' (*quod et oculis uidimus*).[27] The same work was commenced before the death of Ailred of Rievaulx (1167), to whom it is dedicated, but continues to describe the invasions of England by William the Lion of Scotland in the war of 1173–4.[28] The *Vita S. Oswaldi* is explicitly dated to 1165 (c. 55, p. 382). The *Vita S. Godrici* was obviously completed after the hermit's death in 1170, and a cure on Friday 15 June (p. 385) most likely dates to 1177. Reginald's connection with Coldingham is asserted in the fourteenth-century York manuscript of the miracles of Cuthbert, which gives the work the title 'the little book of the powers and miracles of the glorious pontiff Cuthbert according to Ailred, the venerable abbot of Rievaulx, and Reginald, monk of Coldingham'.[29]

These details fit reasonably well with the internal evidence of the *Vita et miracula S. Ebbe* printed here. One of the central events recounted, the foundation of a new oratory to St Æbbe, is explicitly dated to 1188, and the author, writing soon afterwards, was therefore active *c.*1190. The preface and other passages make it clear that the work was written by a monk of Coldingham who was homesick for the mother house of Durham. In discussion of Æbbe's ancestry, it becomes clear that he has been consulting Anglian royal genealogies and noting their discrepancies, just as Reginald of Durham does in his *Vita S. Oswaldi*. A stylistic comparison between Reginald's known works and this text produces rather inconclusive results: although there are no striking similarities, there is nothing to make it completely implausible that the same author produced both. For instance, a comparison of the frequency of some common words in this text and in a comparable sample of Reginald's (with the miracles of Margaret edited below and a sample of Henry of Huntingdon as controls) produces the following results:

---

[26] Richard Sharpe, 'Were the Irish annals known to a twelfth-century Northumbrian writer?', *Peritia*, ii (1983), 137–9; the text is edited by J. Raine, *De ortu sancti Cuthberti*, *Miscellanea biographica* (Surtees Soc. viii, 1838), 63–87.

[27] Reginald, *Libellus*, l, p. 104.

[28] Ibid., i, cxxvii, cxxix, cxli, pp. 1, 272, 275, 290.

[29] York Minster MS XVI. I. 12, fo. 16.

	ut	igitur	enim	-isse	tandem
Æbbe	1:229	1:289	1:316	1:561	1:1263
Reginald	1:274	1:183	1:260	1:470	1:3292
Margaret	1:127	1:1064	1:650	1:1300	1:585
H. Hunt.	1:215	1:117	1:566	1:1037	1:1131

Stylistic analysis is complicated by the fact that the *Vita et miracula S. Ebbe* is a composite work, consisting of four elements of unequal length:

(1) a short preface, in sermon form and taking as its text a passage from Isaiah, addressed to the brethren at Durham, as from Coldingham;

(2) a Life of Æbbe, over a fifth of which is taken verbatim from Bede;

(3) an account of the discovery and translation of her body in the twelfth century and the construction of an oratory in her honour on St Abb's Head (this latter is precisely dated to 1188);

(4) the record of 43 miracles.

The author states in the preface that he is using an earlier book 'on the subject of the virgin's life and works' and also mentions that details of the first translation of the saint (discussed below) were recorded in 'a little book'. He therefore had earlier written sources, in addition to Bede and Anglian royal genealogies. The line between his reworking of this material and his own original composition is difficult to establish, although it may be that everything after the reference to the 'little book' is original. The text from Isaiah—'He calls to you from Seir'—is repeated not only in the prefatory sermon but also in the Life proper and, once, in the account of the translation. Hence the 'sermon-writer' was certainly revising both the earlier texts he had acquired.

The different parts of the text represent different genres and this too is important for their style. The sermon is marked by elaborate parallelism, including emphatic anaphora ('De terra longinqua et deserta, de terra rufi, de terra pilosi et hispidi . . .'), heavily biblical language, and apostrophe. Grammatical subordination is absent or simple ('in qua', 'de qua', etc.). In the account of the translation, by contrast, the sentences are longer and articulated more fluently, with

free use of the ablative absolute and subordinating and co-ordinating conjunctions. The parallelisms are more elaborate and elegant ('nulla certitudinis sentencia oriri sed potius dubietatis perplexitas soleat foueri', 'timorem accedendi et amorem inspiciendi'), and biblical language far less prominent.

It should be remembered, however, that Reginald was not the only member of the community of Cuthbert writing at this time. Geoffrey, sacrist of Coldingham, wrote a history of the church of Durham from 1152–1215 (perhaps originally stopping at 1199), and he may be identical both with the Geoffrey, monk of Durham, who wrote a Life of Bartholomew of Farne, and Geoffrey, monk of Durham, who edited and conflated two earlier Lives of Godric of Finchale.[30] The *Vita S. Bartholomaei* dates to the period 1193–1212, the former year being the date of the death of Bartholomew and the latter that of the death of the dedicatee, prior Bertram of Durham, while the *Vita S. Godrici* is dedicated to Thomas, prior of Finchale, who was appointed in 1196 and had been succeeded by 1211.[31] In terms of chronology and interests, Geoffrey too might thus be a possible candidate for authorship of this text. Moreover, yet another Durham monk produced a collection of miracles of Cuthbert in the early years of the thirteenth century.[32] It is obviously safest not to publish the text edited here under the name of Reginald, even though there is a case for his authorship.

The two translations of the body

The text tells how, centuries after her death and the destruction of her monastery, Æbbe's coffin was discovered at St Abb's Head by shepherds. They tried to open it with their crooks but were blinded, and it was then brought to the priory church of St Mary, Coldingham, where it was placed on the south side of the altar. 'Some say', reports the text, that it was wooden and that one of the brethren broke

[30] *De statu ecclesiae Dunelmensis*, ed. J. Raine, *Historiae Dunelmensis scriptores tres* (Surtees Soc. ix, 1839), 3–31; *Vita Bartholomaei Farnensis*, Symeon, ed. Arnold, i. 295–325; *Vita Godrici eremitae*, *AASS*, Maii, v. 70–85. Alan Piper's suggestion about the original terminal date of the history is mentioned in Richard Sharpe, *A Handlist of the Latin Writers of Great Britain and Ireland before 1540* (Turnhout, 1997), p. 122.

[31] Dates of Bertram and Thomas from David Knowles, C. N. L. Brooke, and Vera London, *The Heads of Religious Houses: England and Wales 940–1216* (2nd edn., Cambridge, 2001), pp. 43–4, 89.

[32] H. H. E. Craster, 'The miracles of St Cuthbert at Farne', *Analecta Bollandiana*, lxx (1952), 1–19.

into it and put his hand in, but was struck down and soon died. The brethren decided to enclose the coffin in stone. They left a written record of all this. At an unspecified later date uncertainty about the contents of the tomb led to the decision to open it: 'some asserted that her bones had been taken from there and removed elsewhere and that the coffin contained nothing but her robe or veil' (as we have seen, Durham did indeed claim to have acquired at least some of her bones in the eleventh century). The decision to translate was supported by a vision of Æbbe herself, who, in the words of the text, 'appeared to a certain older monk, who is still alive'. The surrounding stones were removed, revealing a stone coffin with stone lid, which broke when levered off. Inside was dust in the shape of a human body, cinders, which some thought must be the remains of incense, and some bones, most of which soon crumbled. The monks dried and sieved the remains, placed them in a new shrine on the altar, and moved the stone tomb to a place in the church 'where the devotion of the faithful could revere and embrace it'. There are no dates in this section of the text but clearly the first discovery took place after the Durham monks had established themselves in Coldingham, while the second trans-lation was within the lifetime of someone still alive when the author wrote (*c*.1190).

Henry 'the man of St Æbbe'

The revival of Æbbe's cult was not, however, to be centred in the church at Coldingham. The crucial impetus came from a local layman, Henry, a poor man of servile condition, who came to be nicknamed 'the man of St Æbbe' (*homo sancte Ebbe*) because of his devotion to the saint (compare the musician Elward, cured through the intercession of St Dunstan, 'whom everyone agreed in calling the man and little slave of Dunstan' (*Dunstani hominem . . . servulum-que*)).[33] As a young man Henry had had a lover, but tired of her and transferred his affections to another, whereupon the spurned mistress poisoned him. As a result he lost his senses and was brought to the shrine of St Michael in Coldingham priory church, where he was cured. However, many people thought a trace of his illness remained in his 'startled eyes and simple talk', perhaps seeing his devotion as a sign of simple-mindedness. Henry's assertively lay piety was

---

[33] Osbern of Canterbury, *Vita et miracula sancti Dunstani*, ed. William Stubbs, *Memorials of Saint Dunstan* (RS, 1874), pp. 69–161, at p. 135.

expressed in an austere plain style. He always went either barefoot or shod but with bare soles, and he instructed his wife to bury him not in a muslin shroud, 'as is the custom for lay people', but in his layman's hood and shoes, 'so that the earth should receive his dead body in the same clothes in which he had served God while alive'. He was instructed in a vision to build an oratory to St Æbbe on St Abb's Head and, although he was mocked, he did so, using old stones and clay as the mortar, even ignoring his servile obligations. The Coldingham monks, many of whom were originally sceptical, eventually came around as miracles abounded and crowds gathered; they rebuilt the oratory. The story fits perfectly the model of cult development advanced by Pierre-André Sigal: the starting point of miraculous cults is spontaneous popular piety, but this lay initiative, if it is to endure, has to be taken up by monastic or clerical communities.[34]

The text dates Henry's vision explicitly to 1188 and this fits well with other evidence of the revival of the cult. The first beneficiary of Æbbe's revived power was the daughter of a 'Master Merlin', who appears in charters of the bishop of St Andrews and of Coldingham 1160 × 1203. A document of Bertram, prior of Durham (1189 × 1212), encourages donations 'for the construction of our church of Coldingham, for the love of the blessed Mary and of St Æbbe the virgin, by whose merits many miracles have abounded in that place in our own day, to stir up the good-will of the faithful'.[35] Some of the present remains of the church represent this rebuilding of c.1200. As already mentioned, earlier in the twelfth century, when the monks of Durham had taken possession of St Mary's church, Coldingham, Cuthbert had been added to the dedication; so now, in the later twelfth century, the revival of Æbbe's cult led to her addition to the dedication. A charter of Edward of Restalrig, who was active in the 1170s, makes a grant 'to God and St Mary and St Æbbe and prior Herbert and the monks of Coldingham'.[36] In the thirteenth century Æbbe appeared regularly though not invariably, alongside God, Mary, and Cuthbert, in grants made to Coldingham priory.[37]

---

[34] Sigal, *L'Homme et le miracle*, pp. 167–76.
[35] Raine, *North Durham*, pp. 95–6, no. 534.
[36] Ibid., p. 40, no. 171.
[37] e.g. ibid., pp. 14, 28–30, 37, 43, 46, nos. 64–5, 125–8, 133–4, 158–9, 180, 196.

The miracles

The text records 43 miracles benefiting 42 individuals. All bar one of them were healing miracles, and that one involved the miraculous inability of sceptical women to see the water taken from Æbbe's well. There are no punitive miracles. The sex and ailment of the beneficiaries are always described (even if in the former case it is only by indication of the Latin endings of *alius* and *alia*) and their social class and place of origin are also quite often specified (in a quarter and a third of cases respectively). Age is not usually given in miracle accounts, but in the case of Æbbe's there is a distinctive patterns, as we shall see.

Sex

Of the 42 individuals healed by Æbbe 26 (62%) were female, 16 (38%) male. This ratio is the exact opposite of the usual balance of the sexes at healing shrines in this period, as revealed in the analysis of Finucane, Sigal and others.[38]

Ailment

Types of affliction

Ailment	Number cured	Percentage
Paralysis	12	30
Dumbness	9	21
Blindness	9	21
Swellings	7	16
Insanity	4	9
Other	2	5
TOTAL	43	

Ailments were of the usual type, although dumbness was perhaps more common than usual.

Social class

In 11 cases (26%) there are indications of social standing. Some of the beneficiaries of Æbbe's miracles were upper class: the daughter of a

---

[38] e.g. Finucane, *Miracles*, p. 143, Sigal, *L'homme et le miracle*, p. 300.

knight, the daughter of Master Merlin, a noblewoman, a Welsh girl formerly rich although now impoverished. Some are lower class: a smith, a pedlar of needles, a minstrel. Four are explicitly described as 'poor'. It has been argued that those who kept records of miracles at shrines had a tendency to record higher-class visitors dispropor-tionately, but there does not appear to be any desire to disguise poverty and low social station in the case in Æbbe's cult. One pair of miracles is especially noteworthy in this regard (4. 13): a poor young girl comes to the oratory with a crippled hand, and a young noble-woman arrives in her carriage with a similar complaint; Æbbe appears in a vision, in the company of the Virgin Mary, touches the poor woman's hand, then the noblewoman's, healing them both. 'And so it was that those who shared the same ailment were partners also in receiving the same grace; and this should be noted, that she visited the poor woman first and then went back to the noblewoman, for God's saints are no respecters of persons when heavenly gifts are manifested.'

Geography

There are indications of place of origin in 14 cases (exactly a third). Most of those whose geographical origin is recorded were from Scotland south of the Forth or from the north of England. In addition to named places, several more general indications are found: *Scocia*, meaning Scotland north of the Forth; Lothian; the bishopric of Durham; Wales. If one tabulates ultimate place of origin of the beneficiaries the result is as follows:

Scotland south of Forth	6
Northern England	5
Scocia	2
Wales	1

In several cases the ultimate place of origin had been left many years earlier and so no direct journey from that place to Æbbe's shrine is indicated. There are also several mentions of other shrines that had been visited unsuccessfully prior to the trip to St Abb's Head or were the intended destination of those actually healed by Æbbe: St Thomas Becket at Canterbury (twice) and London; St Margaret at Dunfermline (twice); St Andrews (as an intended destination); St Lawrence at Berwick (only suggested).

The Gaelic presence in the cult was not quite as faint as these

figures suggest, with only two beneficiaries from *Scocia*, for the Gaelic language could certainly be heard in the oratory at St Abb's Head. After a cure of dumbness, which occurred on a major feast day, a girl was tested by being made to recite the Lord's prayer; 'the priests recited to her the Lord's Prayer, the English in English speech, the Scottish in Scottish speech (*Scotticum sermonem*)' (4. 7). This implies the presence of Gaelic-speaking priests.

Age

Most remarkably, 19 (45%) of those healed by Æbbe are specifically described as youthful. The most common terms used are *puella* (girl) or *adolescens* (youth) (Isidore of Seville, the encyclopedist of the Middle Ages, says an *adolescens* is between 14 and 28). Some specific ages are also given: 'new-born'; 'almost 12'; 15; 18; 22 (an *adolescens*).

Hence the analysis of the text reveals a local healing shrine of the late twelfth century, marked by the unusual prominence of pilgrims who were female, poor, and young.

Cult

In addition to throwing light on the clientele of the shrine, the *Vita et miracula S. Ebbe* also give details of the physical foci of the cult and the way its liturgical customs were built up. Three centres of supernatural power were to be found in the vicinity: Æbbe's tomb and shrine in the priory church at Coldingham, the oratory on St Abb's Head, and the two healing springs nearby, where 'Many weak and infirm people have recovered their former health by drinking'. The oratory at St Abb's Head is always clearly distinguished from the priory church at Coldingham. The great majority of the miracles—34 out of 43 (79%)—are explicitly or implicitly located at the oratory, though pilgrims often then come to the church to give thanks afterwards. St Æbbe's fountains play a role in six miracles, usually alongside the oratory. The triptych of oratory, fountain, and church is illustrated in the case of a poor blind woman, who had visited St Thomas's shrine at London in vain, and came to Coldingham 'because she had heard that cures were taking place there'. She goes to the oratory, prays, Æbbe appears to her in a dream telling her to wash in her fountain; this she does and returns cured to Coldingham, where she swears to the details and the monks fill the church with praise (4. 2).

Only six of the miracles (14%) take place at the tomb in the priory church. All of these are in the second half of the miracle collection, and the first of them stimulates the comment 'through this it was made known that the ancient place of her repose had not been emptied of the glory of miraculous power by the absence of her body' (4. 20). It is possible to see here a desire on the part of the monks to divert pilgrims and miraculous activity from the windswept oratory founded by Henry 'the man of St Æbbe' to the more convenient location of their own church. As far as the small sample allows one to conclude, there are no differences between those cured in the church and those at the oratory, the former group also containing women, the poor, and the young.

The creation of the cult of St Æbbe in the twelfth century involved not only miraculous healing and pilgrimage but also liturgical innovation, for there was no continuity of tradition in her case, as there had been notably in the case of Cuthbert. The present text reveals some of the details of this process. It mentions the customary Saturday night vigils when people flocked 'from the surrounding hamlets to the mountain and oratory' (4. 5), and also shows the creation of an annual liturgical cycle: 'Crowds throng here from far and wide on the nativity of the blessed precursor of the Lord, because on this day the brethren began to celebrate divine service here after the place had been long abandoned' (4. 7). This reference to the feast of St John the Baptist on 24 June brings us very close to the date given in the late-thirteenth-century Coldingham Breviary, under 22 June: 'dedication of the altar of St Æbbe in Coldisburh'.[39]

Liturgical initiative originating from the laity is revealed in the story of a female pilgrim who claimed that St Æbbe had appeared to her in a vision and given her precise instructions about her commemoration. The saint had commanded her to say 'that those who wished to visit her place should come also in commemoration of the faithful departed and should recognize that that was the day of her feast on which she cast off the garment of earthly life and put on the cloak of eternal happiness' (4. 19). The 'faithful departed' were commemorated on All Souls Day, 2 November. The date of 2 November is indeed given in the Coldingham Breviary as a feast of Æbbe (fo. 131). Since the text printed here is absolutely explicit both that 2 November was to be celebrated as the day of Æbbe's death and that it needed to be initiated, the natural conclusion would be

[39] BL, Harley 4664, fo. 128ᵛ.

that there had been no fixed day for her commemoration before the construction of the oratory in 1188, and that 2 November was then introduced as her feast day. This simple hypothesis encounters a difficulty, however. The Winchcombe Kalendar, dated on palaeo-graphical grounds to c.1130–1160, records the feast of St Æbbe on 25 August.[40] Since this predates the revival of the cult at Coldingham and occurs at a religious house in Gloucestershire, 250 miles away, it presents a conundrum. One explanation might be that the Æbbe commemorated at Winchcombe was not the Northumbrian abbess but a homonym, plausibly the saint to whom the church in Oxford was dedicated (see above, pp. xiv–xv).

Æbbe's feast of 25 August occurs in the Coldingham Breviary alongside that on 2 November (fo. 129ᵛ). If this date was originally that of a south English Æbbe, the northern cult clearly took it over. The evidence of MS Cambridge, Jesus College 23 (Q. B. 6), a twelfth-century calendar from Durham (earlier than 1170), may be evidence for such a development. The manuscript originally con-tained no entry for Æbbe. Her feast—on 25 August—has been entered in a thirteenth-century hand, marked for twelve lessons; in the fifteenth century 'cappis' (to be celebrated in copes) was added.[41] Hence the feast of 25 August was introduced in the thirteenth century and given greater solemnity in the fifteenth. Another, fragmentary, thirteenth-century calendar with a possible Coldingham provenance, BL Harley 4747, records the 25 August feast marked 'albis xii', i.e. to be celebrated in albs and with twelve lessons.[42]

The establishment of Æbbe's cult involved effort. Indeed, the composition of the text edited here was part of a campaign to secure her reputation as a saint, sometimes in the face of scepticism. Hagiographic literature is, of course, a great treasure house of stories of medieval scepticism. The sceptics always learn their lesson, at least in the texts, but their existence has first to be attested. Æbbe's miracles contain several instances. The Welsh girl, Quinciana, was cured at Æbbe's oratory, 'But because she was poor and unknown, many people had doubts about her recovery. They said she was not telling the truth but had made up things contrary to the truth, in

[40] BL, Cotton Tiberius E. iv, fo. 38ᵛ ; the opinion on date was kindly supplied by Richard Sharpe and corroborated by Martin Kauffmann.

[41] Francis Wormald (ed.), English Benedictine Kalendars after A.D. 1100 (2 vols., Henry Bradshaw Soc. lxxvii, lxxxi, 1939–46), i. 175.

[42] Fo. 1; November is missing, so it is uncertain whether the feast on 2 November was also included.

order to obtain relief in her temporal life' (4. 7). Doubts extended beyond the specific case of opportunistic paupers, however, and the author of the text is explicit about the probative function of some of the miracles. After recounting a miracle in Æbbe's lifetime, he adds, 'I say this to demonstrate the foolishness or madness of those who reject or ridicule as impossible the miracles of the saints of old.'

An especially weak point was the identity of the relics that had been found. Here the vindication through miracles was essential: 'if anyone doubts that these remains of bones and dust are those of the blessed virgin, let him consider the revelation that occurred about her translation. If he contends that the larger bones have been taken away, let him bring to mind the intact dust. If he denies that it is her tomb, let him think over the miracles that have been performed there through her merits.' Thus doubts about the identity of the relics, individual cures, and even the miraculous in general had to be silenced by the reiteration of Æbbe's power in the present. The text thus not only records the establishment of a cult but is itself part of that process.

The edition

The edition gives the text as in Fairfax 6, with some minor editorial emendations. The numbering of books and chapters is editorial, though based on an obvious distinction between the four sections of the work (Preface, Life, Translation, Miracles) and clearly marked chapters in the case of the Miracles (the varying length of these chapters thus reflects the author's or scribe's practice rather then the editor's).

The following three abbreviations have also been collated and their readings cited on the few occasions it is appropriate:

(1) The Coldingham Breviary has lessons for Æbbe's feast day of 25 August, some drawn from the *Vita et miracula S. Ebbe* printed here; the rhythmic sections of the Office were published in *Analecta Hymnica Medii Aevi*, xiii, ed. G. M. Dreves (Leipzig, 1892), no. 42, pp. 114–17.

(2) John of Tynemouth's version in his *Sanctilogium* (*BHL* 2358) survives in three manuscripts:

(a) BL, Cotton Tiberius E. i, vol. 2, fos. 54^{v}–56 (s. xiv) from St Albans.

(b) Oxford, Bodleian, Tanner 15, pp. 171–5 (AD 1499) from Christ Church, Canterbury.

(c) York Minster XVI. G. 23, fos. 135ᵛ–136 (AD 1454) from York.[43]

This version was printed by Wynkyn de Worde in the *Nova legenda Anglie* of 1516, reprinted in *AASS*, Augusti, v. 196–8 and edited from (a) and (b) by Horstman in 1901.[44]

(3) *Breviarium Aberdonense* (2 vols., Edinburgh, 1509–10, repr. Bannatyne Club Pubs. xcvi, 1854), *pars estivalis*, *sanctorale*, fos. lxxxvii–lxviii, has lessons drawn from the *Vita et miracula S. Ebbe* (*BHL* 2359).

THE MIRACLES OF ST MARGARET OF SCOTLAND

The historical Margaret

St Margaret was a member of the old royal dynasty of Wessex and England, being the daughter of Edward Atheling, who was himself the son of King Edmund Ironside.[45] After Edmund's brief reign in 1016, his victorious successor, Cnut, sent the late king's young sons to Sweden, with instructions that they should be killed. Instead, the king of the Swedes sent them on to Hungary, and this is where Edward Atheling grew up, marrying a high-born member of either the Hungarian or German royal family (the evidence is complicated) and having at least three children, Margaret, Christine, and Edgar.[46]

---

[43] Described in N. R. Ker and A. J. Piper, *Medieval Manuscripts in British Libraries*, iv (Oxford, 1992), 705–6.

[44] *Nova legenda Anglie*, ed. C. Horstman [alias Horstmann] (2 vols., Oxford, 1901), i. 303–11.

[45] The crucial source for Margaret's life is the *vita* by her confidant Turgot, prior and archdeacon of Durham and subsequently bishop of St Andrews (d. 1115): for bibliographical details see p. xi n. 1 above. Margaret is discussed at greater or lesser length in all histories of Scotland in her period. See esp. R. L. G. Ritchie, *The Normans in Scotland* (Edinburgh, 1954), pp. 70–83; Barrow, *Kingdom of the Scots*, pp. 165–7, 189–96; A. A. M. Duncan, *Scotland: The Making of the Kingdom* (Edinburgh, 1975), pp. 117–25. Other discussions include Derek Baker, ' "A nursery of saints": St Margaret of Scotland reconsidered', *Medieval Women*, ed. Derek Baker (Studies in Church History, Subsidia i, 1978), pp. 119–41, to be corrected by Lois L. Huneycutt, 'The idea of a perfect princess: the Life of St Margaret in the reign of Matilda II (1100–1118)', *Anglo-Norman Studies*, xii (1990), 80–97; Valerie Wall, 'Queen Margaret of Scotland (1070–93): burying the past, enshrining the future', *Queens and Queenship in Medieval Europe*, ed. Anne Duggan (Woodbridge, 1997), pp. 27–38. There are also several popular biographies of Margaret, e. g. Alan J. Wilson, *St Margaret, Queen of Scotland* (Edinburgh, 1993).

[46] JW, s.a. 1017 (1039), ii. 502–4. For discussion of Margaret's parentage, see Ritchie, *Normans*, pp. 389–92; Gabriel Ronay, *The Lost King of England: The East European Adventures of Edward the Exile* (Woodbridge, 1989), pp. 109–21.

In 1057 Edward returned to England with his family but died almost at once. Margaret and her siblings were then brought up by the king, Edward the Confessor.[47] In the great crisis of 1066, Margaret's young brother, Edgar Atheling, was acknowledged as king by many leading English prelates and nobles after the battle of Hastings, but he was never crowned and soon submitted to the Norman conqueror, William I. This situation endured only for a short period before Edgar, along with his mother and sisters, took flight to Scotland, where they were welcomed by the king of Scots, Malcolm III 'Canmore'. His welcome extended so far as a proposal to take Margaret as his wife, and so the doubly exiled English princess married the Scots king in or around 1070.[48]

Margaret emerges from the pages of the contemporary *Vita S. Margarite* by Turgot as an active and determined Christian lady, enforcing what she saw as the proper norms of religious life and court etiquette. She attempted to change Scottish practice regarding the observance of Lent, she prescribed annual communion and abstention from manual labour on Sunday, she sought to modify Scottish marriage customs to bring them into line with the canon law of the western Church. At the same time she presided over a court marked both by a new ceremony and formality and by public piety and devotion. Her personal religiosity was deep: she prayed constantly, she studied the Bible, and she cared for the poor and the enslaved. Also, however, she fulfilled her dynastic duties, producing six sons (three of whom became kings of Scots after her) and two daughters. When she died in 1093, a few days after her husband, her reputation as a saint was already in existence.

One of Margaret's many acts of devotion was the foundation of a monastery at Dunfermline, the place where she had married Malcolm. It is probable that this was initially a daughter house of Canterbury, with Benedictine monks sent from England, but was raised to the status of an independent abbey in 1128.[49] Margaret was herself buried in the church, which served henceforth as a mausoleum of the Scottish kings. The body of her husband, Malcolm Canmore, was brought back from England, where he had been killed, to lie near

[47] ASC (D and E), s.a. 1057; Orderic Vitalis, *Historia ecclesiastica*, i. 24, ed. Marjorie Chibnall (6 vols., OMT, 1968–80), i. 157.

[48] ASC (D and E), s.a. 1067; for the date of the marriage see E. A. Freeman, *The History of the Norman Conquest of England* (6 vols., Oxford, 1867–79), iv. 782–6.

[49] Barrow, *Kingdom of the Scots*, pp. 193–8; *Charters of David I*, nos. 22, 33, pp. 63–4, 70–2; JW, s.a. 1128 (1150), iii. 184.

his queen, while her sons Edgar, Alexander I, and David I, were interred there, as was David's successor Malcolm IV.

Margaret's son, David, not only probably raised Dunfermline to the status of an abbey but also supported a major reconstruction of the church. Margaret's foundation was rebuilt on a larger scale, to produce a magnificent Romanesque church, the nave of which still stands as one of the most impressive examples of medieval architecture in Scotland. The new church was dedicated in 1150, and it was this building that was to be the centre of Margaret's cult and the scene of her miracles. Fortunately a collection of accounts of Margaret's miracles does exist.

The text

The collection of Margaret's miracles has not previously received scholarly attention, since it has not been edited and survives in a solitary manuscript in Madrid (Madrid, Biblioteca del Palacio Real, II. 2097, fos. 26–41ᵛ). The manuscript contains (1) Turgot's *Vita S. Margarite*, in a heavily interpolated form with many variations from the printed edition, followed by miscellaneous historical material; (2) the *Miracula S. Margarite Scotorum regine*, edited here; (3) Jocelin of Furness's *Vita S. Valleui abbatis de Melros*, a hagiographic account of Waltheof, abbot of Melrose, who died in 1159, in a text much better than that printed in the *Acta Sanctorum*; (4) miscellaneous devotional pieces (there is a full listing of contents below). The date of the manuscript can be established fairly exactly. A regnal list of the kings of Scots, which is written in the same hand as the main text, gives each ruler's name, length of reign, place of death, and place of burial. It concludes, on fo. 25ᵛ, with the words, 'His son, James II, succeeded him and reigned twenty-two and a half years. He died in Roxburgh and was buried at Edinburgh in the abbey of Holyrood. His son, James III, succeeded him and reigned . . .' The text breaks off here, leaving blank space. The obvious implication is that the book was written during the reign of James III (1460–88), and there is nothing in the contents or script that would make this improbable, although the clear, regular hand has struck several scholars, including the nineteenth-century cataloguer of the Madrid library, as being earlier.[50] The late fifteenth century saw considerable

---

[50] *Bibliotheca patrum latinorum hispaniensis*, i (Vienna, 1887), ed. Wilhelm von Hartel from descriptions by Gustav Loewe, p. 480; N. R. Ker, *Medieval Libraries of Great*

copying in the Dunfermline scriptorium and an interest there in both historical and devotional writing.[51] The miscellaneous religious pieces in the manuscript reflect interests similar to those exemplified in the list of books from Dunfermline drawn up in the early fourteenth century, where patristic and monastic texts predominate.[52]

Madrid, Biblioteca Real II 2097 (olim II 4 N)

240 mm × 160 mm, 112 fos., two columns, ruled throughout for 35 lines, rubricated, expert textura

fos. 1^v–17^v:	Turgot, *Vita S. Margarite*
fos. 17^v–26^r:	Historical & legendary miscellany, including Scottish regnal list to James III
fos. 26^r–41^v:	*Miracula S. Margarite Scotorum regine*
fos. 41^v–68^r:	Jocelin of Furness, *Vita S. Valleui abbatis de Melros*
fos. 68^v–70^v:	(Thomas of Ireland), *Liber de tribus punctis Christiane religionis* (completed on fos. 81^r–84^v)
fo. 71^r:	Final part of *exempla* begun at fos. 90^{r-v}
fo. 71^r:	*De litteris huius nominis 'monachus'*
fo. 71^r:	*Pene infernales*
fos. 71^v–77^r:	Ps.-Augustine, *De miseria hominis*
fo. 77^r:	*Terribile quoddam*
fos. 77^v–79^r:	*Speculum claustralium*
fo. 79^r:	*Altercatio inter cor et oculum*
fo. 79^r:	*Duodecim abusiones claustri*
fos. 79^{r-v}:	*Admonicio ualde utilis et bona*
fo. 79^v:	*Vt homo cognoscat seipsum quod sit*
fos. 79^v–80^r:	*De contemptu omnium uanitatum*
fos. 80^{r-v}:	*De contemptu mundi et que sunt eius*

Britain: A List of Surviving Books, Supplement to the Second Edition, ed. Andrew G. Watson (Royal Historical Soc. Guides and Handbooks, xv, 1987), p. 16; the manuscript is there dated 's. xiv in.'. Prof. Richard Sharpe of Oxford and Dr A. I. Doyle of Durham were kind enough to offer palaeographical advice on this matter.

[51] The *Liber Pluscardensis* was compiled at the instigation of the abbot of Dunfermline in 1461, and two manuscripts of the work (Glasgow, University Library, Gen. 333, and Oxford, Bodleian Library, Fairfax 8) were copied there in 1479–97 and 1489 respectively: *Liber Pluscardensis*, i, ed. Felix J. H. Skene (The Historians of Scotland, vii, Edinburgh, 1877), pp. xxvii; Ker/Watson, *Medieval Libraries*, p. 16. A Psalter (Boulogne, Bibliothèque municipale 92) and a *Compendium theologice veritatis* (Edinburgh, University Library 72) also have a late 15th-cent. Dunfermline origin: N. R. Ker, *Medieval Libraries of Great Britain* (2nd edn., London, 1964), p. 59.

[52] *Registrum Anglie de libris doctorum et auctorum veterum*, ed. Richard H. and Mary A. Rouse (*Corpus of British Medieval Library Catalogues*, ii, 1991), p. 308.

fos. 80^v:	Bernard, *Exhortacio* (completed on fos. 91^{r-v})
fos. 81^r–84^v:	Completion of *Liber de tribus punctis Christiane religionis*
fos. 84^v–87^r:	*De confessione secundum magistrum Thomam Hibernicum*
fos. 87^r–89^r:	*Sermo de gaudiis paradisi*
fos. 89^r–90^r:	*Sermo de penis inferni*
fos. 90^{r-v}:	*Exempla* (completed on fo. 71)
fos. 91^r–91^v:	Completion of Bernard, *Exhortacio*
fos. 91^v–92^r:	Short extracts; *fercula celi*; *fercula inferni*
fos. 92^v–93^r:	*Quod nullus differat tempus penitencie et confessionis* ('Hanc ystoriam sicut a uenerabili antistite Pechtelmo didici . . .') (Bede, *HE* v. 13)
fos. 93^r–95^v:	*Disputacio inter corpus et animam predicti militis* (i.e. of the preceding story)
fos. 95^v–106^v:	*De imitacione Christi et contemptu mundi et omnium uanitatum*
fos. 106^v–107^v:	Story of Augustine in Oxfordshire ('Est uicus in pago Oxinfordensi . . .')[53]
fo. 108^r:	Story of two Oxford scholars ('Duo scolares ualde speciales . . .')
fos. 108^v–110^v:	*Destructio ciuitatis Ierusalem* ('Refert Iosephus . . .')
fo. 110^v:	Half-a-dozen citations from Hugh of Saint-Victor, Augustine, Caesarius.
fo. 111^r:	blank
fo. 111^v:	*Quidam clericus in nimia tristicia*
fo. 112^r:	scribbles, draft calendar

The provenance of the manuscript is certain, with the contemporary *ex libris* inscription on the first folio 'Est Margarite de Dunfermlyn liber iste', identical in wording to that in the thirteenth-century *Registrum de Dunfermelyn*.[54] The first two pieces in the book, Margaret's *Vita* and *Miracula*, would make a Dunfermline origin plausible even without such direct evidence. Moreover, Professor Donald Watt of St Andrews has demonstrated that the chronicler

---

[53] Cf. Thomas D. Hardy, *Descriptive Catalogue of Materials relating to the History of Great Britain and Ireland* (3 vols., RS, 1862–71), i. 199–200; Bower, *Scotichronicon*, iii. 33 (ed. Watt, ii. 92).

[54] Edinburgh, National Library of Scotland MS Adv. 34. 1.3a, fo. 41; *Registrum de Dunfermlyn*, ed. Cosmo Innes (Bannatyne Club, Edinburgh, 1842), p. 3, with facsimile between pp. 8 and 9.

Walter Bower, writing his *Scotichronicon* in the 1440s, had access to texts identical to those in the Madrid manuscript. Bower was abbot of Inchcolm in the Firth of Forth and could have consulted an exemplar of the manuscript at Dunfermline.[55]

The route that the manuscript took from Dunfermline to Madrid can be retraced in part. At some time between 1626 and 1642 the Spanish Cistercian Angel Manrique saw the manuscript in the library of the Counts of Gondomar in Valladolid. He described it as 'a very old book, written in an ancient script, that was brought from England to Spain by the illustrious Count of Gondomar, who was more than once Philip III's ambassador in that country. It was kindly shown to us by his son, Don Antonio Sarmiento, who has it in his library at Valladolid. The book is a parchment volume containing the *Life of Waltheof* among other things.'[56] The Count of Gondomar referred to was ambassador to the court of James VI and I in 1613–18 and 1620–22 and died in 1626. He was friendly with Sir Robert Cotton, but there is no definite evidence as to how, where, or when he acquired the manuscript. The Gondomar collection passed in its entirety into the Spanish royal library in 1807. The transmission of the manuscript has been discussed in an article by John Durkan, who placed it in the general context of Spanish interest in Scottish saints, an interest reaching its most notable manifestation in Philip II's acquisition of relics of St Margaret and Malcolm Canmore, for which he constructed a shrine in the Escorial.[57]

The *Miracula* were composed about two centuries before the date of the extant manuscript. The exact dating presents problems. The collection certainly reached its present form after 1263, for one miracle is associated with the battle of Largs, which took place in that year.[58] At first glance, this would suggest a date of composition after 1263, since, at the close of ch. 8, the author writes, 'I can inform readers categorically that, up to this point, I have placed nothing in this little book except what I have seen with my own eyes. What now

[55] Bower, *Scotichronicon*, iii, pp. xvii–xviii.

[56] *Cisterciensium seu verius Ecclesiasticorum Annalium a condito Cistercio tomus II* (Lyons, 1642), p. 336 (ch. 3, no. 3, under the year 1160, not 1168 as stated in *AASS*, Augusti, i (Paris, 1867), p. 247).

[57] 'Three manuscripts with Fife associations: and David Colville of Fife', *Innes Review*, xx (1969), 47–58. Durkan's attention had been drawn to the manuscript by George McFadden, who had worked on the *Life of Waltheof*.

[58] Ch. 7. All numbering of chapters is editorial, taking the first chapter after the prologue as ch. 1. There are forty-two chapters. The Largs miracle is recounted in almost identical words in Bower, *Scotichronicon*, x. 15 (ed. Watt, v. 336–8).

follows I have learned from trustworthy informants . . .' The miracles recounted in the first eight chapters, of which the author is supposedly an eye-witness, include the Largs incident. If his categorical assurance be accepted, this is the *terminus post quem* for the completion of the work in its present form. Other miracles are dated to 1257 and (indirectly but probably) to 1250, and thus support the picture of composition going on in the middle decades of the thirteenth century.

One major enigma complicates the story. If the *Miracula* were completed in the 1260s or later, it is quite remarkable that they make no mention of the papal canonization of Margaret of 1249 and the solemn translation of her relics in 1250. This is an astonishing silence. An author whose main concern is the glorification of St Margaret and who gives a detailed account of an earlier translation in 1180 (see below), makes no reference to what most would consider the ultimate endorsement of Margaret's standing as a saint. Frankly, there is no entirely plausible explanation. One hypothesis would be that the bulk of the collection was assembled before 1249 and that the chapters demonstrably later than that date are interpolations, but this is patently an argument of convenience. Alternatively, one might hazard the argument that, for some monks of Dunfermline, the continuing local miraculous cures were of far greater import than the approval of outside powers, be they popes or kings. After all, to take a vaguely analogous case, there is an enormous literature on why the main chronicler of the tenth-century German kings, Widukind of Corvey, seems to have forgotten to mention the revival of the imperial title by Otto I in 962. In order to explain why a fact mentioned in every historical textbook is not found in the prime contemporary source, German scholars have had recourse to complex and abstruse argument, including the postulation of a conscious anti-Roman stance on Widukind's part.[59] Perhaps a Dunfermline monk of the thirteenth century might be less impressed by papal bulls and royal visits than we would presume and assertively recorded local cures while disregarding the official side of the cult. On the other hand, perhaps the theory of interpolation is safer. The fact that the author claims to

---

[59] There is a large literature in German of which an old but standard instance is H. Beumann, 'Das imperiale Königtum im 10. Jahrhundert', in his *Wissenschaft vom Mittelalter: Ausgewählte Aufsätze* (Cologne and Vienna, 1972), pp. 241–54. There is a brief discussion in English in James A. Brundage, 'Widukind of Corvey and the "Non-Roman" imperial idea', *Mediaeval Studies*, xxii (1960), 15–26.

have received information directly from a monk cured in 1180 might also lend weight to a date for primary composition earlier than 1250.[60]

It is not entirely impossible that the collection of miracle accounts may have had some connection with the attempt to procure Margaret's canonization. The documents regarding this are four, all of them letters of Pope Innocent IV:[61]

(1) A letter of the pope to the bishops of St Andrews, Dunkeld, and Dunblane, dated 27 July 1245, reporting that the king of Scots had requested the canonization of Margaret and instructing them to conduct an enquiry into her life and miracles.

(2) A letter of the pope to the bishops of St Andrews and Glasgow, dated a year later, 13 August 1246, complaining that the report submitted by the bishops of St Andrews, Dunkeld, and Dunblane did not contain the statements or the names of the witnesses and stating that hence he is unwilling to proceed to a canonization. The two bishops are commanded to make a fuller enquiry and report to him.

(3) A letter of the pope to the abbot of Dunfermline, dated over three years later, 16 September 1249. The pope says that he has been favourable to the abbot's petitions. He goes on to report that H., cardinal priest of S. Sabina, to whom the pope committed the examination of the enquiry into the life and miracles of Margaret, has written certain things about the case to the bishop of St Andrews. Lest there be any doubt about what the cardinal wrote, the pope confirms that they proceeded from his (i.e. the pope's) will and good pleasure.

(4) A letter of the pope to all the faithful in Scotland, dated five days later, 21 September 1249. He grants an indulgence of 40 days to all who visit the church of Dunfermline 'on the feast of St Margaret'.

Two things are notable about this little dossier, first the absence of a bull of canonization, second the vexing allusiveness of the third item. Although Margaret is regularly referred to as Scotland's only canonized saint (of the medieval period), there is no clear and explicit

---

[60] The miracle in ch. 9 is dated 1180 and was the immediate inspiration for that in ch. 10, whose beneficiary, a monk, was the author's direct source—'protestatus est nobis'.

[61] *Registrum de Dunfermlyn*, ed. Cosmo Innes (Bannatyne Club, Edinburgh, 1842), nos. 281, 285, 290–1, pp. 181, 183, 185–6; the Utrecht Legendary, which is no longer extant, contained a narrative account of the canonization proceedings, a fragment of which is printed in *AASS*, Iunii, ii. 338.

written evidence for the actual canonization, although it can be safely inferred from item 4.[62]

What the correspondence does show is that not merely one but two inquests were held into Margaret's miracles during the second half of the 1240s. This may have stimulated the monks of Dunfermline to assemble a collection of miracle accounts, a collection that does not mention the canonization of 1249 and translation of 1250 because originally composed prior to those events, but one which was later supplemented in a piecemeal fashion. In any event, the collection as it now stands is not in chronological order, for ch. 7 dates to 1263, ch. 9 to 1180, and ch. 42 to 1257.

The author of the text is anonymous, but was certainly a monk of Dunfermline. Some of the miracles have been told to him by those 'who are at present monks in *our* church' (ch. 8); a miracle in the refectory can be attested 'by us who were there' (ch. 22); the account of a demoniac who had been brought bound to the site of Margaret's first tomb includes the phrase, 'I, who relate this miracle to you, and two brethren with me, came to the sick man . . .' (ch. 16); the author witnesses a cure 'while we were celebrating the solemn feast (of Margaret's translation)' (ch. 23).

Whoever the author was, he had an impressive command of Latin prose, exhibiting great narrative verve and stylistic energy. Sentences are woven together by skilful use of participles (especially present participles), the ablative absolute, and subordinate clauses. The text is enriched with rhetorical flourishes without being swamped by them. Alliteration ('felici furto furatus est ad feretrum', ch. 15) and hyperbaton ('huic sacre se conferunt solennitati', ch. 6; 'piis illorum pulsata precibus', ch. 13) are used effectively. An especial vividness is created by extensive use of direct speech. These passages often involve the imperative or interrogative, and can form extended dialogues or even internal monologues (e.g. ch. 42). Together with the occasional interjection ('ecce!', 'mirabile dictu!') and a free use of superlatives, this gives the text a highly animated tone.

Prose rhyme can also be found not infrequently, as in the prologue ('imitatores accionum . . . coheredes mansionum', 'assimilata . . . glorificata'), and this is sometimes combined with other effects, such as tricolon abundans in asyndeton: 'ex aqua gustauit, caput et oculos lauit, fiducialiter agens coram altari obdormiuit' (ch. 19). The

---

[62] This oddity was noticed by Robert Folz, *Les Saintes Reines du Moyen Age en Occident* (Brussels, 1992), p. 103.

vocabulary is not exotic though choice of word is sometimes distinct-ive. The author's frequent use of forms of *afflictio* and *affligere* (16 instances) might be considered unsurprising in an account of healing miracles, but it is brought into sharper focus by a comparison with the miracles of Æbbe, which have not a single example. Even more striking is the author's especial partiality for female agentive nouns in '-trix', again a natural thing in the hagiography of a female saint but here taken to extremes. We find *adiutrix*, *amatrix*, *auxiliatrix*, *consolatrix*, *consultrix*, *genetrix*, (the very rare) *instigatrix*, *liberatrix*, *mediatrix*, and (the also very rare) *sustentatrix*. In the *Vita et miracula S. Ebbe*, by contrast, there are only three such words (*liberatrix*, *operatrix*, *saluatrix*).

We have, then, a collection of the miracles of St Margaret of Scotland composed by a monk of Dunfermline in the middle decades of the thirteenth century. What we can learn from it may be conveniently considered under three headings: a general profile of the cult of St Margaret—its 'clientele', geography, and special features; specific information about the cult sites and activities within the abbey church of Dunfermline; incidental and miscel-laneous evidence for social history.

The miracles

The *Miracula S. Margarite* is a clearly organized work. The usual pattern is one miracle per chapter (there are 42 chapters). Two exceptions are ch. 6, which describes three separate miraculous cures, and ch. 8, which recounts two individual cures and then mentions the healing of 'thirteen men and women of diverse illnesses'. (Since these thirteen cures are mentioned in such a general fashion, they have been excluded from the following analysis.) In addition, chs. 14 and 15 refer to two different miracles involving the same individual, the monk John. All in all, then, 45 miracles are described, affecting 44 individuals.

Sex

Of the 44 individuals involved in the miracles, 17 are female, 27 male. Such a ratio (39% to 61%) is entirely typical for a cult of the period. It is not at all implausible that women might be attracted to a female saint and evidence from the later Middle Ages shows that St Margaret's help was sought during the dangers of pregnancy and

childbirth,[63] but, in clear contrast to the cult of Æbbe, the cult of Margaret in the twelfth and thirteenth centuries was as dominated by men as most other cults.

Ailment

Types of affliction

Ailment	Number cured	Percentage
Paralysis and strokes	11	24
Other	10	22
Insanity, possession	6	13
Dumbness	4	9
Swellings	4	9
Toothache	3	7
'Moral miracles'	3	7
Swallowing lizards	2	4
Blindness	2	4
TOTAL	45	

'Other' includes individual cases of: cures of dropsy, elephantiasis, abscess, fever, flux, and missing finger-nails; saving from a fall, the threat of shipwreck, and the burns of the ordeal iron; and one unspecified 'serious illness'. 'Moral miracles' are those in which the saint appears in order to encourage her monks, although no physical illness or danger is involved.

The pattern revealed by this analysis is not particularly atypical, although Margaret does appear to have cured fewer blind people than average. A figure of 7 per cent for toothache is also perhaps distinctive, and it has been noted that beneficiaries of cures of toothache are often clerks or monks with easy access to the shrine, as in two of these three cases.[64]

---

[63] Her 'sark' or chemise was used by Scottish queens to assist in the births of James III (1451) and James V (1512): *Exchequer Rolls of Scotland*, ed. John Stuart, George Burnett *et al.* (23 vols., Edinburgh, 1878–1908), v. 447, 512; *Accounts of the Lord High Treasurer of Scotland, iv: 1507–13*, ed. James Balfour Paul (Edinburgh, 1902), p. 334. Steve Boardman kindly supplied these references. The former reference confirms that James III was born in 1451, not 1452, as often asserted: see the discussion in Christine McGladdery, *James II* (Edinburgh, 1990), p. 76.

[64] Sigal, *L'Homme et le miracle*, p. 251.

Social class

The fact that more men than women benefited from Margaret's powers is in part explained by her readiness to aid her own monks. Nine monks are mentioned in the text as receiving healing or spiritual help from the saint (Reginald, Roger, John, Adam, Prior Gregory, Lambert, Adam a novice, and two unnamed monks). In several cases it is explicitly stated and in all cases it is probable that these were monks of Dunfermline. The author sometimes states that he had heard the story from the brother concerned (*protestatus est nobis*; *ut asseruit*). The monks' awareness of Margaret and proximity to her shrine made them natural potential clients, although in one case, that of the novice Adam (ch. 34), there was an inhibiting factor too: 'A monk who had often experienced the favours of St Margaret advised him to go to her tomb and pray devoutly for his recovery. He replied that he dare not do this, since if his master knew, he would denounce him derisively before them all as moved by hypocrisy.' Adam needed special permission before he had the courage to spend the night at the tomb and win his health. This is a nice light on the novice-master's stark rein on any signs of religious presumption among his charges.

The secular clergy are not so well represented. They include Robert, a clerk, the son of a knight, who eventually became a monk at Dunfermline, and William of Inverkeithing, a clerk who went mad through too much study, as well as a priest, 'Dovenaldus', bearing the only Gaelic name in the entire work. The remaining 32 people who experienced Margaret's miraculous power were layfolk.

These lay people vary widely in social rank, from the noblewoman Helen, an unnamed nobleman in Galloway, and the knight, John of Wemyss, through millers, sailors, carpenters and painters, to servant girls and labourers. There are occasional cases of poor people and young people, but they do not have the unusual prominence that they do in the cult of Æbbe.

Geography

The geographical range of the cult extended from Aberdeen to East Anglia. Six of those healed are specifically described as coming from England, two of these from Northumbria and one from 'the eastern regions of that people' (she is a devotee of St Edmund). In addition there is an Englishwoman married to a man from Lothian, where she had settled. One man, the merchant William of 'Dylton', has a

specific place of origin that may be the English village of Dilton in Wiltshire (ch. 23). Nine people, excluding monks, are from Dunfermline or its environs, as far as Inverkeithing, Clackmannan, and Wemyss. From farther afield in Scotland came two Aberdonians and individuals from Galloway and Glencorse in Lothian. One pilgrim is designated simply 'a Scot' (*Scotus*) and explicitly contrasted with 'a local woman' (*indigena*)—clearly the monks of thirteenth-century Dunfermline did not see themselves unequivocally as 'Scots' (even though the *Vita et miracula S. Ebbe* describes the shrine of Margaret as *in Scocia* (4. 39)).

Of the beneficiaries of Margaret's miracles whose origins we know, (31 in total), 9 (or 10 if we include the convert Robert) were monks of Dunfermline, 9 others came from the immediate hinterland of the abbey, 6 came from further afield in Scotland, and 7 came from England. The overall geographical pattern is thus of a strong local core, with a more limited field of influence ranging as far as 100 miles away (Aberdeen, Galloway, Northumbria) and at least one exceptional case from three times that distance (it is over 300 miles from Bury to Dunfermline). It has been established for French cults that a large majority of pilgrims came from less than 35 miles from the shrine. In the case of Margaret, if we deem the monks and those from the hinterland and from Lothian to belong to such a category, it includes 65% of the *miraculés*.

As far as division between the sexes, ailments cured, social class, and geographical origins are concerned, the cult of St Margaret is thus a typical regional cult with a strong monastic core.

Cult

Naturally, the subject about which the miracle collection gives us most information is the cult of St Margaret itself. Much new light is shed on the cultic practices and procedures within the abbey church of Dunfermline, though not all of it is easy to interpret.

One of the more noteworthy sections of the work is an account of a previously unrecorded translation of St Margaret's relics in 1180. The date is established in the text not only by a dating *anno Domini*, which might, of course, have suffered the confusion attendant upon Roman numerals, but also by a specific contemporary allusion—'the first year after the consecration of Master John at Edinburgh', i.e. John, bishop of St Andrews, who was consecrated in Holyrood, near

Edinburgh, on 15 June 1180.[65] The narrative, found in ch. 9, tells how the monks resolved 'that they should move the tomb of St Margaret the queen from the place in which it was situated'. They employed a skilled artist, named Ralph, to construct a reliquary: 'To increase devotion to her, they had already employed an artist (*pictor*) called Ralph, a man of great reputation and most renowned as a creator of carvings. He prepared a reliquary (*theca*) for the blessed queen, covered with gold leaf and with carved images, as can still be seen from the object itself . . .' (This may be the earliest reference to a named artist active in Scotland.) During the translation ceremony the monks lay prostrate in the choir, reciting the seven penitential psalms and the litany. Eventually the relics were re-enshrined 'on the north side of the altar', elevated on a stone slab covered with a splendid cloth. As is made explicit in the account of a miracle that follows, the new location was within the east end of the church (*interiora sanctuarii*).

This account of the translation of 1180 not only gives interesting details of the artistic, liturgical, and indeed logistical aspects of such a ceremony, but tells us also that it is now necessary to posit at least three successive positions for Margaret's remains in the abbey church at Dunfermline: the first from 1093 to 1180, in 'the old church' as the text calls it; the second from 1180 to 1250 'on the north side of the altar'; the third, after the translation of 1250, in the especially constructed east-end chapel, where remains of the shrine base can be seen today.

Harmonizing the description of the translation of 1180 in the *Miracula S. Margarite* with that of the translation in 1250 to be found in John Fordun's fourteenth-century chronicle, and, at greater length, in Walter Bower's fifteenth-century elaboration of it, is a delicate matter.[66] The Fordun narrative simply describes how the king, prelates, and other great men 'raised the bones of the blessed Margaret, once queen of Scots, from the stone tomb in which they had rested for many years, and placed them in a shrine of wood . . .' There is no mention here of the reliquary constructed by Ralph in 1180. Bower adds that the previous location of the bones was the 'outer church', and describes their transport through the chancel arch

---

[65] On him see D. E. R. Watt, *Series episcoporum ecclesiae catholicae occidentalis*, vi (1): *Ecclesia Scoticana* (Stuttgart, 1991), pp. 87–8, with references.

[66] John of Fordun, *Chronica gentis Scottorum*, annal xlix, ed. W. F. Skene (2 vols., Edinburgh, 1871–2), i . 295; Bower, *Scotichronicon*, x. 3 (ed. Watt, v. 296).

into the choir. Clearly the implication of his account is that in 1250 Margaret's bones were moved from a tomb in the nave. The *Miracula* account, on the other hand, has them, from 1180, in a shrine 'to the north of the altar' in the east end of the church.

Reconciliation of the account here with Bower's does not seem possible, and the probability lies in the error being Bower's. He is recording a legendary accretion to the translation account given in Fordun and seems to have pictured the ceremony of 1250 as a simple translation of Margaret's remains from her original resting place to the chapel he knew in his own day. Although he was familiar with a manuscript that was the exemplar of the Madrid manuscript, he does not appear to have paid attention to its account of the 1180 translation.

Margaret's tomb was originally, as Turgot's *Vita S. Margarite* recounts, 'opposite the altar and the sign of the holy cross' in the church which she herself constructed and whose foundations were revealed and surveyed in 1916–17. The later building sponsored by her son, David I, and consecrated in 1150 was raised around it.[67] The 'altar' north of which the remains were placed in 1180 would have been the high altar of the new and larger church. In 1250 the relics were taken from this position into the new chapel beyond the high altar.

Because there were three successive locations for Margaret's remains and because the text here records miracles from different periods, but not in chronological order, there is often difficulty in interpreting some of its references. Mention of a 'translation' may refer to that of 1180 or that of 1250, while the references to the place where the saint's body 'first rested' or 'rested for a time' are likewise ambiguous. A passage in ch. 16 complicates the picture further. In this chapter a demented sailor from Aberdeen who has run amok in Dunfermline has to be restrained. He is brought into the monastery 'to the place where the queen had lain for eighty years'. The period of eighty years corresponds exactly neither to 1093–1180, when Margaret lay in her first tomb, nor 1180–1250 when she lay in her second.

---

[67] Turgot, *Vita sanctae Margaritae Scotorum reginae*, xiii, Symeon, ed. Hinde, p. 254; on the work of 1916–17, see Royal Commission on Ancient and Historical Monuments and Constructions of Scotland, *Eleventh Report with Inventory of Monuments and Constructions in the Counties of Fife, Kinross, and Clackmannan* (Edinburgh, HMSO, 1933), pp. 106–7; the most recent discussion of the building history of the church is by Eric Fernie, 'The Romanesque churches of Dunfermline Abbey', *Medieval Art and Architecture in the Diocese of St Andrews*, ed. John Higgitt (British Archaeological Association, Conference transactions, xiv, 1994), pp. 25–37.

It may plausibly be taken as referring to either (as well as making us grateful that the translation of 1180 is dated by a confirmatory event rather than just by an easily corruptible numeral).

What is clear is that the author of the *Miracula S. Margarite* was familiar with a cult in which an empty tomb or former burial site played an important role. Such a situation, in which both old tomb and new shrine were centres of supernatural power, is not unusual—Swithun in Winchester is an example that has been studied extensively.[68] Margaret's cult, however, seems to have gone further. The multiplicity of cult foci in the church is brought out by the account of a miraculous cure in ch. 13. A girl who is possessed is brought 'before the altar of St Margaret the queen' (which we know from elsewhere in the text was in the nave); while she sleeps the saint appears to her and says, 'go to the place where my bones rested'; she obeys, sleeps 'on the stone of the queen's tomb' (*super lapidem tumuli regine*), and again sees a vision of the saint. She wakes cured and her family take her 'to St Margaret's shrine' (*ad feretrum sancte Margarite*), where they shave her hair and vow her to God (the girl eventually became a nun at the Cistercian house of Elcho). In this one story, we see the altar, the empty tomb, and the new reliquary, all important sites for requests to the saint, the receipt of supernatural visions and power, and making promises to God.

In addition to tomb, altar, and reliquary, there was also, within the church, 'St Margaret's well', which is mentioned eight times in the text. Pilgrims drank from it, bathed their eyes in it, while one poor crippled girl who was just beginning to walk very weakly after her cure was thrown into it by the devil. It seems natural to identify this well with that still visible beneath the modern flooring of the nave of Dunfermline abbey. It is situated in the south aisle, in the third bay from the west end. This position indicates that it lay outside the church built by Margaret, but it was incorporated within the structure when this was rebuilt by David I.

The only doubt concerning this identification arises from the way the text describes the location of the fountain. On more than one occasion it is said to be near Margaret's original tomb: 'the well which

---

[68] Martin Biddle, 'Archaeology, architecture and the cult of the saints in Anglo-Saxon England', *The Anglo-Saxon Church: Papers on History, Architecture and Archaeology in Honour of Dr H. M. Taylor*, ed. L. A. S. Butler and R. K. Morris (Council for British Archaeology Research Report, lx, 1986), pp. 1–31, at pp. 18–25. See also John Blair, 'St Frideswide's monastery: problems and possibilities', *Oxoniensia*, liii (1988), 221–58, at pp. 249–51.

is near the tomb and is called St Margaret's fountain' (ch. 2), 'When he was brought to the place where her most holy body first lay buried, he tasted some of the water from the well next to the tomb' (ch. 27). The examination of Margaret's church undertaken in 1916–17 revealed five tombs in the eastern part of the building, one of which was presumably the queen's own. However, none of them is less than 12 metres from the well, and the two in the prestigious position behind the main altar (often seen as Margaret's and Malcolm Canmore's) are a good 20 metres from it. Perhaps, seen from the monk's eye view in the choir, the well and the old tomb were close, but it is possible that the dispositions of the existing evidence are not the whole story.

Queen Margaret died on 16 November and that date was celebrated as her feast. There is a vivid account by Reginald of Durham of the crowds assembling at Dunfermline at some point in the 1160s to celebrate 'the festive natal day of St Margaret the queen . . . for there rests the holy body of the queen, whose power of sanctity the whole region of Scotland venerates and reveres.'[69] The translation of 1250 took place on 19 June and that was also celebrated.

It is clear, however, that there had previously been a translation feast commemorating the relocation of the relics in 1180. Ch. 5 contains the words, 'The feast of the blessed queen approached, which is celebrated each year in her memory and in veneration of all the saints whose relics are in the church, on which day the translation of her holy body from the former church to the high altar, as described above, is commemorated with a great celebration of psalms and hymns.' The precise reference to the relics' being moved from 'the former church' to the high altar, and the cross-reference, make it clear that this must refer to the translation of 1180. The passage is also explicit that this feast of Margaret's translation coincided with the Feast of the Relics, a commemoration held on different days in different churches to commemorate all the saints whose relics were located in the church. It is not known on what day this was celebrated in Dunfermline. Whether this earlier translation feast was replaced by that of 19 June in 1250 or whether, as sometimes happened, the translation of 1250 was timed to coincide with the date of the earlier one is not known.

Margaret's feasts of 19 June and 16 November are mentioned in the late thirteenth-century Coldingham Breviary and the early

[69] Reginald, *Libellus*, xcviii, pp. 217–18.

sixteenth-century Aberdeen Breviary (with lectiones for the two Offices).[70] The feast day of 10 June, as found in the *Martirilogium Romanum*, was apparently introduced by error in the sixteenth century; in 1677 Innocent XI transferred it to 8 July, but 10 June was again approved by Innocent XII in 1693 as a compliment to James VII and II, whose son 'the Old Pretender' was born on that date.[71]

There was only a modest distribution of relics beyond the main cult centre of Dunfermline. Fourteenth-century relic lists from Durham mention relics 'of the flesh and hair of Margaret, glorious queen of Scots', and that of 1383 also refers to 'a cross called that of St Margaret queen of Scotland', presumably to be identified with the one inventoried at the Reformation as 'the Cross of St Margaret, supposed to be good for those lying-in'.[72] This kind of help was also the function of her 'sark' or chemise, used by Scottish queens of the later Middle Ages (see above, n. 63). In 1379 the monks of Durham were accused of taking 'bones of St Æbbe and relics of St Margaret, queen of Scotland, furtively from Coldingham', and, if true, the charge demonstrates a continuing interest in building up relics of these saints.[73] Relics could be found further south. The king of England possessed a portable reliquary containing, amongst other relics, 'bones of the blessed Margaret, queen of Scotland', according to an inventory of 1344.[74] The inventories of treasures and relics in St George's Chapel, Windsor, drawn up in 1384 and 1410, also mention 'a bone of St Margaret, queen of Scotland',[75] while a list from Worcester of about the same period mentions a relic from Margaret's head.[76]

---

[70] BL, Harley 4664, fos. 128ᵛ, 131; Aberdeen Breviary, unfoliated Kalendar, Offices in *pars estivalis, sanctorale*, fos. i–iᵛ (incomplete due to printer's error), clxii–clxiii.

[71] *AASS*, Junii, ii. 320–2; Propylaeum ad Acta Sanctorum Decembris, p. 231.

[72] *Historiae Dunelmensis scriptores tres*, ed. J. Raine (Surtees Soc. ix, 1839), p. ccccxxviii; *Extracts from Account Rolls of the Abbey of Durham*, ii, ed. J. T. Fowler (Surtees Soc. c, 1899), pp. 426–7; *Letter and Papers, Foreign and Domestic, of the Reign of Henry VIII*, x (1536), ed. James Gairdner (London, 1887), no. 364, p. 142.

[73] Raine, *North Durham*, p. 103, no. 591.

[74] *The Antient Kalendars and Inventories of the Treasury of His Majesty's Exchequer*, ed. Francis Palgrave (3 vols., London, 1836), iii. 207.

[75] *The Inventories of St George's Chapel, Windsor Castle, 1384–1667*, ed. Maurice F. Bond (Windsor, 1947), pp. 58, 112.

[76] Worcester Cathedral Priory MS A22, fo. 18ʳ⁻ᵛ, as cited by I. G. Thomas, 'The Cult of Saints' Relics in Medieval England', Ph.D. thesis (London, 1975), p. 428, who notes the omission of this item from published editions of the list.

The edition

The edition gives the text as in the Madrid manuscript, with some minor editorial emendations. The numbering of chapters is editorial. Only ch. 7 has appeared in print before, being incorporated in Bower's *Scotichronicon*.

Topics Common to the Two Collections

Social history

As historians are aware, miracle stories form a rich source for social history. Their protagonists are often of relatively humble level, and the amount of incidental detail given is great. Hence we can learn about such things as mealtimes, dress, games and entertainments, wedding and funeral customs, oaths, and much more, all in vivid individualized detail. The *Miracles* of Æbbe and Margaret offer many such snippets.

In one story in the *Miracula S. Margarite*, for example, involving the exorcism of demons, we see how unsurprising it is that a landed gentleman can produce a psalter at home and, moreover, read from it (ch. 13). In ch. 37, the affection that a nurse would have for the children in her care is highlighted. When a monk is troubled by doubts about his vocation, a vision appears to his nurse 'who had suckled him and thus loved him more deeply'. St Margaret, speaking to the nurse, even refers to the monk as 'your son'. It is no surprise that deep affective bonds would grow up between wet-nurses and their charges (we know that Richard I of England rewarded his, Galiena, with land)[77] but it is good to have concrete instances rather than general assumptions. On a rather different subject, trade routes, the story in ch. 40 shows the import of grain from Berwick to Dunfermline by ship, although whether this is overseas produce from an entrepôt or the surpluses of the Merse taking the cheapest route to Fife is not clear.

There is also a reference (ch. 20) to the practice of tying mad people to the cross at *Lochorfrech* (the old name for Borthwick in Lothian) in the hope of a cure. Such a practice is also mentioned by

---

[77] R. W. Hunt, *The Schools and the Cloister: The Life and Writings of Alexander Nequam* (Oxford, 1984), pp. 1–2.

Jocelin of Furness in his *Vita S. Kentigerni*, written between 1175 and 1199. According to Jocelin, the saint erected many crosses, including a stone one in the cathedral cemetery to which those possessed by demons were tied and left overnight, in the morning being either cured or dead, and one at *Lothwerverd* (a variant of *Lochorfrech*), which was made miraculously out of sand. 'To this cross also', he writes, 'many people suffering from various ailments, and especially the insane and those possessed by demons, are tied at night and in the morning many of them are found sane and healthy and return freely home.'[78]

These passages, and others like them, give us, of course, only small fragments of information, but our knowledge of twelfth- and thirteenth-century Scotland is not so extensive that we should not be grateful even for such tiny addenda on subjects such as lay devotion, child-rearing, trade, and the treatment of the insane.

The *Vita et miracula S. Ebbe* offer similarly rich incidental information. On the subject of medicine, which was, of course, the great rival to miraculous healing cults, there are several interesting passages. The use of herbal ligatures is mentioned in one story, concerning a child with a black swelling on his side: 'They treated him with medicines tied onto him with cords but as soon as they were tied on they fell off again as if untied by heavenly power, so that thereby they might understand that he could not be cured by the power of herbs but would be healed by the blessing of heavenly mercy' (4. 8). A similar attitude is shown in the story of an Edinburgh man, who was completely crippled; 'He frequently applied fire and iron to cure his body, so that he had covered his sides with scars, and, feeling that no help would come from earthly medicine, he was inspired by God to take refuge in divine medicine' (4. 5). Scepticism about doctors is also expressed in the laconic comment in the *Miracula S. Margarite* about a sick woman who, 'because doctors promise what doctors do, spent almost her whole wealth on doctors' (ch. 17).

The *Vita et miracula S. Ebbe* also provide what must be the earliest reference to a Scottish fiddle player (4. 6), a nice counterpoint to the first mention of a named Scottish artist (Ralph) in the *Miracula S. Margarite*. In the tale of the Welsh girl Quinciana, we learn of the effects on one family of Henry II's incursions into Wales: 'When king

[78] c. 41, ed. Alexander Penrose Forbes, *Lives of St Ninian and St Kentigern* (Edinburgh, 1874), pp. 233–4.

Henry II sent his army against the Welsh and devastated them with fire and sword, the woman's husband and three sons were burned together in their house, while her father and other relatives were killed by the enemy's sword' (4. 7).

One story in the *Miracula S. Margarite* that repays close attention concerns trial by ordeal (ch. 24). A carpenter by the name of William had raped a woman. Arrested and held in chains until trial, he was then brought before the judges. They decided that he should undergo trial by hot iron (*ferro iudiciali adiudicatur*). On the appointed day he carried the hot iron and felt 'a dreadful burning'. The hand was bound and sealed, 'as the custom is', and then followed the waiting period, after which the hand would be inspected and guilt or innocence decided by its appearance. On the first night the culprit went to St Margaret's tomb and prayed for her help. She appeared to him, in her customary way, told him to stretch out his hand and blew on it. Immediately he felt the pain disappear. When he was brought to the place where the judges were to decide his fate, he exhibited his hand 'in which not a trace of burning was seen to appear'. Upon his release the grateful carpenter took the cross and went off to the Holy Land.

The passage is remarkable for various reasons. First, it is the only known account of a trial by ordeal in Scotland. All other references are general prescriptions or formulae. This, on the other hand, is a narrative. Secondly, it shows the institution of the ordeal flourishing and unquestioned, and, in a text from this period, this is noteworthy, given the debate among historians on the timing and causes of the demise of the ordeal.[79] A law attributed to Alexander II (1214–49) and hence very close in time to the events of this story prohibited ordeal in cases of theft.[80] Thirdly, the miracle benefits a guilty man—the text leaves no doubt that he committed the rape. Like the virgin Mary, St Margaret of Scotland could be invoked to save the culpable from the consequences of their actions as well as help those afflicted through no fault of their own.[81]

---

[79] On which see the present writer's *Trial by Fire and Water: The Medieval Judicial Ordeal* (Oxford, 1986), pp. 34–102.

[80] *Statuta regis Alexandri*, vi. *Acts of the Parliament of Scotland*, i, ed. T. Thomson and C. Innes (Edinburgh, 1844), 70 (400).

[81] On this aspect of the Virgin Mary, see e.g. Benedicta Ward, *Miracles and the Medieval Mind: Theory, Record and Event 1000–1215* (Aldershot and Philadelphia, 1982), pp. 163–4.

Apparitions, incubation and demons

If one set the cults of Æbbe and Margaret, as revealed in these miracle stories, alongside the typical healing cults of the period, two distinctive features emerge, one concerning the process of the cure, the other the causes of the afflictions:

> Incubation, i.e. sleeping at a cult centre prior to healing, and visual apparitions of the saint (and others) are extremely frequent.
> Afflictions in which demonic intervention or activity play a part are also common.

Of Æbbe's 43 miracles, 24 involve apparitions of the saint (plus 2 of apparitions of a visionary dove) while 25 involve incubation, thus in each case approaching 60 per cent of the total. Of Margaret's 45 miracles, 29 involve a visionary appearance (or, in one case, the saint's commands being heard) and 30 involve incubation, thus accounting for approximately 65 per cent of the total.

These figures, of 60 and 65 per cent, are remarkably high. The French historian Sigal, who analysed 2,050 accounts of posthumous healing miracles from eleventh- and twelfth-century France, found that only 255 cases, or 12 per cent, involved the appearance of the saint in a vision.[82] When we take into account the fact that some of Margaret's miracles (and one of Æbbe's) were not healing miracles, the significance of visionary apparitions is even greater. As the author of the *Vita et miracula S. Ebbe* himself remarked of the saint, 'she who wished to heal wished also to be seen manifestly and recognized by her whom she healed' (4. 10).

The frequency of visionary appearances is obviously linked with the frequency of incubation, i.e. the custom of sleeping at the cult centre prior to healing. 'Permission to spend the night in the church' had to be sought (as in *Miracula S. Margarite*, ch. 1), after which a night or several nights was spent either awake in prayer or asleep. The custom is expressed in the verb *pernoctare*, 'to pass the night', which occurs five times both in the *Vita et miracula S. Ebbe*, and in the *Miracula S. Margarite*. Significantly, in 1199, when William the Lion, king of Scots, was debating with himself whether to invade England, he 'passed the night' (*pernoctavit*) at Margaret's shrine, obtaining in a dream the advice not to attack.[83]

[82] Sigal, *L'Homme et le miracle*, pp. 134, 255.
[83] Roger of Howden, *Chronica*, ed. William Stubbs (4 vols., RS, 1868–71), iv. 100.

The usual pattern of the saint's appearances was that, while a pilgrim was sleeping in the church, a 'venerable virgin' or 'venerable matron' would appear or suddenly be standing there (*apparuit* and *astitit* are used in this context twenty times in the *Miracula S. Margarite* and sixteen times in the *Vita et miracula S. Ebbe*). This often took place on the third night of vigil. Almost invariably, the saint addresses the pilgrim, sometimes promising aid, occasionally uttering reproaches for some sin. Margaret, unlike Æbbe, identifies herself, some half-a-dozen times, in the words 'I am Margaret, queen of the Scots'. Often the saint touches the pilgrim. For instance, in one story Margaret appears to a girl who had lost her wits and the power of speech after being struck by a demon. She takes the girl's head in her hands, then places her finger in the girl's mouth and withdraws it again. 'Most holy mother,' says the girl, 'I give you deep thanks for the mercy you have shown me. I feel that I have recovered my senses and the power of speech. If you would be willing to touch the place where I was struck by the demon, I know that I would be completely restored to health.' This the saint does, and the girl awakes fully cured (ch. 13).

Some of this visionary activity involves figures other than Æbbe and Margaret. On three occasions Æbbe is accompanied by other saints (Mary, Margaret, and Michael), on two occasions visionary doves play a part in the healing at her oratory. In ch. 42 of the *Miracula S. Margarite*, a woman from Glencorse in Lothian, suffering from paralysis of a hand and a foot, tours the shrines of England and Scotland, eventually returning to St Katherine's chapel in the Pentlands. One night, while she sleeps, 'three matrons, dressed in magnificent clothes, appeared to her and promised that if she devoutly sought out the place where the body of St Margaret, queen of the Scots, lies translated, without a doubt she would recover the blessing of health.' Others who appear in visions include a monk's dead father, sent by St Margaret to strengthen the monk in his wavering profession. This deceased but still disciplinarian father beats his son until the blood flows (ch. 28). In another story a dead father returns to chastise his son's mistress: 'You shameless little whore, it is your fault that my son lies in peril of his soul!' (ch. 33).

Both cults thus exhibit a very high level of visionary activity, coupled with the prominence of the custom of incubation.

Demonic activity

It is, of course, fairly common for medieval authors to attribute misfortune to the actions of demons. The Miracles of Æbbe and Margaret seem especially ready to do this. Moreover, they give some details of the forms which these demonic figures took and the situations which were most perilous for humans. In some cases they seem to be reporting popular beliefs about figures who are much closer to conventional ideas of wicked fairies than of Christian demons.

A particularly chilling example from the *Miracula S. Margarite* (ch. 5) concerns a man who had been dumb since the age of five. At this age, while he was

out in the fields tending the young grazing stock, he became sleepy and laid his limbs down in the green grass to take a peaceful sleep. Three women—or, as their actions showed, figures in female form—approached him. These wicked apparitions spoke to each other: 'What shall we do with this male? Where shall we carry him off to?' When two of them had given their opinion, proclaiming shamelessly that he should be killed, the third, as if more devout, but in fact most evil, dissented and said, 'It will be enough for this one if we throw an apple in his mouth and condemn him to perpetual silence.'

The magic apple was eventually removed by St Margaret, but only many years later.

The three ominous women are described as approaching the boy *phantastice*, that is 'like spectres or phantasms'. The word has overtones both of ghosts and unreality. Peter Comestor, discussing the appearance of the dead Samuel to King Saul in his *Historia scholastica* of *c.*1170, says that 'some people say that a wicked spirit appeared in the shape of Samuel or that his image appeared there *phantastice*, which was called Samuel'.[84]

A more definite identification of eerie women as demons occurs in the case of the teenage boy, John, who 'met two wicked women, or rather, demons in the shape of women. One of them was dressed in green and the other in white linen. They ran quickly to the boy and snatched away a charm he was carrying around his neck and hid it in a nearby thorn-bush. When he was released by them, the boy ran towards his father's house, throwing stones at them as fast as he could to defend himself . . .' (*Miracula S. Margarite*, ch. 26). Here the

---

[84] *Historia scholastica, Historia libri I Regum*, xxvi (*PL* cxcviii. 1321).

demonic nature of the figures is asserted explicitly. Yet the icon-
ography is hardly that of traditional Christian devils: two women, one
in green and one in white linen, encountered while out walking.

Another tale (*Miracula S. Margarite*, ch. 13) in which the element
of the uncanny seems stronger than the demonic is the story of the
noble girl Christine, who hears 'a voice like that of a little child' and
encounters 'a boy who was just like her brother, who had died a little
time before'. He asks for a kiss but she refuses, saying 'I know that
you are my brother, but because you have gone the way of all flesh, I
am not allowed to kiss you.' He knocks her down and she is found
almost senseless. When she is brought into the house, her father reads
the psalter over her. The girl calls out that she sees the house full of
people singing. 'Behold how beautiful that queen is,' she cries, 'how
fair of face, how lovely in appearance, how sweet the song of those
leading the choir.' After her father compels her to recite the Creed
and Lord's Prayer, she says that all have now gone except her brother
at her feet. When her father recites psalms at her feet the brother also
goes, but she says 'my ears are still filled with the sound of their
singing'. Half a dozen questions spring to mind: was the figure of her
brother really her dead brother? how does she know it is forbidden to
kiss the dead? who are the people singing? what are they singing? are
they as malign as the women with the apple or those who tear the
charm from the neck of the boy John? was there a contemporary
vernacular word to describe these figures?

The *Vita et miracula S. Ebbe* also have information on dangerous
women. While a six-year-old Scottish boy was in the fields asleep,
'Behold, four women approached, who gave him so much to drink
that the great quantity they poured into him more than made up for
his prior thirst. But, after such a great drink, he thought that his
insides would burst and he would give up the spirit. When he
eventually awoke, he lay there with his whole body distended . . .'
(4. 39). Clearly these women are as phantasmal as those in the
Miracula S. Margarite.

Dangerous figures are not always uncanny females, however, and
the Miracles have a range of more conventional demonic types,
including dogs, Africans, crows, and riders on black horses.
Humans are particularly vulnerable to demonic attack when out in
the open, especially if they are asleep or have their mouths open.
Even orchards could be dangerous. One girl 'entered an orchard and
put out her hand to pluck an apple, when she suddenly fell to the

ground. It seemed to her that hideous black men hung her in a tree and cut off her arm' (*Vita et miracula S. Ebbe*, 4. 35). Another time 'a gust of wind suddenly blew into the mouths of four youths who were collecting apples at Newbattle and completely deprived them of the power of speech' (*Vita et miracula S. Ebbe*, 4. 12). The causality here is underlined by the author's immediate comment: 'Nor should that gust of wind be believed to be anything other than an evil spirit blowing in their face.'

Remote spots were even worse. One boy, who was struck dumb, had 'incurred this affliction, while he was pasturing sheep in a remote place, from a phantasmal demon who appeared to him in the likeness of a little black boy, because he disdained to consent to the games he suggested to him' (*Vita et miracula S. Ebbe*, 4. 7). A Welsh girl, similarly in a remote place with her father's animals, had gone dumb after spending three nights in a hollow tree. Even snoozing in the shadow of his own mill was dangerous for a miller, who might find lizards creeping into his mouth and down into his body (*Miracula S. Margarite*, ch. 27; cf. ch. 17).

Many of the afflictions which were miraculously cured by Æbbe or Margaret, appearing in visions, were caused by fey ladies or evil spirits who also appeared in visions. The supernatural dangers that surrounded people had supernatural remedies and both involved manifestations from another world. The picture that the Miracles of Æbbe and Margaret reveal is of holy cult centres in a landscape full of phantasmal peril.

VITA ET MIRACVLA
SANCTE EBBE VIRGINIS

(Oxford, Bodleian Library, Fairfax 6, fos. 164^r–173^v)

[1. Preface]

Ad uos clamat de Seyr.¹ Clamat caro mea, clamat et anima mea. De terra longinqua et deserta, de terra rufi, de terra pilosi et hispidi,² ad uos clamat de Seir. Non de terra in qua et de qua factus est Adam, neque de ea de qua manus tue, Domine, fecerunt me et plasmauerunt me, set de terra turpitudinis, de regione dissimilitudinis³ in qua tibi dissimilis factus sum, terra uiciorum et peccatorum que, ne respiciam ad montes unde ueniat auxilium mihi,⁴ semitas mentis mee lapidibus concluserunt. Vos uero felices diximus, uos uere liberos qua libertate donauit Deus, qui deuicto carnis imperio metum non habetis de carne, sed quasdam paradisi delicias interne quietis iocunditate et mutue caritatis dulcedine prelibatis.

Vos corporis beati patris Cuthberti ueneranda fouet presencia, optata muniunt presidia, beata roborant merita, gloriosa letificant miracula et eo securius militatis, quod quasi uiuentem in medio pre oculis ducem habetis. Quod quocius mecum recogito, quasi peregrinus et aduena⁵ ad propriam suspiro. Qui igitur uestre glorie interesse non ualeo, ad beate Ebbe matris nostre, ubi infirmi etiam acceperunt uirtutem, protectionem confugio, de cuius uita et uirtutibus exiguum uestre sanctitati sermonis dirigo munusculum, ut cum habueritis quare laudetis, sciatis certius quantum amare debeatis. Venit mihi quandoque liber in manibus de conuersacione et operibus eiusdem uirginis editus, in quo quam multa uulgo tantum dictante uidebantur inserta; a nonnullis nostrorum ferebantur incerta, quia nulla maiorum auctoritate suffulta.ᵃ Cuius ego pratum opusculi cum legendo percurrerem quosdam flosculos collegi, quorum odore in maiorem tante matris dilectionem corda debeant audiencium attendi.

ᵃ *corr. from* sufflata

¹ Isa. 21: 11; Seir was the dwelling place of Esau.
² Gen. 25: 25, referring to Esau. Jerome interprets Seir as 'pilosus vel hispidus', *Liber interpretationis Hebraicorum nominum* (*CCSL* lxxii. 72).
³ Augustine, *Confessiones*, vii. 10. 16.
⁴ Ps. 120 (121): 1.

Here begins a sermon on the life and miracles of Saint Æbbe the virgin

[1. Preface]

He calls to you from Seir.[1] My flesh calls and my spirit calls too. From a distant and desolate land, from the land of the red man, from the land of the hairy and shaggy man,[2] it calls to you from Seir. Not from the land in which and from which Adam was made, nor from that from which your hands, Lord, made me and formed me, but from a land of wickedness, from a region of estrangement[3] in which I have become unlike you, a land of vices and sins that, lest I look up to the mountains from whence comes my help,[4] have blocked the paths of my mind with stones. We call you happy indeed, truly free with that freedom that God has given, who have conquered the demands of the flesh and have no fear of the flesh, but have a foretaste of some of the delights of paradise in the joyfulness of internal peace and the sweetness of mutual charity.

The venerable presence of the body of our holy father Cuthbert supports you, his much desired guardianship protects you, his blessed merits strengthen you, his glorious miracles delight you, and you fight the fight with much greater confidence since you have your leader, as it were, before your eyes in your midst. Whenever I consider this, I pine for my own land like a wanderer and a stranger.[5] I, who cannot participate in your glory, therefore fly to the protection of St Æbbe, our mother, where the infirm also obtain strength. I am sending to your holiness the little gift of a sermon about her life and miracles, so that when you have something showing why you should praise her, you may know more certainly how much you should love her. A book happened to come into my hands on the subject of the virgin's life and works, in which a great deal seemed to be included only on the basis of popular report and was said by many of our people to be uncertain, because not supported by the authority of our predecessors. While I was running through the meadow of this little work in my reading, I collected some flowers, by whose scent the hearts of the hearers should be directed to greater love of such a mother.

[5] Cf. Gen. 23: 4; Num. 9: 14; Ps. 38 (39): 13 (and similar phrases elsewhere).

[2. Life]

Regali ex progenie claram duxit originem. Erat enim regis Oswyu soror uterina, Egfridi Deo deuoti regis amita.[6] Quorum temporibus uelut mater regni et decus tante nobilitatis enituit. Sicut enim, ut ait quidam, uitis uuam profert in uinea aut florem ex se producunt lilia,[7] sic ex nobili regum prosapia, felix Ebbam felicem protulit[a] Britannia. Beda in hystoria gentis sue de patre eius et matre nichil uidetur interserere. De claritate tantum sui nominis et subuersione sui monasterii quasi ad alia festinans pauca perstringit,[8] eo forte animo quod in illo opere maluisset breuitate succingi quam prolixitate diffluere, uel pocius aliis eius sanctitatis opera reliquid scriptoribus et posteritatis relationi commisit. Vnde est quod auribus nostris multa audiuimus et patres nostri narrauerunt nobis opus quod operata est in diebus eorum in diebus antiquis.[9] Tradunt autem cronica de genealogia regum Deirorum et Berniciorum Ethelfridum, Ethelrici Ide regis Berniciorum filii filium, de regina sua Aycha, Elle regis Deirorum filia, septem sustinuisse filios et unam filiam, scilicet Enfridum, Oswaldum, Oswyu,[b] Oslaf,[c] Oslac, Offan, Oswdum et sanctam Ebbam abbatissam.[10] E contra dicunt aliqui eum duos ex ea filios Eanfridum et Oswaldum habuisse, Oswyu autem et reliquos de concubinis suscepisse.[11] In diebus illis summa nobilium ingenuitas habebatur in qua Christi seruitus probaretur, nec aliquam celsitudinis gloriam se credebant attigisse quos humilitatem dominice crucis non constitit induisse. Propterea clamat de Seir, ubi hodie sapiens, ubi scriba, ubi conquisitor huius seculi,[12] ubi sacerdos aut princeps populi qui omnia relinquat que possidet, et post Christum crucem baiulet?[13] Hoc profecto in religiosis despiciunt quod ipsi pocius in seipsis amplecti debuerunt. Vtraque tunc Domini familia, uirorum scilicet sacre multitudinis conuentus et innumerabilis uirginum chorus,

---

[a] perfudit MS   [b] Oswyum MS. Bede uses 'Oswiu' as the nominative, accusative, and genitive forms of the name. The form 'Oswyu' below is accusative   [c] Olaf MS

---

[6] Oswiu, king of Bernicia and Deira (d. 670); Ecgfrith, king of Northumbria (670–85). Both relationships are mentioned by Bede (see Introduction).

[7] Unidentified.

[8] HE iv. 25, pp. 420–6.

[9] Ps. 77 (78): 3; 43 (44): 2.

[10] ASC (E), s.a. 617, lists the sons of Æthelfrith as Eanfrith, Oswald, Oswiu, Oslac, Oswudu, Oslaf, and Offa; JW, s.a. 593 (615), ii. 70, gives Eanfrith, Oswald, Oslaf, Oswiu, Offa, Oswudu, Oslac, and Æbbe; the De primo Saxonum adventu gives Eanfrith, then, as sons of Acha, Oswald, Oswiu, Oslac, Oswudu, Os(l)af and Offa; Symeon, ed. Arnold, ii. 365–84, at p. 374.

[2. Life]

She had a distinguished origin from royal stock, for she was the half-sister, through her mother, of king Oswiu, and the aunt of king Ecgfrith, who was so devoted to God.[6] In their time she shone forth as the mother of the kingdom and the glory of such great nobility. For just as, as someone says, the vine brings forth grapes in the vineyard or lilies produce flowers from themselves,[7] in the same way happy Britain brought forth happy Æbbe from a noble line of kings. Bede appears to put nothing about her father or her mother in the history of his people. He refers only to the celebrity of her name and the downfall of her monastery very briefly, as if he wanted to hurry on to other things.[8] Perhaps his reasoning was that in that work he preferred to deal with matters briefly rather than expand on them at length, or rather he left her saintly deeds to other writers and entrusted them to narration by posterity. Hence we have heard with our own ears many things and our fathers have told us the work she worked in their time in ancient days.[9] The chronicles of the genealogy of the kings of the Deirans and Bernicians relate that Æthelfrith, son of Æthelric, son of Ida, king of the Bernicians, had by his queen Acha, daughter of Ælle king of the Deirans, seven sons and one daughter, namely Eanfrith, Oswald, Oswiu, Oslaf, Oslac, Offa, Oswudu, and St Æbbe the abbess.[10] On the other hand, some say that he had two sons by her, Eanfrith and Oswald, while he fathered Oswiu and the rest from concubines.[11] In those days the highest nobility of the well-born was regarded as that manifested in the service of Christ, nor did they believe they had attained any degree of heavenly glory unless they had put on the humility of the Lord's cross. On that account he calls from Seir, where is now the wise man, where the scribe, where the disputer of this world,[12] where the priest or prince of the people who would leave all that he possesses and follow Christ bearing his cross?[13] Certainly, they despise in the religious what they ought rather to embrace in themselves. At that time both of the Lord's families, the congregation of the holy multitude of men and the innumerable chorus of virgins, served

---

[11] Exactly this is asserted in Reginald of Durham, *Vita sancti Oswaldi regis et martyris*, Symeon, ed. Arnold, i. 326–85, at p. 340. JW, s.a. 672 (694), ii. 120, in an addition to Bede's text, calls Æbbe the *germana* of Oswald and Oswiu.

[12] 1 Cor. 1: 20.

[13] Luke 14: 27.

fo. 164ᵛ   sparsim per Angliam militabant, et in uno loco sub unius | patris siue matris regimine diuersis diuisi monasteriis degentes,ᵃ contra potestates tenebrarum, gladio spiritus accincti,[14] prelia castitatis exercebant. Impletum est etiam illud in Canticis, 'Flores apparuerunt, uinee florentes odorem dederunt et uox turturis audita est in terra nostra.'[15] Flores enim erant merita confessorum, uinee trophea martirum, uox turturis castitas uirginum. Castrorum suorum in montibus adhuc excelsis et paludibus lutosis relinquuntur uestigia et in scriptis patrum eorum inperpetuum reperietur memoria. Horum beata uirgo gloriosos intuens exitus, fidei profecto imitabatur profectus. Regnum igitur mundi et omnem ornatum seculi cum flore iuuentutis contempsit propter amorem filii Dei, quem mundo corde uidit, quem casto corpore quesiuit, in quem tota mente credidit, quem tota uirtute dilexit, et a sancto Finano Lyndisfarnensi episcopo sancte conuersacionis uelamen accepit.[16] Dominicam nobilitati pretulit seruitutem, spiritualem diuiciis paupertatem, spontaneam honoribus abiectionem. Claris siquidem exorta natalibus, mundum fide et formam moribus et sexum uicit uirtutibus.

Petebatur autem a quodam Scottorum tiranno Eadano. Cuius Beda in sua, id est Anglorum, meminit hystoria.[17] Quo demum ob sui contemptum raptum meditante et amore simul et uiolencia eam persequente, traditur ad montem Colludi confugisse et ad preces eius mare se a meridie in altum erigens, subiecte uallisᵇ alueum transcurrens, hosti triduo continuis fluctibus obstitisse et, cooperante Domino, municionis presidium uirgini prestitisse. Quod, quia uulgo tritum est et a maioribus traditum, assertione uidetur dignum; cum etiam ex loci qualitate uideatur habere uestigium.[18] Et quidem pene simile apud Lyndisfarniam olim gestum est et ad fidem plerumque facilius admittuntur quo aliqua similitudine comprobantur. Si enim mare plenum portitoribus corporis beati Cuthberti siccum iter prebuisse dicerem, non esset forte qui crederet, nisi simile admiracionis opus in mari rubro factum ante legisset.[19] Fugienti etiam cum

---

ᵃ degentis *MS*; degentes *John of Tynemouth*   ᵇ ualles *MS*; uallis *John of Tynemouth*

[14] Eph. 6: 17.   [15] S. of S. 2: 12–13.
[16] Finan, bishop of Lindisfarne, 651–61.
[17] Bede indeed refers to 'Aedan rex Scottorum qui Brittaniam inhabitant' (*HE* i. 34, p. 116), but places him around the year 603.
[18] A very similar story is told of St Æthelthryth, who was a nun under Æbbe (see below), in the *Liber Eliensis*, i. 11, ed. E. O. Blake (Camden, 3rd ser., xcii, 1962), 27–8. The 'Coldeburcheshevet' of the *Liber Eliensis* is clearly St Abb's Head, and there is a similar appeal to the evidence of the local topography.

throughout England, and in one place under the rule of one father or mother, distributed among various monasteries, they fought the battles of chastity, girded with the sword of the spirit,[14] against the powers of darkness. And that passage of The Song of Songs was fulfilled which says, 'Flowers appeared, flourishing vines gave off a fragrance, and the voice of the turtledove was heard in our land'.[15] For the merits of the confessors were flowers, the trophies of the martyrs vines, the chastity of virgins the voice of the turtledove. They left the traces of their castles on the high mountains and in the muddy marshes until now, and their memory will be found in the writings of their fathers forever. When the blessed virgin saw the glory of their final state, she fully imitated their progress in the faith. So, in the flower of her youth, she turned her back on the kingdom of this world and all the splendours of secular things, for love of the son of God, whom she saw with a pure heart, whom she sought with a chaste body, in whom she believed with her whole spirit, whom she loved with all her strength, and she received the veil of the holy way of life from Finan, bishop of Lindisfarne.[16] She preferred the service of the Lord to nobility, spiritual poverty to riches, voluntary humiliation to honours. Born, as she was, of noble descent, she conquered the world by faith, her beauty by goodness, and her sex by virtue.

She was sought in marriage, however, by a tyrant of the Scots called Aidan, whom Bede mentions in his History of the English.[17] Because she rejected him, he eventually decided to take her by force and pursued her with both love and violence. It is said that she took refuge at St Abb's Head and that, at her prayers, the sea, raising itself up from the south and overflowing the course of the adjacent valley, for three days obstructed the enemy and provided the protection of a fortification for the virgin, with the Lord's help. This is a familiar story among the populace and has been handed down by our forefathers, so it seems right to maintain it, since, in addition, it seems to have left a trace in the nature of the terrain.[18] Indeed something quite similar once happened at Lindisfarne, and things are believed more easily if they can be supported by a similar happening. For, if I should say that the brimming sea provided a dry path for those carrying St Cuthbert's body, nobody would perhaps believe it, unless they had previously read of a similar work of wonder performed in the Red Sea.[19] Once also a thief was fleeing with a

---

[19] Two such miracles are recorded. The drying of the sea before those bearing

equo furi, siccis circumquaque patentibus harenis, mare subito cum fluctibus occurrit, sed eo ad insulam regresso et ad se per penitentiam reuerso, quia ipse tumorem mentis in humilitate deposuit, ipsum ex feruore ire sue detumuit. Denuo uenienti harenas siccas reddidit.[20] Quid igitur mirum si crudeli tyranno uiam obstrueret et, eo recedente, aquas suas in se recolligens ad locum suum reddidit? Quid mirum si hoc sue contulit uirgini, qui illud suo contulit confessori? Hec ad arguendam eorum insipienciam uel insaniam dixerim, qui signa ueterum tanquam impossibilia repellunt et irrident, quod eis ex infirmitate fidei prouenit, dum credere nolunt quod ea que quondam ad conuersionem malorum facta sunt, bonis ad laudem transmissa sunt, cum nec mundus credidisset nisi maiores uirtutes factas conspexisset.

Erat olim mons ille edificiorum sublimitate preclarus, postea a malicia habitancium in eo in solitudinis planiciem conuersus. Est autem rupes mari superposita ad instar oui situ rotunda, que, a facie aquilonis fronte sua grossior et ad austrum paulatim in longum lateribus producta tandem angustior, desinit pene in acutum. Adeoque in sublime erigitur quod eam propria altitudine nature gracia precingat et asperitatis circuitu premuniat. A circumpositis montibus amplissima ualle se iungitur. Suaque solitudine ita uidetur superbire quod sociorum equalitatem montium dedignetur et nominis sui priuilegio quodam modo preesse glorietur. Difficilis illo ascensus et accessus. Ab aquilone enim et meridie per angustas semitas uenientibus patet nec sine metu precipitii quod deorsum imminet. Ad fo. 165ʳ occidentem in exigue collis | tumulum altius exurgit et inde ad orientem in gibbosam descendit planiciem, in qua beate uirginis oratorium conspicitur, ita silencio et quieti milicie spiritualis secretum, ut nichil in eo carnalis oculus intueri queat, cuius luxuria cordis obtuitu a desiderio supernorum reflectat. Duos fontes ad sue solitudinis et heremitice conuersacionis habet solacium, irriguum uidelicet superius et irriguum inferius. Vnus enim ad radices eius latice perpetuo madet, alter in cacumine[a] eius ad calores estiuos quandoque arescit et querentibus aquam fossam exhibet. Horum

---

[a] acumine *MS*; cacumine *John of Tynemouth*

Cuthbert's body from Lindisfarne in 875 is described in Reginald, *Libellus*, xii, pp. 16–19, also with invocation of Moses' parting of the Red Sea. The drying of the sea before those bearing Cuthbert's body to Lindisfarne in 1069, also with invocation of the parallel of Moses, is described in *De miraculis et translationibus sancti Cuthberti*, vi, Symeon, ed.

horse, with dry sands stretching out on all sides, when suddenly the sea sent its waves against him, but when he returned to the island and came to himself through penitence, since he turned the inflation of his spirit to humility, he emptied the sea of the fervour of its anger. When he came again, it restored dry sands for him.[20] Why, therefore, should it be amazing that the sea obstructed the cruel tyrant's path and, when he went away, gathered its waters together and restored them to their place? Why should it be amazing if He granted this to His virgin, when He granted that to His confessor? I say this to demonstrate the foolishness or madness of those who reject or ridicule as impossible the miracles of the saints of old. This stems from their lack of faith, for they are unwilling to believe that what was once done for the conversion of the wicked has been handed down to the good for praise, for the world would not have believed unless it had seen greater miracles.

That headland was once resplendent with tall buildings but afterwards was turned into a level wasteland by the wickedness of those who lived there. There is a rock situated above the sea, round in shape like an egg, its northern face being larger, while to the south its sides slowly converge almost to a point. It rises so high that the favour of nature girds it with its own height and defends it by the rough surroundings. It is connected to the surrounding hills by a very wide valley. It seems to pride itself in its solitude so much that it disdains to have an equal among the other hills and it glories in a kind of pre-eminence accorded by its distinguished name. It is hard to climb and hard to reach, for to the north and south it is approached by narrow paths, not without fear of the precipice which plunges downward, while to the west it rises to a peak in a little hill and thence slopes eastwards to an uneven flat surface, where the oratory of the blessed virgin can be seen. It is so secluded, in the silence and quiet of spiritual striving, that the material eye can see nothing in it at whose sight the wanton heart might be deflected from the desire for heavenly things. It has two fountains as a comfort to its solitude and hermit life, a higher spring and a lower spring. For one furnishes perpetual moisture with its waters at the roots of the hill, the other at the top of the hill sometimes dries up in the summer heat and presents only a ditch to those seeking water. Many invalids and sick

Arnold, i. 229–61; ii. 333–62, at i. 245–7; also in Symeon, ed. Hinde, pp. 158–201, at pp. 170–2, whence it was borrowed by Symeon, *Libellus*, iii. 15, p. 186.

[20] *De miraculis*, xv, Symeon, ed. Arnold, ii. 350–2; Symeon, ed. Hinde, 183–5.

haustu salubri multi debiles et infirmi pristinam consecuti sunt salutem. Ex hiis beata uirgo et sue congregationis sacri bibere conciues, nec mirum si tot ora sanctorum et tam frequentes haurientium et abluencium attactus uirtutem impresserint aquis. In huius uastitate deserti utrum, spiritu sancto preuenta, religionis cultum prima instituerit an ab antecessorum studiis institutum repererit, incertum est. Nichil autem uerius quam quod ibi sobrie, iuste et pie conuersata sit et beatum celo spiritum, relicta terre sancti corporis gleba, intulerit.

Aliud autem monasterium feminarum ex dono fratris sui Oswyu secus ripam Dirwentionis fluminis construxit eique ex nomine suo Ebcestre, id est castrum Ebbe, uocabulum indidit.²¹ Quod quale quantumque in se olim fuerit dum staret ex ruinis suis manifeste nunc docet, mutato namque ut solet statu temporum, interfectis habitatoribus suis temporibus nefandorum principum Hyngwar et Vbbe, qui miserandas longe lateque in Anglos cedesᵃ perempto rege eorum Edmundo exercebant.²² Subuersum est et in plurimamᵇ nemorum uastitatem et animalium pascua, sicut hodie uidetur, commutatum.

In priori uero monasterio prefuit congregacioni uirorum et uirginum. Contigua utrique ibidem habebant habitacula. Qui diuino conducti federe, cum summa anime et spiritus iocunditate sub ea gaudebant uiuere, que se admirabili discrecionis gracia et puellis matrem exhortacionis instancia, et uiris patrem exhibuit animi constancia, propterea clamat ad uos de Seyr, nec clamoribus silencium imperat. Stupendum etenim est in uirginea teneritudine uirilem reperiri fortitudinem. Nos igitur uiri profectu uirtutis esse debuimus; succumbendo uiciis uiri nomen non habemus. Nos enim uel iuuenes barbatuli, qui quasi fortiores grauioris pugne cursum suscepimus in armorum, uictus scilicet durioris et uestitus, asperitate, molliciem querimus, uel senes prouecti, qui carnem senio

---

ᵃ corr. from scedes   ᵇ plurima MS; plurimam John of Tynemouth

---

²¹ Ebchester, Co. Durham, on R. Derwent. The name is otherwise first recorded in the Pipe Roll for 1230 (Allen Mawer, *The Place-names of Northumberland and Durham* (Cambridge, 1920), p. 71) and therefore later than the time of the composition of this text; it means 'Æbbe's *chester*' but Æbbe was a common Old English name and the connection with the saint may well be a late and retrospective deduction.
²² Ingvar and Ubba were traditionally regarded as the leaders of the Viking army that invaded England in 866, and Ingvar was blamed for the killing of Edmund king and martyr

people have obtained their former health though drinking their healing waters. The blessed virgin and the holy companions of her congregation drank from these fountains, and it is no wonder if the mouths of so many saints drinking so frequently and their touch when washing have impressed the waters with special power. Whether, with the Holy Spirit going before, she was the first to establish the religious life in this empty waste, or whether she found it already established by the efforts of predecessors, is uncertain. But nothing is truer than that in that place she lived soberly, justly, and piously, and rendered her blessed spirit to heaven, leaving the clay of her holy body to the earth.

Through the gift of her brother Oswiu she built another nunnery by the banks of the river Derwent and called it Ebchester, that is, Æbbe's castle, after her own name.[21] Its ruins teach us today quite clearly what it was once like and how great it once was when it was standing. For, times changed, as they do, and its inhabitants were killed in the time of the wicked chieftains Ingvar and Ubba, who committed appalling slaughter far and wide amongst the English after they had killed their king, Edmund.[22] Ebchester was destroyed and turned into forested wastelands and grazing places for animals, as it appears today.

In the earlier monastery she presided over a congregation of men and virgins. They lived in dwellings adjacent to each other. Assembled together in God's covenant, with the greatest happiness of soul and spirit they rejoiced to live under her, who, with wonderful powers of discretion, showed herself a mother to the girls in the tenacity of her exhortations and a father to the men in the constancy of her mind. On this account she calls to you from Seir, nor does she command silence to those who call out. It is amazing to find masculine strength in a virgin's tenderness. Therefore we should be men in the pursuit of virtue; by yielding to the vices we do not have the name of men. For the young and almost beardless men among us, who have, like the stronger warriors, sustained the course of a harder battle, with harsh weapons, namely rougher food and clothing, seek softness. We older men, who believe we have conquered the flesh

in 869: see the notes in ASC, ed. Plummer, ii. 84; *Chronicon Aethelweardi*, ed. A. Campbell (London, 1962), pp. 35–6; Abbo, *Passio sancti Eadmundi*, v, ed. Michael Winterbottom, *Three Lives of English Saints* (Toronto, 1972), p. 71, and *passim*. JW, s. a. 995 (1017), ii. 444–5, explicitly connects the abandonment of Lindisfarne by Cuthbert's community with the devastation wrought by Ingvar and Ubba; cf. also Reginald, *Libellus*, xv, p. 23.

triumphasse credimus, nobis ueniam*a* ex canicie, otium*b* ex annorum longitudine deberi censemus. Non sic, karissimi, non sic. Donec in cinere uiuit igniculus, non erit secus dormiens ab igne securus. Quoad uiuitur, bellum quod cum carne gerimus, uinci quidem potest, finiri non potest. Ecce uirgines feliciter mundum uincunt et beate de prelio redeunt, que post uictoriam uinci non norunt. Ecce de qua loquimur uirgo sapiens, uirgo prudens, cum adhuc delicata libere mundo uti potuisset, non consideracione deuicta originis, non teneritudine detenta etatis, non infirmitate depressa carnis, non fragilitate seducta sexus, sed contra cunctos hostis uiriliter dimicauit impetus, contempsit aulas regias, famulatu multo perstrepantes, thalamos ornatu uario et mollicie luxuriam redolentes, at, intra breuissime solitudinis angustias se concludens, hanc omnibus deliciis preposuit leticiam: uidere uirgines Deo dedicatas contra carnis illecebras spiritualem exercere militiam. Cum enim uirtutibus succresceret et fama operum et fragrancia sanctitatis eius se circumquaque diffunderet, confluxerunt ad eam multe nobiles, florentem mundum eius exemplo mentis despectu calcantes. Virgo etiam illa nobilis Etheldritha, Coludensis olim discipula, Heliensium nunc gloria, lecti regalis societate contempta, tante magistre rudimentis se subdidit, et tradente Wilfrido episcopo sanctimonialis habitus uelamen accepit.[23] Beatus quoque pater Cuthbertus, licet consortia |

fo. 165ᵛ mulierum uelut quamdam pestem ab infancia uitauerit, ad huius colloquia uenire et ad habitancium informationem aliquot dies manere consueuit.[24] Sed et sanctorum quorumlibet delectabatur frequencia quorum doctrinis et exemplis instrui posset congregatio sibi commissa. Videbatur locus ille quidam paradisus deliciarum ante subuersionem esse, cum habitantes in eo diuersarum uirtutum fructibus corda fouerent et, illecebra carnalium passionum edomita, in quandam impassibilitatis quietem in carne positi transirent.

Sed erat serpens in paradiso.[25] Quis enim in sinu sponsi securus ita dormiet contra quem Leuiathan non sibilet? Propterea ad nos clamat de Seir, ne susciteris eum.[26] Dormit enim sed non nobis. Dormit in

---

a corr. from uineam   *b corr. from* ostium

[23] Æthelthryth, wife of king Ecgfrith of Northumbria, foundress of Ely (d. 679). Her reception of the veil at the hands of Wilfrid and her entry into Coldingham are mentioned by Bede (*HE*, iv. 19, p. 392).
[24] A visit by Cuthbert to Coldingham is described in both the Anonymous *Vita S. Cuthberti* (ii. 3) and in Bede's *Vita S. Cuthberti* (c. x): Colgrave, *Two Lives*, pp. 80–2, 188–90. On his 'misogyny', see n. 47 below.

with old age, consider we should have indulgence because of our white hair and repose because of the length of our years. It is not so, dearest, it is not so. While the slightest spark is alive in the ashes, he who sleeps alongside will not be safe from the fire. As long as we live, the war which we fight against the flesh can be won but cannot be finished. Behold, virgins happily conquer the world and return blessed from the battle, who after victory do not know how to be beaten. Behold the wise virgin of whom we are speaking, the prudent virgin. Although hitherto she had been used to a soft life and had been able freely to enjoy the world, she was not defeated by consideration of her high origin, nor held back by the tenderness of her age, not cast down by the weakness of the flesh, nor led astray by the fragility of her sex, but she fought valiantly against all the attacks of the Enemy. She despised royal halls resounding with their crowds of servants, and beautifully adorned beds, redolent of soft luxury, and shut herself up within the narrow confines of her solitude, preferring before all pleasures this happiness: to see virgins dedicated to God fighting a spiritual fight against the enticements of the flesh. For as she grew in virtue and the fame of her deeds and the fragrance of her sanctity spread all around, many noblewomen flooded to her, following her example and disdainfully trampling the flourishing world beneath their feet. The noble virgin Æthelthryth, too, once a disciple at St Abb's Head, now the glory of Ely, spurned the royal bed, subjected herself to training under such a mistress, and received the nun's veil at the hands of bishop Wilfrid.[23] The blessed father Cuthbert too, although from childhood he had shunned the company of women like the plague, used to come to talk with her and spend some days instructing those who lived there.[24] The visits of any saints whose teaching and example could instruct the congregation committed to her were a source of delight. The place seemed to be a kind of paradise of delights before the fall, with its inhabitants fostering in their hearts the fruits of various virtues and, after conquering the enticements of bodily passion, passing into a kind of quiet impassability while still in the flesh.

But there was a serpent in paradise.[25] For who can sleep so soundly in their spouse's lap that Leviathan does not hiss against them? Wherefore he calls to you from Seir, do not arouse him.[26] For he sleeps but not for us. He sleeps in moist places and in the covert of

[25] Cf. Gen. 3: 1–5   [26] Cf. Job 3: 8.

locis humentibus in secreto calami.[27] Dormit in dormientibus. Vigilat contra uigilantes et circuit querens quos deuoret uigiles.[28] Sicut enim primorum parentum uiri et femine emulabatur gloriam, ita uirorum et feminarum aggressus est diripere continentiam. Ad antiqua ergo sue calliditatis arma conuersus est, primos, ut dixi, parentes per illicite commestionis excessum de regalibus sedibus in luteas mansiones deiecit; sodomitas, quorum regio antequam subuerteretur speciosa sicut paradisus effloruit, crapula et feda commixtione corporum, ignis et sulfuris pena dignos reddidit;[29] populum Domini Israel per Madianitas[30] et ueteranos iudices et pene exhaustos senes[31] sepius[a] delusit. Ita et hic. Habitacula enim, que ad oracionum, lectionum et alia spiritualis uite exercitia fuerant facta, in commessationum confabulacionum et aliarum illecebrarum conuertebantur cubilia.[32] Ipse tetendit archum et ex eorum pharetra, ipsi sibi erant iacula. Ipse parauit foueam et ipsi inciderunt in eam.[33] Virginum species imperiosa uiros allexit et inquieta uirorum cupido uirgines attraxit. Quociens uacabat texendis subtilioribus indumentis indulgebant, quibus aut se in contumeliam superni sponsi ad uicem sponsarum laicarum adornarent aut externorum uirorum amicitiam compararent.[34] A sui denique status rectitudine ad equinos motus, quibus non est intellectus, utrique incuruati sunt et quasi stelle de celo cadentes in ceno uoluptatum inuoluti sunt. Hec autem illusionum Ebbam latebat iniuria.

Libet enim paucis ad memoriam reducere que uenerabilis Beda de eorum latius disserit subuersione.[35] Anno igitur ab incarnacione Domini sexcentesimo octogesimo[36] *monasterium uirginum, quod Coludi urbem cognominant, per culpam incurie flammis assumptum est. Quod tamen a malicia habitancium in eo,*[37] *et precipue illorum qui maiores esse uidebantur, contigisse, omnes qui nouere facillime potuerunt aduertere. Sed non defuit puniendis admonicio diuine pietatis, qua,* si *correcti per ieiunia et fletus et preces* fuissent, *iram a se instar Niniuitarum*[38] *iusti iudicis auertissent. Erat* enim *in eodem monasterio uir* exsimie sanctitatis,

---

[a] species MS, corr. from septies (emendation suggested by Dr Greti Dinkova-Bruun)

[27] Job 40: 16. [28] Cf. 1 Pet. 5: 8.
[29] Gen. 13: 10–13, 18–19. [30] Num. 25.
[31] Presumably a reference to the *senes iudices* of the Susanna story: Dan. 13: 5 (Sus. 5).
[32] Cf. Bede, *HE* iv. 25, p. 424.
[33] Cf. Prov. 22: 14; Eccles. 10: 8.
[34] *HE* iv. 25, pp. 424–6.
[35] *HE* iv. 25, pp. 420–6 (words cited directly or very closely from Bede in the following passage are italicized).

the reed.[27] He sleeps for sleepers. He watches against those who watch and goes around seeking whom of the watchers he might devour.[28] For just as he envied the glory of our first parents, the man and the woman, so he has attacked in order to destroy the continence of men and women. Therefore he turned to the old weapons of his cunning, casting out our first parents from their royal seats, as I have said, and bringing them to dwellings of mud through the sin of eating what was illicit; he made the Sodomites, whose beautiful land flourished like paradise before it was overthrown, deserving of the penalty of fire and sulphur because of their drunkenness and foul forms of intercourse;[29] he often deluded Israel, the people of the Lord, through the Midianites[30] and elderly judges and almost exhausted old men.[31] So also in this case. For he turned their dwellings, which had been constructed for prayer, reading, and other spiritual exercises, into dens of feasting, gossip, and other seductions.[32] He charged his bow from a quiver of them, for they were arrows for him. He prepared a pit and they fell into it.[33] The irresistible beauty of the maidens attracted the men, and the restless desire of the men drew the maidens. Whenever they had spare time, they indulged in weaving fine garments, with which they might adorn themselves as if they were lay brides, in contempt of their heavenly spouse, or with which they might procure the love of men outside the monastery.[34] At length both sexes declined from the uprightness of their position to movements just like those of horses in which there is no understanding, becoming enmired in the mud of pleasure like stars falling from the sky. This outrage of delusions, however, lay hidden from Æbbe.

It is right to bring to mind briefly what the Venerable Bede wrote at greater length about their fall.[35] In the year of the Lord 680,[36] *the monastery of virgins, which they call St Abb's Head, was consumed by flames because of carelessness. All who knew could easily perceive that this had happened because of the wickedness of its inhabitants,*[37] *and especially of those who seemed more prominent. But the divine goodness did not fail to give those who were about to be punished a warning, by which, if they had corrected themselves through fasting and weeping and prayers, they would have turned away from themselves the wrath of the just judge, just like the people of Nineveh.*[38] For *there was in that monastery a man* of

[36] For the dating, see the Introduction, p. xiv.
[37] Cf. Ps. 106 (107): 34.
[38] Jonah 3.

nomine *Adamnanus, de* nacione *Scottorum* oriundus.[39] Hic *in adoles-*
cencia sceleris aliquid commiserat quod, si sibi reconciliacio sacerdocis
et penitencie non subueniret remedium, eternis cruciatibus grauius a
Deo nouit *puniendum.* Quemdam ergo magne religionis presbiterum
consuluit et si quid rursum *salutis* haberet humiliter expeciit,
'*Adolescencior sum etate*', inquiens, '*et uegetus corpore et quicquid mihi
imposueris* libenter *feram, dummodo in die Domini saluus fiam, si totam
noctem stando in precibus peragere, si integram septimanam iubeas
abstinendo transigere.*' Presbiter respondit, '*Multum est, sed biduanum
aut triduanum satis est obseruare ieiunium. Hoc facito donec redeam et
quamdiu huic penitencie insistere* et quid deinceps agere debeas *plenius
ostendam.*' *Abiit igitur sacerdos, descripta penitencie* forma, et, *secedens
in Hyberniam unde originem duxit,* eodem anno humanis rebus
excessit. Quod cum accepisset, Adamnanus nec secretum suum
fo. 166ʳ alteri committere uoluisset, | ipse sibi sacerdos factus omni tempore
quoad uixit nichil *cibi uel potus* in ebdomada iuxta *descriptum sibi
penitencie* modum nisi *in die dominica et quinta sabbati percepit,* hoc ex
propria uoluntate adiuncto, quod *noctes integras sepe uigilando
transegit. Et quod causa diuini timoris semel ob reatum ceperat, iam
causa diuini amoris delectatus* semper *agebat* et quod *ex necessitate
emendande prauitatis obuenerat, in uoluntarie consuetudinis* usum
*conuertebat. Quod dum multo tempore sedulus exequeretur, contigit eum
die quodam de monasterio longius egressum, comitante secum uno de
fratribus, peracto itinere redire. Qui cum monasterio propinquarent et
edificia illius sublimiter erecta conspicerent, solutus est in lacrimas uir Dei
et tristiciam cordis uultu indice prodebat. Quod intuens comes, quid faceret
inquisiuit. At ille, 'Cuncta', inquid, 'hec que cernis edificia publica uel
priuata in proximo est ut ignis absumens in cinerem conuertat.' Quod ille
audiens mox ut monasterium intrauere matri congregacionis curauit
indicare. At illa de tali merito turbata presagio, uocauit ad se uirum et
diligencius unde hoc nosset inquirebat. Qui ait, 'Nuper occupatus noctu
uigiliis et psalmis, uidi astantem mihi subito quemdam incogniti uultus,
cuius presencia cum essem exterritus, dixit mihi ne timerem et quasi
familiari me uoce alloquens, "Bene facis", inquid, "qui tempore nocturne
quietis non sompni indulgere, sed uigiliis et orationibus maluisti insistere.
Tibi namque et multis aliis opus est peccata sua bonis operibus redimere et*

---

[39] Although a contemporary and namesake, not the famous abbot of Iona.

outstanding sanctity, *Adomnán* by name, *born from the Irish nation.*[39] *As a young man he had committed some crime which* he knew would be *punished* by God with heavy and eternal torments unless reconciliation through a priest and the remedy of penance came to his aid. So he consulted a priest of great faith and asked humbly if he yet had any hope of *salvation. 'I am young and strong of body,' he said, 'and I will* willingly *bear whatever you impose upon me, if only I may be saved in the day of the Lord: if you command me to spend the whole night standing in prayer, or to pass the whole week fasting.'* The priest replied, *'That is a great deal, but it is enough to observe a two-day or three-day fast. Do this until I return and then I will show you more fully how long to maintain this penance* and what you should do thereafter.' *So the priest went away after prescribing* the form of *his penance and withdrew to Ireland, which was his place of origin,* where, in that same year, he departed from this world. When he had learned this, Adomnán had not wished to impart his secret to another, and, he himself now becoming a priest, for the whole time that he lived *took no food or drink* during the week, according to *the* mode *of penance prescribed for him,* except *on Sunday and Thursday,* adding this from his own will, that *he often passed whole nights in vigils. What he had once begun out of fear of God and on account of his guilt, he now did* constantly *out of love of God and from delight,* and what *had originated from the necessity of correcting wickedness he converted* into a voluntary and habitual *practice. When he had been following this way of life continuously for a long time, it happened one day that he went far from the monastery, accompanied by one of the brethren, and returned when the journey had been completed. As they drew near to the monastery and saw its buildings raised on high, the man of God dissolved in tears and betrayed the sadness of his heart by the indications on his face. His companion saw this and asked what he was doing. 'All these buildings that you see,' he said, 'public and private, will soon be turned to ash by consuming fire.' As soon as they entered the monastery, he took care to inform the mother of the community of what he had heard. She was naturally troubled by such a prophecy, called the man to her and inquired with great diligence how he knew this. He said, 'Recently, when I was keeping vigil and reciting psalms at night, I suddenly saw standing by me someone whose face I did not recognize and whose presence terrified me. He told me not to be afraid and spoke to me in a familiar tone, saying, "You do well, preferring to devote yourself to vigils and prayers in the period of nocturnal quiet rather than to indulge in sleep. For you and many others need to redeem your sins with good works*

cum cessatum est a laboribus rerum temporalium tunc pro appetitu eternorum bonorum liberius laborare. Set hoc tamen paucissimi faciunt. Siquidem totum hoc monasterium perlustrans, singulorum casas ac lectos inspexi et neminem preter te erga sanitatem anime sue occupatum repperi sed omnes prorsus et uiri et femine aut sompno torpent inherti aut uigilant ad lapsum *peccati. Vnde huic loco et habitatoribus eius grauis de celo uindicta flammis seuientibus preparata^a est." ' Dixit autem abbatissa, 'Et quare non cicius hoc compertum mihi reuelare uoluisti?' Qui respondit, 'Timui propter reuerenciam tuam ne forte nimium turbaberis et tamen hanc consolacionem habes, quod in diebus tuis hec plaga non superueniet.*[40] *Qua diuulgata uisione, aliquantulum loci accole paucis diebus timere et, intermissis facinoribus, seipsos ceperunt castigare.* Propter hoc clamat ad nos ille de Seir. Dicit enim Deus Abrahe, 'Non delebo omnem locum propter iustos decem'.[41] Ecce propter unius meritum uniuersitatis protelatur exitium.^b Eidem quoque patri que futura erat in Sodomis diuina seueritas ostendit et beatum Benedictum de monasteriorum suorum subuersione premonuit.[42] Pensandum itaque est cuius ista meriti fuerat, quam ad ipsius consolacionem de loci sui desolacione per seruum suum Dominus dignatus est edocere. Sed ad equalitatem beati Loth creditur peruenisse. Eo namque de Sodomis egresso, quos relinquerat sulphureus ignis absumpsit. Ita ista corpore exuta et ad Segor[43] que paruula est,[44] id est regnum celeste quod paruulorum est,[45] translata, *ad pristinas sordes* reuersos *prefate ulcionis* clades inuoluit. Conuersus est exinde locus ille in heremi solitudinem et qui remanserant corde soluti per loca diuersa sunt metu compellente dispersi et quod eis contigit ad ruinam, multis ad castigationem profuit et medelam. Clamat ergo ad nos de Seir. Liquet namque ex hiis quam uitanda sit bonarum etiam cohabitacio mulierum. Perpendite quanta seruis suis prelia malignus spiritus earum familiaritate intulerit, quot urbes incenderit, quot monasteria subuerterit, quot demum corda sublimia et ad celum per contemplacionis graciam erecta, solo conspectu earum, tamquam conspectu reguli, ad profundum iniquitatis inclinauerit.

Beatus pater Cuthbertus tunc in solitudine Farnensi adhuc in

---

^a preperata *MS*   ^b excicium *MS*

[40] The dating of the fire to 680 and Æbbe's death to 683 is inconsistent with this statement.
[41] Gen. 18: 32.
[42] Gregory I, *Dialogi*, ii. 17 (*Sources chrétiennes*, cclx. 192).
[43] The city where Lot took refuge: Gen. 19: 22–3.

and when the time for the work of the world is over, then to work more
freely from desire for eternal goods. But very few do so. Indeed, wandering
through this whole monastery, I have inspected the rooms and beds of
everyone here and found nobody except you busy with the health of their
soul. Every single one of them, male and female, is either drowsing in
sluggish sleep or awake in order to sin. Hence heaven has prepared the
severe punishment of raging flames for this place and its inhabitants."'
The abbess said, 'And why did you not wish to reveal this information to
me sooner?' He replied, 'I was afraid for your reverence, lest you perhaps
be greatly disturbed. But you have this consolation, that this disaster will
not occur in your time.[40] *After the vision had been made known, the*
inhabitants of the place began to be somewhat afraid for a little while and,
giving up their sins, they punished themselves. On account of this he of
Seir calls to us. For the God of Abraham says, 'I will not destroy the
whole place for ten just men.'[41] Behold, for the merit of one, the
destruction of them all is delayed. The divine severity showed to that
same patriarch what was to befall the inhabitants of Sodom and
forewarned St Benedict of the downfall of his monasteries.[42] Think
what her merit was, whom, for her consolation, the Lord deigned to
inform through His servant of the desolation of her place. One can
believe that she was the equal of the blessed Lot. For after he came
out of Sodom, the sulphurous fire consumed those whom he had left
behind. So, when she left the body behind and was conveyed to
Segor,[43] which is 'little',[44] for the kingdom of heaven belongs to the
little ones,[45] they returned *to their original filth* and the destruction of
the *vengeance we have mentioned* overwhelmed them. Thereafter that
place was turned into an empty wilderness and those who had
remained pure at heart were driven by fear to disperse to many
different places. What had befallen them to their ruin was of profit to
many as a chastisement and a remedy. Therefore he calls to us from
Seir. For it is clear from this how important it to avoid living with
women, even good women. Consider how great are the battles that
the evil spirit inflicts on his servants through familiarity with them,
how many towns he burns, how many monasteries he destroys, how
many lofty hearts, raised to heaven through the grace of contempla-
tion, he turns into the depths of iniquity simply by their glance, as if
by the glance of a kinglet.

At that time the holy father Cuthbert was still dwelling in the body

[44] Jerome, *Liber interpretationis Hebraicorum nominum* (*CCSL* lxxii. 72).
[45] Matt. 18: 3–4; 19: 14; Mark 10: 14–15.

fo. 166ᵛ corpore | degebat.[46] Qui, accepto quanta facta fuit in domo Domini
per feminas confusio, creditur, etsi non legitur, celebre condidisse
decretum, lege perpetua seruis suis obseruandum, quo non solum eis
quocumque sui sancti corporis presencia fuerit consortia feminarum
prohibuit, uerum etiam earum introitus et accessus et aspectus
abscidit.[47] Clamat adhuc ad nos de Seir ut horum, de quibus
supradictum est, miserabilem aduertentes interitum, pessime conuersacionis uitemus exemplum. Et isti uiri erant pilosi et hispidi,[48]
uiri certe de Seir, uiri sanguinum et peccatorum. Clamat et apostolus
ad nos et ipse aliquando de Seir, persecutor scilicet et blasphemus,
'qui stat uideat ne cadat'.[49] Isti in culmine religionis steterunt et
celum bonorum operum oppinione pulsare uidebantur sed, fallente
diabolo, per immundiciam carnis et habundanciam iniquitatis cor-
ruerunt et opprobrium sempiternum nomina sua in terris suis
relinquerunt. Gulam igitur ieiunia superent, luxuriam uigilie edo-
ment, linguam silencia temperent, uisum pudor et mundi contemptus
humilient, carnem parcitas edomet, animum constancia roboret,
motus omnes et affectus mater caritas ordinet et conformet. Hec a
summo bono, sine quo nichil boni, petenda sunt, ab ipso patre
luminum, cuius est omne datum optimum et omne donum perfec-
tum. Clamat et nunc ad nos de Seir, 'Custos, quid de nocte, custos
quid de nocte?'[50] Dicit custos, 'Nisi Dominus custodierit ciuitatem
nostram, frustra uigilat qui custodit eam. Frustra domum edificabit,
nisi Dominus coedificauerit.'[51] Sed quid nostris meritis edificando et
uigilando non ualemus, huius matris nostre patrocinio consequi nos
posse credamus.

[3. Translation]

Transiit beata Ebba temporibus Egfridi regis, memoratum patrem
quatuor annis precurrens ad regnum.[52] Cuius quidem mausoleum
apud nos est. Et id suum profecto esse non tam ex traditione
seniorum quam frequencia didicimus uirtutum et beneficio consola-
tionum. Vtrum uero aliquas sacri corporis reliquias contineret an

---

[46] Farne Island, Northumberland.

[47] The association of Cuthbert's 'misogyny' with the destruction of Coldingham is made
earlier in Symeon, Libellus, ii. 7, pp. 104–8; see Victoria Tudor, 'The misogyny of St
Cuthbert', Archaeologia Aeliana, 5th ser., xii (1984), 157–67; ead., 'The cult of St Cuthbert
in the twelfth century: the evidence of Reginald of Durham', St Cuthbert, His Cult and
Community to A.D. 1200, ed. Gerald Bonner et al. (Woodbridge, 1989), pp. 447–67, at
456–8.   [48] Gen. 25: 25.   [49] Cf. 1 Cor. 10: 12.

at the hermitage of Farne.[46] Learning of what great confusion had
arisen in the house of the Lord through women, he enacted the
famous decree (as we believe, even though it is not recorded in
writing), to be observed as a perpetual law by his servants, according
to which not only was the company of women forbidden to them
wherever his holy body was present but even the entry, access, and
sight of women were prohibited.[47] He calls to us from Seir that we
should attend to the miserable destruction of those mentioned above
and avoid the example of wicked living. And these men were hairy
and shaggy,[48] truly men of Seir, men of blood and sin. The Apostle
also calls to us and he sometime of Seir, namely a persecutor and
blasphemer, 'let him that stands take heed lest he fall'.[49] These stood
at the height of the religious life and seemed to knock at heaven's door
in their reputation for good works but, tricked by the devil, they fell
through the foulness of the flesh and the abundance of iniquity and
their names left a note of perpetual disgrace in their lands. Therefore
let fasting overcome gluttony, let vigils tame lust, let silence restrain
the tongue, let modesty and contempt for the world humble the
eyesight, let deprivation subjugate the flesh, let constancy strengthen
the mind, let mother charity order and shape all movements and
feelings. These things are to be sought from the highest good,
without whom there is no good thing, from the very father of light,
whose every grant is wonderful and whose every gift is perfect. He
calls now to us from Seir, 'Watchmen, what of the night, watchmen,
what of the night?'[50] 'Unless the Lord watches over our city, the
watchmen stand guard in vain. He builds a house in vain unless the
Lord builds too.'[51] But what we are unable to build and guard
through our own merits, let us believe we can attain through the
patronage of this our mother.

[3. Translation]

St Æbbe passed away in the time of King Ecgfrith, preceding the
father already mentioned to the kingdom by four years.[52] Her tomb is
in our midst. We have learned that it is indeed hers not so much from
the tradition of our elders as from the frequency of miracles and the
gift of aid. But ancient tradition had left no certain information for

---

[50] Isa. 21: 11.   [51] Cf. Ps. 126 (127): 1.
[52] Cuthbert died in 687 and hence this statement implies a date for Æbbe's death of
683; Ecgfrith reigned 670–85.

penitus illius depositi thesauro careret, nichil certum posteris assertio
relinquerat uetustatis. Ossa siquidem eius inde sublata et alias
translata et ibidem preter peplum nichil contineri affirmabant. In
urbe quoque Coludi a pastoribus post multa temporum curricula
repertum. Qui cum illud manibus leuassent et baculis—non enim alia
eis aderant instrumenta—aperire satagerent, iuxta exemplum Osam
qui archam Dei indigne tetigit et indignacione diuina correptus
interiit,[53] repentina sunt cecitate percussi et insanis motibus diucius
agitati. Quo comperto, loci illius incole illud in ecclesiam Sancte
Marie de Coldingham tulerunt et ad meridianam partem altaris
reuerenter deposuerunt. Ferebant quoque aliqui illud ligneum esse
et quendam fratrem, qui id a parte pedum confregerat, si quid in ea
contineretur immissa manu attemptasse et lintheum ibi et ossa minuta
sensisse, sed non impune, quia subito membrorum dolore correptus
infra paucos dies ad extrema deductus est. Quo fratres agnito, lapide
illud undique et desuper diligenter concluserunt, ne si quis denuo
simile negocium attemptaret, consimilem sue presumpcionis iram
incurreret. Et hec quidem quasi omnibus manifesta et ueritati
consentanea in libello maiores redegerant.

Cum igitur ex diuersis opinionibus nulla certitudinis sentencia
oriri sed potius dubietatis perplexitas soleat foueri, placuit fratribus
uenerandum sarcofagum aperire et quod ibi inuenissent ad omnium
noticiam transferre. Sed ne id auderent et timor eis ex peccatorum
consciencia et memorati fratris et pastorum quam ex presumpcione
meruerant repellebat offensa. Nullus ad id temporis ex metu
similium ad apercionem manum audebat apponere nec circa
eundem locum quippiam operis sine sui status periculo presump-
sisse. Suadebant ergo quidam, saluti fratrum pie sed trepide
consulentes, | quatinus sarcophagum ita intactum in loco relinque-
rent et, muro usque ad pauimentum erecto, admota deforis humo,
tabulam lapideam quasi super os putei desuper componerent, que et
ea que subter erant operiret et tumbe similitudinem artuato opere
protenderet.[a] Cumque inter utrumque et timorem accedendi et
amorem inspiciendi animo suspensi hererent,[b] dies statuerent, nec
propositum accelerarent. Apparuit uenerabilis abbatissa cuidam

fo. 167[r]

---

    [a] corr. from pertenderet   [b] corr. from haberent

[53] 2 Kgs. (2 Sam.) 6: 6–7; 1 Chr. 13: 9–10

posterity as to whether it contains any relics of the holy body or completely lacks that treasured deposit. They affirmed that her bones had been removed from there and taken elsewhere and that it contained nothing except her veil. The tomb was found on St Abb's Head after a long passage of time by some shepherds. When they had lifted it up with their hands and were trying to open it with their crooks—for they had no other tools—they were struck by sudden blindness and for a long time agitated with insane movements, just like Uzzah who touched the Ark of God unworthily and died struck down by divine anger.[53] When they learned this, the inhabitants of the place brought it into the church of St Mary of Coldingham and deposited it reverently on the south side of the altar. Some also said that it was wooden and that one of the brethren, who had broken it at the foot, put his hand in to see if it contained anything and felt some linen there and small bones, but not without punishment, for he was struck by sudden pain in his limbs and met his end within a few days. When the brethren learned this, they enclosed it carefully in stone, on every side and above, lest anybody trying a similar thing again should incur similar anger for his presumption. Our elders put all this, as apparent to everyone and consonant with the truth, into a little book.

Because differences of opinion do not give rise to a definite view of a matter but tend instead to foster doubt and uncertainty, the brethren wished to open the venerable coffin and bring what they found there to the notice of everyone. But they were deterred from daring to do it both by the fear that sprang from their own consciousness of sin and because of the injuries that the monk and the shepherds whom we have mentioned had earned for their presumption. Nobody at that time dared to lay his hand to opening it, out of fear of something similar happening, nor did they believe they could undertake any kind of work around the spot without danger to their well-being. So some of the brethren, being mindful of their safety in a way both devout and anxious, recommended that they should leave the coffin intact where it was and, raising a wall all the way to the pavement and bringing earth from outside, they should place a stone slab over it, as if over the mouth of a well, and this would both cover what was underneath and present the likeness of a vaulted tomb. While they were stuck in their minds between the fear of approaching and the desire to look in, they named a day but did not hasten their plan. A venerable abbess appeared to a certain older

ueterano qui adhuc superest, qui etiam quod refero sciscitantibus referre cum lacrimis consueuit, imperiose inungens quatinus propositum noui operis constanter admoneret, ne ipsam leuare et transferre titubaret, sed omnem deponeret metum, siquidem id sine dubio haberet acceptum.

Concepta igitur ex diuina reuelacione fiducia, quidam frater, adhibito sibi eiusdem operis proposito, accessit nec sine tremore cordis et corporis, qui ei*^a* inerat ex consciencia peccati et metu supplicii. Deiectisque qui*^b* desuper coartabant siue contegebant et circumquaque concluserant lapidibus, inuenerunt saxum sepulcri pergrande pondere et longitudine mirandum eiusdemque longitudinis et latitudinis lapide coopertum studio artificis diligenter coaptatum et ad instar cratere insertum. Quo instrumentis ferralibus tandem leuato, pro sui mole confractum est. Et cum particula quedam multorum inde manibus fuisset ablata, apparuit subterius uelut croceo colore respersa. Et introspicientes uiderunt puluerem ad similitudinem corporis humani extentum et manibus hucusque intemptatum, carbones quoque paucos superpositos in humacione eius, ut quidam auctumant de turribulo eiectos. Nulla illic adhuc ossa apparebant. Iniectis igitur manibus forma illa cum fauilla decidit. Pulueremque illum perscrutantes, ossa deorsum multa reppererunt, quorum quedam inter manus tractancium in cinerem ex diutine corrupcionis uetustate resoluta sunt, quedam uix sue integritatis graciam reseruarunt, puluerem autem illum, qui suum hucusque cum frigiditate seruauerat humorem, in facie solis siccantes et cribrantes et ossa colligentes, in theca noua recondebant et digne ueneracionis gracia super altare collocabant partemque pulueris quem cribrum reliquerat in sarcophago reposuerunt. De quo fratres non nulla pulsabat sollicitudo. Quidam enim, quia minime pre ponderis magnitudine moueri posse credebant, illic decernebant sepeliri, alii*^c* uero alibi in ecclesia quo illud deuocio fidelium uenerari posset et amplecti, saniori consilio iudicabant quantacumque uirium adhibito conamine transferri; quod et factum est. Sed nec illud pretereo, quod cum de loci sui angustia et tenebris traheretur in lucem et medio itinere uix sui integritate seruata confractionis detrimentum pateretur, apparuit in fundo per girum, quasi grossioris similitudo funiculi, quoddam pinguedinis recentissime uestigium, que profecto de resolucione sacri corporis effluxit et in longum et latum stature prebebat indicium.

^a eis *MS*   ^b que *MS*   ^c aliis *MS*

monk, who is still alive, and who also has been accustomed to tell with tears what I am relating to those who inquire, and she imperiously commanded him constantly to encourage the planned new work and not to hesitate to elevate and translate her, but to put aside all fear, since without a doubt she was in favour of it.

Given confidence by this divine revelation, the brother to whom this work was assigned drew near, not without trembling of the heart and the body, which beset him from his consciousness of sin and the fear of punishment. When they had taken down the stones that pressed together above or covered and enclosed the coffin on every side, they found the stone of the tomb, of immense weight and astounding length, covered by a stone of the same length and breadth, carefully fitted by the efforts of the mason and inserted like a bowl. Once this had eventually been raised by iron bars, it broke from its own weight. When a small part had been removed from it by the hands of many, underneath it appeared as if it was sprinkled with a yellow colour. Looking inside, they saw dust in the shape of a human body and untouched until now by human hands, also a few coals on top of her burial, incense from thuribles in the opinion of some. No bones appeared there as yet. When they put their hands in, the shape of dust dissolved. They searched through the dust and found many bones underneath, some of which turned to dust from age and decay in the hands of those touching them, some of which were barely preserved complete. They dried the dust, which had been kept moist until now because of the cold, in the sunshine and sieved it, and collected the bones together, then arranged them all in a new shrine which they placed on the altar where it could be revered worthily. They replaced in the tomb that part of the dust which the sieve had left. The brethren were very concerned about the tomb, for some, who believed it could not be moved on account of its weight, considered that it should be buried where it was, but others, of wiser counsel, judged that, whatever effort was required, it should be transferred to another location in the church, where the devotion of the faithful could revere and embrace it. This was done. But I must not omit to say that, as it was dragged from its narrow corner and out of the shadows into the light and, in the middle of its course, looked as if it could scarcely be kept intact and was about to shatter, because of the motion there appeared in the bottom the trace of very fresh fat, looking like a thick rope, which indubitably flowed from the dissolution of the holy body and gave an indication of its height and width.

Si quis igitur prefatas reliquias ossuum et pulueris beate uirginis fuisse dubitat, reuelacionem de ipsius subleuacione factam recogitet. Si ossa grandiora inde sublata contendit, puluerem intactum ad mentem reducat. Si tumbam illius esse denegat, uirtutes que ibidem meritis eius facte sunt perpendat. Alii igitur sacras eius reliquias sibi blandiantur—et habere gaudeant et uenerari letentur;[54] nos earum immunes non esse gaudeamus et manibus tractasse gratulemur, quos sua iugiter constat protectione muniri et in omnibus tribulacionibus nostris uberibus sue consolacionis lactari. Clamat ergo de Seir: ut dum huius uirginis cineres scrutamur, de nostre quoque condicionis fragilitate meditemur. Quod enim in ea factum uidemus, in nobis futurum non dubitemus. Nec illam debitum carnis soluisse uilescat, quam in celestibus uiuere uirtutum gloria clamat. Presens etiam semper esse credenda est ubi eius manifesta sunt beneficia et fo. 167ᵛ signorum florent insignia, cuius pio interuentu Dominus | culpas nostras abluat et iram sue indignacionis a nobis protinus auertat et que sunt bona in nobis enutriat ac pietatis studio que sunt nutrita custodiat.

Fuit uir magne simplicitatis et innocencie nomine Henricus, omnibus in uilla de Coldingham notissimus, qui ex rerum euentu homo sancte Ebbe a uulgo dictum est. Pauperem cum uxore et liberis uitam duxit. Hanc autem sibi religionis formam constituit, quod omni tempore peregrinacionis sue in corpore aut nudis pedibus aut calciatus nudis plantis incederet. Cumque appropinquerent dies eius ut moreretur,[55] precepit uxori sue ne corpus eius in sindone, sicut mos est secularibus, obuolueret sed cum cuculla sua laica et calciamentis sepeliret, quatinus in quali habitu Deo uiuens seruierat, in tali quoque mortuum telluris gremium exciperet. Hic cum adhuc iunior mundum cum flore teneret, mulierem quendam adamauit, cuius post potitos aliquamdiu amplexus consortium fastidiens, ad alterius amorem animum contulit. Quo illa comperto, potum pestiferum miscuit et uiro dedit, qui ex eo protinus sensus officium funditus perdidit. Conuersus itaque in rabiem et loris constrictus ad memoriam sancti Michaelis,[56] que ibidem ab incolis deuota ueneracione recolitur, amicorum manibus ducitur ibique meritis beati archangeli et eorum

---

[54] See the Introduction for Durham's claim to have Æbbe's relics.

[55] Cf. 3 Kgs. (1 Kgs.) 2: 1.

[56] Celebration of the 'dedication of the altar of St Michael in Coldingham' on 29 April is recorded in the Kalendar of the late-13th-cent. Coldingham Breviary, BL, Harley 4664, fo. 127ᵛ; Francis Wormald (ed.), *English Benedictine Kalendars after A.D. 1100* (2 vols., Henry Bradshaw Soc. lxxvii, lxxxi, 1939–46), i. 171.

So, if anyone doubts that these remains of bones and dust are those of the blessed virgin, let him consider the revelation that occurred about her translation. If he contends that the larger bones have been taken away, let him bring to mind the intact dust. If he denies that it is her tomb, let him think over the miracles that have been performed there through her merits. Others may flatter themselves that they have her holy relics—let them rejoice to have them and be happy to venerate them;[54] let us rejoice that we are not lacking in them and celebrate having touched them with our hands, we who, it is certain, are defended continually by her protection and in all our troubles fed with the milk of her consoling breasts. So he calls from Seir, so that while we examine the ashes of this virgin, we may meditate on the weakness of our condition. For what we see has become of her, we should not doubt will become of us in the future. Nor does paying the debt of the flesh make her vile, when the glory of her miracles calls out that she is alive in heaven. We should believe that she is always present where her benefits are manifest and the glory of her miracles flourishes. By her kindly intervention may the Lord wash away our faults, turn aside the wrath of His indignation from us, nourish what is good in us and guard by the zeal of His kindness what is nourished.

There was a man of great simplicity and innocence called Henry, well known to everyone in the town of Coldingham, who, because of what subsequently happened, the common people came to call 'the man of St Æbbe'. He lived a poor life with his wife and children. He had adopted the following religious practice, that for the whole time of his pilgrimage in the body, he would go either barefoot or shod in shoes without soles. When the days came that he should die,[55] he commanded his wife that his body should not be wound in a muslin shroud, as is the custom for lay people, but that he should be buried in his layman's hood and shoes, so that the bosom of the earth should receive his dead body in the same clothes in which he had served God while alive. While he was still young and the world and its flower were his, he loved a woman, but, after he had enjoyed her embraces for some time, he grew tired of her and fell in love with another. When she learned of this, she concocted a deadly potion and gave it to the man, who as a result went completely out of his senses and became raving mad. He was bound with thongs and led by his friends to St Michael's shrine,[56] which is venerated there with great devotion by the inhabitants, and there, by the merits of the blessed archangel

fidei interuentu sibi et suis mente integra restitutus est. In oculis tamen attonitis et simplicitate locucionis infirmitatis preterite uestigium aliquod ei semper ab intuentibus putabatur inesse.

Ille ergo quodam tempore in Vrbe Coludi per uisum constitutus, uidit duos senes, amictu candido, uultu splendido et canicie uenerabiles, montem circuire et querentis siue explorantis similitudinem exhibentes, nunc hic, nunc illic adinuicem conferendo subsistere. At ipse appropinquans accessit et de loci solitudine conqueri ex eorum sermonibus agnouit. Et illi conuersi ad eum, 'Quid hic', aiunt, 'agis, Henrice? En deserti huius uastitatem circuimus nec locum diuinis misteriis aptum in eo repperimus. Tu autem oratorium nobis in honorem Domini et sancte uirginis Ebbe construe, ubi sacra officia celebrentur quociens huc nos uel aliquos fideles contigerit aduenire.' Quo scementarie artis impericiam et sue penuriam tenuitatis pretendente, ipsi magis imperando instabant et adiutorium debitamque a Deo remuneracionem promittebant. Noluit interrogare qui essent aut unde uenissent. Pauor enim circumdederat illum. Mane autem facto uisionis ordinem nonnullis exposuit, qui eum mente excedere dicebant et pro deliramento id habentes irridebant.

Elapsis interea aliquot diebus, in sompnis ei uirgo uenerabilis astitit et dudum sibi diuinitus imperata prosequi iussit. Cumque hac semel et secundo et sepius per uisum admoneret et ille ex aliorum incredulitate et duricia cordis negligeret, adierit aliquando dicens, 'nisi hoc feceris, condignam tui contemptus ulcionem experieris'. Quod et factum est. Cum enim de laborum suorum fructu felicius uitam duceret et in rure excolendo uberius proficeret, cepit repente opum illarum copia inopescere, laboribus terra minus solito respondere, adeo quod noti eius et uicini inde stuporem haberent, diuinum tamen flagellum esse non intelligerent. Quia uero sola uexacio intellectum dat auditui,[57] quid erga se gereretur aduertit, oratorium construxit uili quidem materia conditum sed celesti uirtute, sicut postea signorum frequencia claruit, preditum. Rudis enim artifex pro scemento lutum habebat et pro lapidibus sectis saxa dura et aspera, que solo uetustas obruerat et destruentium olim manus relinquerat.

---

[57] Isa. 28: 19.

and through the agency of their faith, he was restored completely sane to himself and his family. However, those who saw him always thought there was some trace of his former illness in his startled eyes and simple talk.

One time, therefore, he was placed on St Abb's Head in a vision and saw two venerable old men in white cloaks with bright faces and white hair, who were going around the hilltop and seemed to be looking for or seeking something, stopping now here, now there, and conferring with each other. He approached them and realized from their conversation that they were complaining about the desolateness of the place. They turned to him and said, 'What are you doing here, Henry? We have gone around the whole of this vast wilderness and have not found any place suitable for the divine mysteries here. But you construct an oratory for us, in honour of the Lord and of the holy virgin Æbbe, where the holy office may be celebrated whenever we or other faithful folk happen to come here.' When he objected that he was ignorant of the mason's art and lacking in means, they insisted all the more on their command and promised help and a due reward from God. He was unwilling to ask who they were or whence they had come, for fear had encompassed him. But in the morning he recounted the course of the vision to many people, who said he had gone out of his mind and mocked him, regarding it as an absurdity.

Some days later a venerable virgin was present to him in his sleep and ordered him to carry out the things that had been divinely commanded him previously. When she had admonished him in this way in a vision once and a second time and several times, and he had neglected it because of the disbelief and hard-heartedness of others, she came to him one time saying, 'Unless you do it, you will experience a suitable punishment for your disregard.' So it happened. For while he had lived a happy life from the fruits of his labours and won rich yields from cultivating the land, suddenly that abundance of means began to turn to want and the land failed to respond to his labours in the usual way, so that his acquaintances and neighbours were amazed by it, not understanding that it was an affliction from God. But since vexation alone makes you understand what you hear,[57] he paid attention to what was happening to him and built an oratory, constructed with humble materials but, as the frequency of miracles afterwards made clear, endowed with heavenly power. For the unskilled craftsman had mud for mortar and, instead of shaped stones, hard, rough rocks that antiquity had covered with soil and the hand of destroyers had left

Aquam in doliolo carro inposito a radice montis per deuexi montis latus itinere scopuloso deferebat, tanteque magnitudinis lapides muro qui iam humeris alcior imminebat solus leuabat, quod, licet uerbis eius credendum non esset, ex hoc incredulus et irrisor quilibet dictis fidem etiam nolens habere potuisset. Cumque ad dominos suos seruili condicione teneretur | astrictus, neque deinceps ad consuetas operaciones compelli nec uexacionibus nec minis ab incepto opere poterat auelli.

Non nulli quoque ex fratribus operantis sollicitudinem deridebant, aliqui uero quorum mens sanior fuerat uenerabantur et laudabant. Crebrescentibus autem ibi miraculis et cateruatim ruentibus populis, transiit infidelitas in fidem, contemptus in reuerenciam, irrisio in laudem, ignorancia in gloriam. Nouumque fratres eodem in loco destructo ueteri oratorium construxerunt, cuius amplitudo prioris angustias dilataret et diuinis obsequiis commodior, sicut in presenciarum cernitur, existeret, ubi et egroti sanitatis beneficia et fideles sue peticionis consecuntur desideria. Facta est autem hec de huius loci restitucione siue reedificacione reuelacio anno ab incarnacione Domini millesimo centesimo octogesimo octauo, qui est annus deposicionis sancte Ebbe quingentesimus sextus.[58] Ad laudem Domini nostri Ihesu Cristi, cui est honor et gloria per seculorum secula amen.

[4. Miracles]

1. Licet plura uirtutum opera temporibus maiorum prestiterit, continuata tamen uirtute in hiis reflorere non desinit, ut fiat assertio ueterum exhibicio nouitatum et fidem reparet operosa nouitas, quam leserat otiosa uetustas. Ea igitur quae nuper contigerunt, ne uicio mihi uerteretur intermissio, noticie fidelium mandare uolui, ut qui socii fuerint discipline, consortes sint et leticie. In multiplici igitur curacionum largicione Ebbe uirtus indefessa crescebat. Ne quid uero in publicum admitteretur uerum, fidei tarditas[a] elaborabat. Ad tenebras igitur dubietatis abolendas, magistri Merlini filia[59] prima

---

^a corr. from traditas

⁵⁸ Again pointing to the year 683 for Æbbe's death.

⁵⁹ Master Merlin appears in documents of the bishop of St Andrews and of Coldingham 1160 × 1203: D. E. R. Watt, *A Biographical Dictionary of Scottish Graduates to A. D. 1410* (Oxford, 1977), p. 390. Several generations of his family are traceable as local landholders

behind long ago. He carried water, in a little cask placed on a cart, from the foot of the mountain up a rocky path across the side of the steep mountain. All alone he raised a wall which now loomed higher than his shoulders, using stones of such great size that, because of this, although his words had not been believed, those who had disbelieved him and mocked him were now able, even if unwillingly, to have faith in what he had said. And although he was bound to his lords by his servile condition, he could not thereafter be compelled to perform his customary labours nor to turn aside from the work he had begun, either by afflictions or by threats.

Many of the brethren also mocked the efforts of this worker, but others, of a wiser mind, revered and praised him. However, as miracles multiplied in that place and people came rushing from all sides, lack of faith was transformed into faith, contempt into reverence, mockery into praise, ignorance into glory. The brethren constructed a new oratory in that same place, after demolishing the old one. Its proportions were larger than the cramped spaces of the earlier one and more suitable for divine service, as can be seen at the present time, and here sick people gained the benefit of health and the faithful the petitions they longed for. This vision concerning the restoration or rebuilding of this place occurred in the year of the incarnation of the Lord 1188, the 506th year after the burial of St Æbbe.[58] To the praise of our Lord Jesus Christ, to whom be honour and glory, world without end. Amen.

[4. Miracles]

1. Although she manifested many miraculous works in the times of our elders, nevertheless she does not cease to blossom in our own times with continued power, so that the promise of those of old should become the experience of our own modern time and that active innovation should restore the faith that idle age had harmed. I wished, therefore, to bring to the knowledge of the faithful the events which recently occurred, so that I should not be blamed as neglectful, and that those who are fellows in discipline might also share in joy. The untiring power of Æbbe grew in granting many cures, but the slowness of faith laboured that the truth should not be made public. So, the daughter of Master Merlin[59] was the first to be admitted to

in Ayton, three miles south-west of Coldingham: Raine, *North Durham*, pp. 46–8, nos. 201, 210–14, 216.

omnium admissa est, que fantastica uexacione demonum unius oculi uisum, auris unius auditum, lingue penitus quindecim diebus perdiderat officium. Eratque miraculum tam teneram uirginem tot malorum agere posse uicissitudinem. Dei tamen uoluntate factum est ut triplex incommodum triplex incommoditatis afferret remedium, scilicet uisus redditus in dubitancium cordibus lucem ueritatis accenderet, auditus audiencium moras disrumperet, sermo irridencium ora in laudem aperiret. Ad oratorium ergo memoratum deducta est, quatinus, si diuina pietas permitteret, uirgo uirgini salutem optatam conferret, miroque modo noctem uigilando duceret. Pre tedio dormitans, super altare columbam niueam stare conspexit, quam sibi, soluto statim uinculo lingue, dari*a* peciit. Et in hac uoce euigilans, omnem pariter cum sopore infirmitatem deposuit. Mane facto quibusdam ex nostris a mulieribus, que eam secute fuerant et hec uiderant oblata, se uidere, audire, loqui libera uoce, professa est. Nos autem credentes pie tamen dubitantes, ex assercione parentum id plenius esse decreuimus cognoscendum. Quibus in crastino uenientibus et quod in filia sua factum fuerat signum cum iuramento attestantibus, ipsa, in medio stans, proprio ore se prefatis languoribus fuisse religatam, per merita uero beate Ebbe coram omni populo asserebat esse solutam. Nos igitur ympno laudis decantato, gracias egimus saluatori omnium Deo, qui illuminat cecos et surdos facit audire et mutos loqui.

2. Eminenciorem in beata uirgine admirari possumus graciam, si cecitatem paupercule mulieris intuemur extrusam. Huic in stratu suo quiescenti apparuit quedam uultus incogniti, admonens eam lectum mutare et ulterius sibi quiescendi locum non habere. Quod illo tercio repetente*b* ipsa contempsit et euiligans exterioris ilico se corporis tenebras incurrisse cognouit. Quid tunc faceret misera, quo se uerteret, ignorabat. Fossas ad instar carnis crude sanguine perfusas habebat ubi paulo ante lumen celi uiderat. Erat quidem de amissione desolacio et de humana subuencione grauius urgebat desperacio. Sola ergo Dei imploranda sunt suffragia, quia sileant necesse est humana ubi constituunt uel ceperunt*c* operari diuina. Memoriam igitur beati fo. 168ᵛ Thome | martiris, que ex fidelium deuotione in finibus Londonie

---

a dare *MS*   *b* corr. from repente   *c* uel ceperunt *marg. add.*

dispel the shadows of doubt. Through the phantasmal aggravation of demons, she had lost sight in one eye, hearing in one ear, and any use of her tongue, for a period of fifteen days. It was a miracle that such a tender young girl could bear the vicissitudes of so many evils. But by the will of God it happened that the triple ailment brought a triple remedy of the ailment, for her restored sight lit the light of truth in the hearts of doubters, her restored hearing destroyed the objections of those who heard, her restored speech opened in praise the mouths of those who had mocked. She was led to the oratory which we have mentioned, so that, if the divine goodness allowed it, the virgin might confer on this virgin the health she desired and, in a wonderful way, would spend the night in vigils. Sleeping through weariness, she saw a snow-white dove standing on the altar, which she begged to be given to her, for the bond of her tongue was immediately released. Awaking at this utterance, she set aside the illness just as she set aside sleep. In the morning some of the women who had accompanied her and seen these blessings declared to some of us that she saw, heard and spoke with ready tongue. We believed devoutly but doubted and decided to learn about it more fully from the account of her parents. Next day they came and attested on oath the miracle that had been performed in their daughter, while she stood in our midst and asserted with her own mouth how she had been bound by those afflictions but had been released through the merits of the blessed Æbbe before all the people. So, after singing a hymn of praise, we gave thanks to God, the saviour of all, who illuminates the blind, and makes the deaf hear and the dumb speak.

2. We can admire a higher grace in the blessed virgin if we consider how the blindness of a poor little woman was driven out. While she was resting in her bed, a woman, whose features she did not know, appeared to her and commanded her to abandon her bed and no longer have a place of rest. She rejected this request three times and, when she awoke, realized she had been struck by darkness of the physical body. The wretched woman did not know what to do next nor where she should turn. She had hollows like raw meat, full of blood, where a little time before she had seen the light of heaven. She was desolated by the loss and deeply oppressed by despair of any human help. So God's help alone is to be sought, for it is necessary that human things should be silent when divine things are appointed or begun to be worked. She went therefore to the shrine of blessed Thomas the martyr, which has been constructed in the London area

constructa est,[60] adiit sed noluit idem martir petitam ei conferre sanitatem, quatinus ostenderet quanta in beata uirgine uirtus curacionis existeret. Ab amicis denique admonita, Coldingham, quia ibi sanitates celebrari audierat, uenit et ibi in domo cuiusdam seruientis nostri mansit. Post hec, filia sua paruula eam ducente et gressus cecos regente, ad montem Coludi perrexit et in oratorium introducta pro sua salute Deo et gloriose uirgini uota precum effudit. Cui illa uestibus albis decenter induta in sompnis apparuit et, assidens humiliter dormienti, infelicitatis eius accidenciam materna pietate consolari cepit. 'Graues', ait, 'ex cecitate molestias hoc in anno perpessa es; nunc autem accede ad radices montis et lauare ex fonte meo et reilluminaberis.' Ad hanc uocem expergefacta, discussis paululum ex facie eius tenebris, uidit, quamuis ea que uiderat clarius agnoscere non posset. Que mox fontem querere statuit et, circuito monte et hiis que subiecta sunt locis, nullo tandem ducente uel indicante, repperit. Et lauit et, omni penitus decessa caligine, pristinam uidendi graciam recepit, eius exemplum secuta qui missus ad natatoria Syloe lauit et uidit et cum uisu corporis lumen quoque optinuit cordis.[61] Quo facto Coldyngham remeauit cum gaudio et, cognito ex ore eius attestantibus cunctis qui aderant et iuramentum prestantibus quod factum fuerat signo, personante in laudem Dei ecclesia, gracias egimus ei qui saluos facit sperantes in se, qui quos uult ad correpcionem excecat et quando uult ad sui nominis honorem illuminat.

3. Referam quoque quoddam uirtutis signum in quodam adolescente meritis eiusdem matris nostre nuper ostensum. Hic enim cum de auca comederet, contigit ut incaute modicam ossis acutissimi particulam in ore sumeret. Quod lapsu facili in guttur subito uenit et illic ex tranuerso fixum hesit. Conabatur deglutire nec poterat; uolebat reicere nec ualebat. Alii, missis in ore eius hastulis, id quidem tangebant nec mouebant. Coartato igitur spiritu, collo in tumorem conuerso, rauce facte sunt fauces eius et defecerunt pre tedio oculi ipsius et in magnam animi diutius inquietudinem singulis quamtocius morituri preferebat ymaginem. Desperacioni

---

[60] There was a chapel of St Thomas of Canterbury on London Bridge: *Victoria History of the Counties of England. London*, i (1909), 572. It was founded before 1205: *Annales de Waverleia*, ed. H. R. Luard, *Annales monastici*, ii (RS, 1865), 256–7.

[61] John 9.

by the devotion of the faithful,[60] but the martyr was not willing to grant her the healing she requested, in order to show how great healing power there was in the blessed virgin. Thereupon, on the advice of her friends, she came to Coldingham, for she had heard that famous cures were occurring there, and lodged there in the house of one of our servants. After this, led by her little daughter who guided her blind steps, she came to St Abb's Head, entered the oratory and poured out her entreaties in prayer for her health to God and the glorious virgin. The virgin, elegantly dressed in white albs, appeared to her in her sleep and, sitting with humility beside the sleeping woman, began, with maternal kindness, to console her for her unhappy accident. 'This year', she said, 'you have suffered great troubles from blindness, but now go to the foot of the mountain and wash in my fountain and your sight will be restored.' Waking at this statement, she found that the shadows had dispersed slightly from her gaze and she saw, although she was unable to recognize clearly what she saw. She soon determined to seek the fountain and, going around the mountain and the places below it without anyone to guide her or show her the way, she found it. She washed, the darkness completely dispersed and she received the gift of sight as before, following the example of him who was sent to the pool of Siloam and washed and saw and obtained light in his heart along with the sight of the body.[61] When this had happened, she returned to Coldingham with joy. When the miracle had been made known from her own mouth, and what had happened had been attested and affirmed on oath by all who were present, the church resounded with praise of God as we gave thanks to Him who saves those who have hope in Him, who blinds whoever He wishes for their chastisement and, when He wishes, gives them sight to the honour of His name.

3. I will tell also of a miraculous happening that was recently manifested in a certain young man through the merits of that same mother of ours. For it happened that while he was eating goose he incautiously took into his mouth a small piece of very sharp bone. This slipped down easily and immediately reached his throat, where it stuck sideways. He tried to swallow it but was unable to, he wished to eject it but could not. Others pushed sticks into his mouth and could touch the bone but not dislodge it. His spirit was depressed, his neck swelled up and his throat became sore, while his eyes failed him because of exhaustion. For a long time he was in great mental distress and presented to everyone the very image of someone soon to die. At

demum derelictus est. Sola mors expectabatur, que finis sue fieret expectacionis. Inspirante autem Deo, quidam eius insolenciam arguere cepit, quod in confinio mortis positus ad suffragia sancte Ebbe confugere non meminerit. At ille, accepto salubri consilio, annuit et, cursu ueloci aduolans, de fonte qui ad radices memorati montis est tercio hausit et, transcenso monte, ingressus oratorium se in oracionem dedit. Mira res et temporibus nostris stupenda uehementer! Sanus namque, acsi nichil mali ante sensisset, de oratione surrexit et, quod miraculo exudit miraculum, ignorabat quo os illud deuenit, quia nec id in uiscera se suscepsisse, neque per os professus est eiecisse. Nec mirum si uirgo uenerabilis opera sanctitatis et misericordie petentibus miseris impendit, que et de sanctis originem duxit[62] et misericordie uiscera[63] circa subiectos sibi dum uiueret gessit.

4. Quedam puella unius brachii officio penitus fuerat destituta. Que ad prenominatum locum a parentibus deducta, duabus noctibus in uigiliis et orationibus transactis, graciam pristine consecuta est sanitatis. Cepitque factam in se uirtutem brachium iactando et digitos diuersas in partes flectendo pandere, in quibus pre nimii rigoris constricione per dimidium fere annum nichil poterat sentire.

5. Ad attolendum alcius uenerande uirginis meritum, quod in quodam de Edenburgensium finibus oriundo gestum est, libet enarrare miraculum. Hunc a planta pedis usque ad uerticem graue fo. 169ʳ dolorum accidens perfudit et a sui status rectitudine | ad beluinam usque similitudinem inclinauit. Curuus enim incedens, usus est baculo tanquam uehiculo. Vnum pedem gerens liberum, alterius autem talo suspenso digitis tangens humum, saltus pocius agebat quam gressum. Ad sui uero corporis redempcionem ferro simul et igne frequenter adhibito renes cicatricibus repleuerat sibique sentiens non adesse medicine carnalis auxilium, inspirante Deo confugit ad diuinum. Terra namque et cognacione et domo relicta,[64] peregrinacionis laborem arripuit et Cantuariam a beato martire Thoma salutem mendicare uenit. Aliorum quoque sanctorum ubi signa florere uirtutum audierat loca circuiens, nec aliquam ab eis beneficii

---

[62] This does not seem to be literally true, although her uncle King Edwin and her possible half-brother King Oswald were both regarded as saints.

[63] Luke 1: 78; Col. 3: 12.

[64] Cf. Gen. 12: 1.

last he gave himself up to despair. Death alone was anticipated, which would bring an end to his waiting. However, at God's instigation, someone reproached him for insolence because, being so close to death, he had not brought to mind the thought of seeking refuge in St Æbbe's aid. But he accepted this salutary advice and, rushing up with a swift pace, he drank three times from the fountain which is at the foot of the mountain we have mentioned, and then, climbing over the mountain, he entered the oratory and gave himself up to prayer. A wonderful thing, truly astonishing in our times, occurred. For he arose from prayer as healthy as if he had never experienced any ill and—what brought forth a miracle from the miracle—he did not know where that bone went, for he declared that he had not received it into his bowels nor had he ejected it through his mouth. Nor is it amazing if the venerable virgin should perform works of holiness and mercy for the unhappy people who petition her, for she traced her descent from saints[62] and, while she was alive, she showed bowels of mercy[63] towards those subject to her.

4. There was a girl who was completely deprived of the use of one arm. Brought by her parents to the place we have already mentioned, she spent two nights in vigils and prayers, and then received the blessing of her former health. She began to demonstrate the miracle that she had experienced by thrusting out her arm and flexing her fingers in different directions. For almost half a year she had been unable to feel anything in them on account of their stiffness and contraction.

5. In order to extol more highly the merit of the venerable virgin, it may be permitted to recount the miracle that was performed for a man from the Edinburgh area. A serious affliction had befallen him that affected him from the soles of his feet to the top of his head and twisted him from his upright stance into the likeness of a beast. Walking bent over, he employed a staff to help himself along. While one foot moved freely, the heel of the other one was twisted upwards and he had to touch the ground with his fingers, making more of a leap than a step. He frequently applied fire and iron to cure his body, so that he had covered his sides with scars, and, feeling that no help would come from earthly medicine, he was inspired by God to take refuge in divine medicine. For, leaving his land and his acquaintances and his home,[64] he undertook the labour of pilgrimage and came to Canterbury to beg health from the blessed martyr Thomas. He also went around to the shrines of other saints where he had heard that

graciam accipiens, cum, iam desperacione magis quam labore confectus, ad sua reuerti disponerat, sugestione quorundam in Berewyci'[65] admonitus est ut memoriam quoque sancte Ebbe in Monte Coludi requireret; fecitque prout imperauerunt[a] et in uilla de Coldingham quindecim diebus moram egit, ut uenture curacionis tot existerent testes quot infirmitatis prius habuerat cognitores.

Irruentibus igitur more solito quodam die sabbati populis et de uillulis ad montem predictum et oratorium properantibus, ipse pariter ire cepit et, testudinis emulans tarditatem, a nona diei hora iter protelans in uesperam illo tandem peruenit. Sedentique cum ceteris iamiamque pre lassitudine dormitanti uirgo memorabilis apparuit et loca dolorum manibus explorans fortiter attrectauit. Ad cuius contactum uoces ipse miserabiles emisit, quia, sicut postea nobis referebat, tantum inde paciebatur angustie acsi membrum aliquid auulsum fuisset e corpore. Nec silencio preterire par est quod, quociens sopor irrepsit, beata uirgo assistens artus pacientis ut dictum est strinxit, quatinus attractu frequenti doceret quam forte malum fuit quod celerius abire contempsit. Aut forte requirebat fidem in hominem et distulit graciam ut probaret perseuerenciam. Omnibus igitur mane recedentibus, ipse non recedebat sed, maiore spe concepta, instancius oracioni uacabat. Et media nocte de sompno sanus consurgens, baculum simul ibi cum dolore deposuit et residuum noctis in graciarum accione transegit et in crastino nobis que gesta fuerant, cum testimonio fidelium qui hec uiderant, aperuit. Quo facto repletum est gaudio os nostrum in laudem Dei, qui salus est omnium se inuocancium et uera subleuacio et fortitudo in se sperancium.

6. Erat alius, multis in prouincia Lodoneie[66] cognitus, qui arte cantandi querens uictum, uidule quoque exercebat officium. Cui licet gutte tumor, que paupertati coniuncta pene mors altera est, tumore pedum sepe nimio prepediret incessum, ad solacium tamen uite uirtus semper inerat lingue. Hic tempore mortalitatis et famis que totum fere ante hoc biennium consumpserant orbem—nam urbes, uicos, agros mortuis, egrotis et egenis repleuerant[67]—simili inter alios

---

[a] imperauit MS

[65] Scotland's most important port at this time; now in Northumberland.

[66] The south-eastern part of the kingdom of Scots, between Forth and Tweed.

[67] Possibly that of 1196, described by William of Newburgh, *Historia rerum anglicarum*, v. 26, ed. Richard Howlett, *Chronicles of the Reigns of Stephen, Henry II and Richard I* (4 vols., RS, 1884–9), ii. 484–5; cf. also John of Fordun, *Chronica gentis*

miracles were abundant, but received no benefit from them. When, worn out by despair more than by his labours, he had determined to return home, some people in Berwick[65] advised him to seek out the shrine of St Æbbe on St Abb's Head. He did as they commanded and spent fifteen days in the town of Coldingham, so that there should be as many witnesses to his forthcoming cure as there were those familiar with his previous illness.

So, one Saturday, when people were flocking with haste from the surrounding hamlets to the mountain and oratory, as was the custom, he too began to go and, travelling painfully like a slow tortoise from the ninth hour of the day until evening, he at last arrived there. While he was sitting with the others and sleeping because he was so tired, the celebrated virgin appeared to him and explored with her hands the places where he felt pain, touching them quite roughly. As she touched them he uttered miserable cries, for, as he afterwards told us, he felt so much anguish as if a limb had been wrenched from his body. It is not right to pass over in silence the fact that, whenever sleep crept up, the blessed virgin was there touching the limbs of the sufferer as we have said, so that by that frequent contact she might teach him how great an evil it was that he disdained to come sooner. Or perhaps she demanded faith in the man and deferred her blessing to test his perseverance. In the morning, when everyone else went away, he did not go away but, conceiving greater hope, pressed on with his prayers more insistently. Rising up from sleep in the middle of the night cured, he put aside his staff there along with his pain and spent the rest of the night in thanksgiving. Next day he disclosed to us what had happened, supported by the testimony of those faithful people who had seen it. After this our mouth was filled with joy in praise of God, who is the salvation of all who invoke Him and the true relief and strength of those who have hope in Him.

6. There was another man, well known in the province of Lothian,[66] who earned his living as a singer and also played the fiddle. Although the swelling of gout, which, when combined with poverty, is almost a second death, impeded his walking because his feet were often greatly inflamed, there was always the skill of his tongue as a comfort in his life. At the time of the mortality and famine which consumed almost the entire world two years ago—for it filled towns, villages, and fields with the dead, the sick, and the starving,[67]

Scottorum, ed. W. F. Skene (Historians of Scotland 1 and 4, 2 vols., Edinburgh, 1871–2), i. 274 (annal 22).

languore percussus est. Interque dira famis et egritudinis flagella pacientis animum grauius urgebat, quia quos crebro dulci modulamine cantus iocundos fecerat auditores et intentes, eorum tunc cura ipsum preteriit et pietas ignorabat. Ex horum tamen malorum uinculis tandem Deo miserante euasit, qui ad maiorem suam gloriam et manifestandam in sua uirgine patrociniam eum sibi reseruauit. Venit igitur Coldyngham debilis et nudus et, a priore loci et fratribus misericorditer exceptus, infra paucos dies largitatis eorum beneficio pristine sanitati restitutus est et officio. Cum uero eum communis pestilencie manus dimitteret, sua protinus ipsum solita uidelicet gutte inquietudo excepit. Adeoque uexabat quod per quatuor ferme menses nec de loco quo sederet uel iaceret sine subleuancium adminiculo moueri potuisset. Putabant etiam nonnulli quod cum fo. 169ᵛ nulla doloris intermissio | fieret, hoc ei continuo cum uita inualitudo cohereret. Tantam denique Dominus uigoris graciam ei contulit quod, sedato aliquantulum tumore noxio, duobus baculis hinc et inde corpus a terra subleuantibus incedere uel pocius saltare potuit. Auxilium uero beate Ebbe uirginis iugiter inuocabat et salutem sibi eius precibus affuturam cum summe spei certitudine palam omnibus predicebat. Nec fefellit fidei meritum celestis gracie donum. Ad oratorium enim memoratum uenit et deuotas in oracionibus excubias egit. Eoque sopore depresso uirgo uenerabilis, candidis induta uestibus, affuit et caput eius et reliquas corporis partes blanda manu pertractauit. Euigilans ad hec ille concito surrexit et factum in se miraculum stupore ingenti uehementer expauit. Exiliit ergo letus et ambulabat glorificans et laudans Deum qui salus est omnium in se confidencium. Relictisque ibi ob tante uirtutis memoriam baculis, sanum se eis crastino obtulit, a quibus sero eger et gressu inualidus recessit.

7. Fuit quedam Gwalensis genere, Quinciana nomine, parentibus locupletissimis oriunda. Hec annorum adhuc septem adolescentula de domo patris in agrum ad greges patris egressa, sola denique, relictis illic sodalibus, rediit et, nemoris interpositi deuia percurrens, in cuiusdam trunci concauitatem se propter timores nocturnos et ferarum incursus proiecit ibique sopore triduano hospicium quietis accepit. Tertio die, a custode porcorum inuenta, parentibus oblata

he, like others, was struck with the same illness. Amid the cruel whips of hunger and disease, it distressed the spirit of the sufferer more deeply that those whom he had often made happy and attentive hearers with the sweet melody of song now did not extend their care to him and failed to acknowledge him kindly. But at last he escaped from the bonds of these evils, by the mercy of God, who had reserved him for Himself, for His greater glory and in order to manifest His virgin's powers of protection. So he came weak and naked to Coldingham and, received with compassion by the prior and brethren of the place, he was restored to his former health and skills within a few days thanks to their generosity. But although he was released from the grip of the general sickness, his usual affliction of gout continued to lay hold of him. It troubled him so much that for almost four months he was unable to move from where he was sitting or lying without the help of men to lift him. Many people even thought that, since there was no remission of the pain, this illness would be with him for the rest of his life. At last the Lord conferred on him the gift of such strength that, as the noxious swelling subsided somewhat, he was able to use two sticks to raise his body from the ground and walk, or rather leap, here and there. But he continually invoked the help of the blessed virgin Æbbe and predicted before everyone with the surest hope that health would come to him through her prayers. Nor did the gift of celestial grace deceive his meritorious faith. For he came to the oratory we have mentioned and spent many devout watches in prayer. While he was sunk in sleep the venerable virgin, dressed in white garments, was present and touched his head and other parts of his body with gentle hands. At this he awoke and quickly arose, overcome with great fear and wonder at the miracle that had been performed in him. He bound forth therefore overjoyed and walked about glorifying and praising God, who is the salvation of all who trust in Him. He left his sticks there as a memorial of this great miracle and on the morrow he came in good health to those whom he had left the evening before sick and weak of step.

7. There was a Welsh girl called Quinciana whose parents were extremely rich. When she was a young girl of seven, she had gone out of her father's house into the fields to her father's flocks and then, leaving her companions there, had returned alone. Going through the remote places of the intervening wood, she had thrown herself into the hollow of a tree, because of her night fears and the attacks of wild animals, and slept for three days in that quiet lodging. On the third day she was found by a swineherd and returned to her parents, who

est, gaudentibus quidem illis quia que periisse putabatur inuenta, lugentibus uero quia uirtute loquendi priuata. Elapsis aliquot annis, petiit eam homo prediues et accepit uxorem, non taciturnitatis eius attendens uicium sed paternarum rerum considerans emolumentum. Rex igitur Henricus secundus cum exercitum in Gualenses dirigeret et eos igne ferroque uastaret,[68] uir huius et tres filii in domo pariter incensi, pater autem et reliqui parentes eius hostili gladio sunt deleti. Quid ageret misera et uidua et tot dolorum mucrone sauciata? De sui tantum corporis salute sollicita, relicta domo rebusque suis, tam Galliarum quam Anglorum regionem summa egestate comite circuiens, sanctorum memorias expetiit, nec eandem salutem donec ad uirginis Ebbe quod in urbe Coludi ⟨illo⟩ tempore constructum est oratorium perueniret optinuit, non quia Dominus sanctis suis potentiam subtrahebat, immo quia eam ad gloriam sui nominis et gloriose sue uirginis in thesauris misericordie sue reseruabat.

Ad hunc quoque locum in natiuitate beati precursoris Domini quam plures, tam de uicinis quam remotis aliarum regionum partibus, cateruatim conueniunt, eo quod ipso die post desolationem loci ipsius ibidem a fratribus diuina celebrari inchoarent.[69] Populis igitur illo uenientibus, uenit et ista pauper pariter et muta, Dominum pro salute tam corporis quam anime etsi non lingua carnis ore cordis rogatura, miroque modo tumore colli cepit uehementer urgeri, adeo quod se subito casuram crederet et mori. Astantium statim oculos in se doloris impaciencia conuertit et in sui compassionem sua compassione commutauit. Inter crebras uero cordis et corporis angustias sopore depressa, uidit sanctam uirginem super sanctum altare sedentem, que duos digitos misit in os eius et tetigit linguam eius, tamquam ei uoce dominica diceret 'Effeta', quod est 'adaperire',[70] tantamque de eorum contactu se dulcedinem professa est accepisse acsi mel sumpsisset in ore. De sompno igitur consurgens, omni inflacione gutturis celitus deposita, cepit in uoces erumpere et uerba proferre. Accurrebant ad tante rei nouitatem qui conuenerant et repleti sunt stupore et extasi in eo quod contigerat illi. Cupientes autem miraculi ueritatem certius agnoscere, presbiteri orationem

---

[68] Henry II invaded Wales in 1157, 1158, and 1165, but if the dumbness lasted only 'eleven years' (as below) and the oratory was constructed in 1188, the reference, if accurate, must be to warfare in the period after 1177. Disconcertingly, these last years of Henry's reign (1177–89) were amongst the most peaceful in the history of relations between Welsh and English.

[69] The feast of John the Baptist is 24 June. The 'dedication of the altar of St Æbbe in

rejoiced indeed that she, whom they deemed to have perished, had been found, but grieved that she had been deprived of the power of speech. Some years later a very rich man sought and obtained her in marriage, disregarding the fact that she was dumb but considering the advantage of her father's wealth. When king Henry II sent his army against the Welsh and devastated them with fire and sword,[68] the woman's husband and three sons were burned together in their house, while her father and other relatives were killed by the enemy's sword. What should she do, this unhappy widow who had suffered so much from the point of the sword? She turned her care to her bodily health alone and, leaving her home and possessions, she sought out the shrines of the saints, travelling around both France and England in the utmost poverty. She did not obtain healing until she came to the oratory of the virgin Æbbe which was built on St Abb's Head at that time, not because the Lord took away their power from His saints, but rather because, in the treasures of his mercy, He was saving her for the glory of His name and of His glorious virgin.

Crowds throng here from nearby and from distant regions on the nativity of the blessed precursor of the Lord, because on this day the brethren began to celebrate divine service here after the place had been long abandoned.[69] So, when the people came there, this poor dumb woman also came, to ask the Lord for health of both body and soul, with the mouth of her heart even if not with a physical tongue. Remarkably, she began to be beset by a terrible swelling of the throat, so that she thought she would immediately fall down and die. Her inability to bear the suffering turned the eyes of the bystanders on her and, through fellow-feeling, turned into compassion for her. In the midst of these frequent torments of heart and body she fell asleep and saw the holy virgin sitting on the holy altar. She placed two fingers in her mouth and touched her tongue, as if she said to her in the Lord's voice, 'Ephphatha', that is, 'Be opened',[70] and she declared that from her touch she experienced so great sweetness as if she had taken honey into her mouth. So she arose from sleep with all the inflammation of her throat completely subdued by heavenly power and began to break out in speech and utter words. Those who had assembled there ran up at such an unusual occurrence and were filled with wonder and amazement at what had happened to her. Desiring to learn the truth of the miracle with greater certainty, the priests

Coldisburh' on 22 June is recorded in the late-13th-cent. Coldingham Breviary, BL Add. 4664, fo. 128ᵛ.   [70] Mark 7: 34; cf. Miracle 35 below.

dominicam Angli Anglicum, Scotti Scotticum quemcumque quique sermonem proponebant,[71] ipsa ex facilitate lingue repetebat quam per undecim annos clausam habuerat, acsi in ore eius omnium eorum qui fo. 170ʳ loquebantur genera nascerent linguarum. Quia | uero pauper et incognita fuit, dubiam pluribus de reddita sanitate fidem reliquid. Dicebant enim eam uera non asserere sed pro solacio temporalis uite sub ueritatis pallio contraria conserere.

Placuit igitur uirgini uenerande tenebris eorum lucernam adhibere et forma simili et casu consimili in sexu licet dissimili idem uirtutis signum iterare, quatinus geminatam credentibus exultacionem afferret, a non credentium autem cordibus dubietatis uulnus amputaret. Quinta etenim nocte sequenti quidam adolescentulus affuit, multis in hac regione notissimus, decem et octo a puericia annis officio lingue destitutus. Hanc et ipse doloris uicissitudinem cum oues in deserto pasceret, demonis illusione qui ei in similitudine nigri pueruli apparuit, incurrit, quia ludis quos ei offerebat assentire contempsit. Habebatur multo tempore multis, et precipue notis suis, ostentui simul et illusioni. Inualitudinis enim sue certitudinem experiri uolentes, alii furcis crura cruentabant et pene perforabant, alii per pollices quandoque manuum quandoque pedum suspendebant, nec ab eo preter clamores horridos et mugitus miserandos extorquebant. Sicut etiam postea iuramentis asserebat. Elegit sepius uitam carnis uoluisse magis excedere quam huiusmodi cruciatus et suspendia diucius sustinere. Quod diuina dispensatione gestum est, ut qui temptatores egritudinis fuerant dubii, uenture curacionis testes fierent probatissimi. Cumque a primis adolescencie sue temporibus surdus esset et mutus, auditum a glorioso Cantuarensis martire ac pontifice Thoma recepit sacrisque aliorum sanctorum liminibus ob salutem lingue perlustratis, ad hanc demum urbem Coludi, Domino miserante, peruenit, quatinus ibi a tam preclare antidoto sanctitatis gustum et ipse perciperet sanitatis. Cum ergo coram altari staret et, cor suum sursum habens, ad Dominum se simul et preces offeret, eisdem quibus et mulier supradicta doloribus in gutture fatigatus est, et iocunde uisionis consolatione recreatus. Et apertum est illico os eius et solutum est uinculum lingue eius et loquebatur, gratias agens gracie diuine[72] qui uult omnes homines

---

[71] Meaning 'the Scots speakers in Scots, the Gaelic speakers in Gaelic'.
[72] Cf. Luke 1: 64.

recited to her the Lord's Prayer, the English in English speech, the Scottish in Scottish speech,[71] and she repeated it with great facility of tongue, a tongue which had been silent for eleven years, as if in her mouth there were produced the kinds of tongues of all those who were speaking. But because she was poor and unknown, many people had doubts about her recovery. They said she was not telling the truth but had made up things contrary to the truth, in order to obtain relief in her temporal life.

So it pleased the venerable virgin to bring light to their darkness and to repeat that miracle in a similar way and a comparable case but in a different sex. In this way she might bring a double joy to believers and remove the wound of doubt from the hearts of those who did not believe. For on the fifth night following, a poor young man was there, well known in the region, who had been deprived of the power of speech for eighteen years, from boyhood. He incurred this affliction, while he was pasturing sheep in a remote place, from a phantasmal demon who appeared to him in the likeness of a little black boy, because he disdained to consent to the games he suggested to him. For a long time many people, especially his acquaintances, held that this was mere show and deceit. Wishing to test whether his incapacity were genuine, some bloodied his legs with forks, almost piercing them, while others hung him up sometimes by the thumbs, sometimes by the feet, but they were not able to extort from him anything other than terrible yells and wretched moaning. So he later asserted on oath. On many occasions he would have preferred to leave the life of this flesh rather than sustain these torments and suspensions any longer. It was by the divine dispensation that this happened, so that those who were doubtful and tested his illness should be the most trustworthy witnesses of the cure he was to obtain. Although he was deaf and dumb from earliest boyhood, he received his hearing from the glorious martyr and archbishop Thomas of Canterbury, and, travelling around the holy shrines of other saints seeking recovery of his tongue, by the Lord's mercy he at last came here to St Abb's Head, where he was to receive a draught of healing from the antidote of such famous sanctity. So, while he was standing before the altar, with his heart raised aloft, offering himself and his prayers to the Lord, he was troubled by the same pains in the throat as the woman we mentioned earlier, and then restored by the consolation of a joyful vision. And his mouth was straightaway opened and the bond of his tongue released and he spoke, giving thanks to the divine grace,[72]

saluos fieri et ad agnicionem ueritatis peruenire.[73] Tantaque similitudo uirtusque fuerat miraculi quod nulli merito in dubium uenire
possit quod sequentis exhibicio uirtutis prioris fuerit probacio
exhibicionis. Hec et hiis similia ibi celebrantur, quatinus ex hiis
quisque fidelis intelligat quod culpam que hactenus sacris locis
solitudinem intulit, diuina bonitas signorum attestacione relaxauit.

8. Affuit illo quedam cum paruulo suo. Huic tumor noxius in latere
succreuerat cuius magnitudinis et nigredinis horribilis aspectus
parentibus quidem metum, sue uero teneritudini celerem minabat
interitum. Quindecim dies cum dolore transegerat insompnes. Appo-
nebant ipsi medicamenta et funiculis circumligabant sed apposita
cicius decidebant quasi celitus dissoluta, quatinus inde daretur
intelligi non ei posse uires herbarum sed celestium mederi debere
graciam miseracionum. Cumque et nunc apponentis matris frequens
deluderet elapsus, tedio tamen conuicta ut saltem eiulatibus imperaret
silencium, suum excepit in gremium, ubi placidum resolutus in
soporem se contra morem, mirante ipsa, reclinauit in requiem. Et
euigilans arrisit matri et uultu letiore gaudium insolitum fecit de
salute. At illa, aliquid accidisse diuinum intelligens, loca doloris
palpauit adeoque latus illud sanum et simile carni relique repperit
quod nec cicatricis uestigium deprehenderet quasi nichil unquam in
eo tumoris apparuisset.

9. Quedam mulier mente capta ad eundem uenture sue reparationis
locum a duabus aliis, comitante uiro suo, ducta est. Abiit autem ille,
fo. 170ᵛ spem salutis | in summo salutari constituens et ei sueque uirgini
curam illius derelinquens. Cumque sederet uinculis quidem corporis
soluta, animo artius a demonio ligata sederentque duo muliercule et
custodie sollicitudinem diligenter impenderent, tres subito mire
magnitudinis corui per hostium uolatu precipiti irruperunt et,
quodammodo furore deuecti, in pacientem rostris et ungulis uelut
ad dilaniandum irruere conati sunt. Quo uiso, mulieres, stupore
femineo exterrite, cum uirtute tamen animi prosiliebant et, contra
impetus illorum manus opponentes, eos tandem fide magis quam
fortitudine effugabant. Erant, ut credimus, insanie spiritus qui in

[73] 1 Tim. 2: 4.

which wishes all men to be saved and to come to knowledge of the truth.[73] So great was the similarity and power of this miracle that nobody could reasonably doubt that the manifestation of the second miracle was a proof of the first manifestation. These and others like them were celebrated there so that anyone of the faithful might understand from them that the divine goodness had alleviated by the attestation of miracles the fault of desolation that the holy places had suffered from.

8. A woman was there with her little son. A malignant swelling had grown up on his side which was so horrible to look at, being huge and black, that it brought fear to the parents and threatened a swift death to the tender young child. He had passed fifteen days without sleep on account of the pain. They treated him with medicines tied onto him with cords but as soon as they were tied on they fell off again as if untied by heavenly power, so that thereby they might understand that he could not be cured by the power of herbs but would be healed by the blessing of heavenly mercy. When they had slipped off many times, mocking the mother who tied them on, she wearily determined that at least she would silence his crying and took him onto her lap, where he fell quietly asleep and, unusually and to her wonder, lay in repose. And when he woke up he smiled at his mother and with a happy face he made unwonted joy from his recovery. But she realized that something divine had happened and touched the place where the pain had been and found that side so healthy and like the rest of his flesh that she cold not detect the trace of a scar, as if he had never had a swelling.

9. A woman who had gone out of her mind was brought to this place of her future healing by two others and accompanied by her husband. He went away, placing hope of her recovery in the highest saviour and leaving her cure to Him and His virgin. While she was sitting down, released from the bonds around her body but bound more tightly in the mind by the demon, and the two little women were also sitting down and vigilantly watching over her, suddenly three crows of enormous size burst through the door in swift flight and, as if carried away by a kind of madness, they tried to attack the sufferer and lacerate her with their beaks and claws. When they saw this the women were frightened and stupefied, as women would be, but nevertheless they jumped up with a bold spirit and opposed their hands to their attacks, eventually driving them off more by their faith than by their strength. We believe that they were spirits of insanity

adiutorum eius qui in ea hospitabatur aduenerant, quatinus posteriora eius deteriora fecerent prioribus et ex periculo mentis periculum quoque totius incurreret corporis. Quod melius ex hiis que gesta sunt perpendi potest. Cum enim hoc tercio fecissent et tociens mulierum instancia repulsi fuissent, cepit misera ex eorum aduentu maiori furore agitari, adeo quod a manibus custodum uix ipsa teneri, uix in ea, ligatis manibus et pedibus, rabies diabolica potuisset coherceri. Tanta etiam sui alienacione tenebatur quod cum a marito sacri uiatici, quod iamiamque moriture coniugis exitum muniret, singulare presidium peteretur, ueniente sacerdote et inter monita pie exhortacionis crucis osculum offerente, crucem illa nutu cum indignacione abiceret et, in uerba blasfemie*a* aliquando prorumpens, ore nefario ad eius conspectum spueret. Domum igitur reducta et secundo illuc a suis adducta, excubias illis pro eius salute celebrantibus et deuotas Deo preces et lacrimas offerentibus, munere diuino et illorum fidei merito se continuo sana recepit nec aliquid in illa postmodum insanie signum apparuit. Sola equum ascendit et, benedicens Dominum et beatam eius ancillam, ad sua secum rediit, que extra se demonis uerbere posita longius a se recesserat. Multorum ex hoc in laudem eiusdem matris nostre corda et ora accensa sunt, dicencium ei 'gloriosa dicta sunt de te ciuitas Dei'.[74]

10. Quedam puella, inter sacra missarum celestia apparente ei beata uirgine et digitum in os eius mittente, loquendi usum accepit, cuius antea beneficium nature ei impotencia a natiuitate subtraxit. Cum uero, sicut eius relacione cognouimus, digito linguam ancilla Christi extraheret, quasi nodum aliquem rupisset in collo crepitum dedit, quatinus per hoc manifestum daretur indicium, natiuum eam cum eodem crepitu uocis rupisse silencium. Stupendumque est et in miraculis precipuum, quod ea que sanare uoluit ab ea quam sanabat uideri quoque manifeste ad cognicionem uoluisset. Abeuntem illa, cursu celeri, protensis manibus et nomine suo eam uocans, ad altare prosecuta est. Sed saluatricem suam minime apprehendit quia ipsam salutem tenuit. Adeoque in oculis astancium repentina erat curacio, quod cum flexione genuum adesse uideretur et ipsa sibi ex facilitate

_____

a blashemie *MS*

_____

[74] Ps. 86 (87): 3.

come to help the one who had taken possession of her, so that they might make her subsequent state worse than her earlier one and that from the danger to her mind she might incur danger to her whole body. This can be better appreciated from what happened, for when they had done this three times, and had been beaten off by the women's efforts three times, the wretched woman began to be agitated at their coming by a greater madness, so that she could scarcely be held by the hands of her custodians and even when her hands and feet were tied the diabolical frenzy in her could scarcely be restrained. She was in the grip of such insanity, that when a priest came (for her husband had sought the last rites for her, as a special protection to fortify the departure of the wife who seemed on the point of death) and amongst words of pious exhortation offered her the cross to kiss, she indignantly rejected it with a shake of the head, broke out into blasphemy and used her wicked mouth to spit at the sight of it. After she had been taken home and brought there by her friends a second time, while they kept vigils for her recovery and offered devout prayers and tears to God, by the divine gift and because of their faith she immediately recovered her health nor did any trace of insanity appear in her afterwards. She mounted a horse by herself and, blessing the Lord and his blessed handmaid, she returned home and to herself, who had long been estranged from herself because the blows of the demon had made her out of her mind. Because of this the hearts and mouths of many were aroused to praise our mother, saying to her, 'Glorious things are spoken of thee, O city of God'.[74]

10. The blessed virgin appeared to a girl during the sacred and heavenly mass and put a finger in her mouth, thus giving her the power of speech, a natural gift she had lacked from birth. As we learned from this girl's own account, when the handmaid of Christ pulled out the tongue with her finger, it gave a crack, as if some knot in the throat had been broken, so that thereby there might be a clear indication that with that crack she had broken her inborn inability to speak. It is amazing and a remarkable thing in miracles, that she who wished to heal wished also to be seen manifestly and recognized by her whom she healed. As she went away, the girl followed her to the altar, with a swift step and outstretched hands, calling her by her name. But she did not grasp her saviour, since she now had her health. So sudden was the cure in the eyes of those present there that it seemed to happen at the bending of the knees and she herself would

locucionis et tumore faucium fidem faceret, si testem etiam curacionis non haberet.

11. Ad reprimendam quorundam qui uirtutibus fidem negabant duriciam et exhibendum uirgini noue exaltacionis obsequium, patratum est in quodam contracto quoddam mirande nouitatis signum. Eadem per quinquennium inualitudine tenebatur. Pedibus contra morem in celum erectis, genibus nitebatur et manibus, quibus lignea supposuerat sustentacula. Et licet manus haberet ad usum, lignum tamen ad incessus adhibebat solacium. Ad hunc igitur locum, licet ad sanctum Andream[75] tenderet, casu diuertit et inopinate rei euentum inuenit. Cum enim sederet, cepit subito quasi febrium estu inualescere et, rapido ad altare reptatu se transferens, Ebbam | inuocare. Cumque hoc secundo ei contigisset, dulcem demum resoluto in soporem, uirgo uenerabilis apparuit et, signo crucis edito, eleuata cum manu benedixit. Et euigilans loca arida cum temptaret extendere, continuo super pedes erexit se, ut nemo dubitet contractionum duriciam ad benedictionem uirginis emollitam, amissam neruorum agilitatem recepisse. Gressuque tremulo et adhuc non solido, sine omni tamen sustentacionis adminiculo, relictis ibi ligneis instrumentis, ad ecclesiam uenit et paulatim deinceps in meliorem soliditatem conualescens, omnium oculos in sui admiracioni conuertit et corda in laudem saluatoris accendit. Nos igitur cum uirtutes huius uirginis legimus, ad eam animos tota deuocione conuertamus, ut que hunc contractum erexit de puluere, contracta corda precibus suis ad ueniam dignetur erigere, largiente Domino, qui soluit conpeditos et erigit omnes elisos.[76]

12. Quatuor adolescencium apud Neubode[77] poma colligencium ora turbo uenti repentinus infudit et omnes protinus loquendi facultatem ademit. Nec eundem aliud flatum credendum est fuisse, nisi in eo quoque spiritum malignum affuisse et in faciem eorum insufflasse. Vnus eorum multis apud Coldyngham diebus mutus permansit, cuius adeo lingua de loco suo introrsus descenderat quod uix eius summitas ab inquirentibus uideri uel etiam tangi potuisset. Illo igitur in oratorio memorato quadam nocte ad oracionem constituto, ei manum in sompnis uirgo beata in os mittens, linguam extraxit et diabolice alligacionis nodum soluit et infusum difficultatis uicium extersit. Qui mane consurgens, loquebatur libere, benedicens Deum qui non deserit confidentes in se.

[75] The famous pilgrimage site in Fife.   [76] Ps. 145 (146): 7–8; cf. Ps. 144 (145): 14.
[77] Midlothian.

convince one, from her facility of speech and the swelling of her throat, if there had been no witness to the cure.

11. To repress the hardness of those who do not have faith in miracles and to demonstrate the duty of a new glorification of the virgin, a miracle of astonishing novelty occurred to a certain cripple. He suffered this affliction for five years. Abnormally, his feet were turned upwards and he got about on his knees and hands, to which he had fixed wooden supports. Although he had the use of his hands, he employed the wooden props to help him walk. He happened to turn aside to this place, although he was on his way to St Andrews,[75] and experienced something unexpected. For while he was sitting, he suddenly began to feel ill, as if he were burning with fever, and, quickly crawling to the altar, he invoked Æbbe. When this had happened to him a second time, and he had at length fallen into a sweet sleep, the venerable virgin appeared and, raising her hand in the sign of the cross, gave a blessing. He awoke and, when he tried to stretch the shrivelled parts, he immediately raised himself on his feet, so that nobody should doubt that it was at the virgin's blessing that the harsh contraction had been softened and the muscles recovered the mobility they had lost. He came to the church with shaky steps that were still not steady, but without the aid of any prop, for he had left behind the wooden supports, and, as he gradually recovered and became stronger, he turned all eyes towards him in wonder and ignited their hearts in praise of the saviour. So, when we read of the miracles of this virgin, let us turn our minds towards her with total devotion, so that she who raised the cripple from the dust may deign to raise our crippled hearts to forgiveness by her prayers, through the bounty of the Lord, who releases those who are shackled and lifts up all those who are cast down.[76]

12. A gust of wind suddenly blew into the mouths of four youths who were collecting apples at Newbattle[77] and completely deprived them of the power of speech. Nor should that gust of wind be believed to be anything other than an evil spirit blowing in their face. One of them remained many days at Coldingham, dumb and with his tongue displaced so far back that its tip could scarcely be seen or even touched by inquirers. One night as he was praying in the oratory we have mentioned, the blessed virgin put a hand in his mouth while he slept, pulled forth the tongue, untied the knot that the devil had tied and removed the defect that had been inflicted. Rising up in the morning, he spoke freely, blessing God who does not abandon those who trust in Him.

13. Venit illuc puella pauper et paruula. Hec quatuor digitos sinistre manus per sex annos in palmam habebat reflexos, ita quod ungues cuti insiderant, ut etiam modo pugnus esse uideretur et non manus. Venit et alia nobilis et etate tenera, in uehiculo posita, tribus fere mensibus medietate sui corporis destituta. Eius quoque uis languoris pollicem dextere manus in palmam retorquebat, quem etiam desuper quatuor digitorum reflexio deprimebat et a suo officio manum coartabat. Per uisum autem uirgo gloriosa, cum beata Maria matre Domini, aduenit et, primo accedens ad pauperem, manu sua manum eius blande pertractans aperuit et, deinde ad nobilem transiens, eiusdem operis beneficium sanando ministrauit. Factumque est ut que fuerant unius egritudinis consortes, unius fierent gracie participes. Et hoc notandum quod primo pauperem uisitauit et deinde ad nobilem rediit. Non enim apud electos Dei personarum est acceptio,[78] ubi diuini muneris exercenda est exibicio.

14. Venerunt quoque mulieres que sicut ex diuerso loco, sic erant et merito. Alie namque ad fontem qui in monte est accedentes aquam minime reppererunt, alie uero uenientes uas quod secum tulerant impleuerunt. Aquam ergo se habere predicabant. Alie uero stupebant et, fidem non adhibentes, cum indignacione aquam iubebant ostendere. Cumque ollam inclinarent, uacuam inuenerunt quam paulo ante plenam habuerant, ut circumspictrices non essent elementi, que despictrices erant fidei. Vas tamen secum domi tulerunt et plenum inuenerunt, de quo qui in eodem uico infirmabantur communicantes et alleuacionem corporum et subleuacionem acceperunt animorum. Reuocandum est igitur ad memoriam illud reuerentissimi et beatissimi Beuerlacensium patris Iohannis archiepiscopi miraculum, cuius meritis fracto uase uinum illibatum pependit in poste.[79] Nec minus est in pleno uase ariditatem inueniri quam uinum in soliditatem conuerti.

15. Venit etiam mulier ceca et post noctem uetuste cecitatis noue
diem | inuenit salutis.

16. Et altera que adeo inflata tumuerat quod se uix cutis extenta teneret; humorem uomitu deponens noxium, pristine gracilitatis consecuta est donum.

17. Neque illud silere libet quod multorum lingua cum fama non

[78] 2 Chr. 19: 7; Rom. 2: 11; Eph. 6: 9; Col. 3: 25.
[79] John of Beverley, bishop of York (d. 721): Folcard, *Vita sancti Iohannis episcopi Eboracensis*, x, ed. J. Raine, *Historians of the Church of York* (3 vols., RS, 1879–94), i. 255–7; cf. ibid. pp. 524–5, 529, 533, 538.

13. A poor little girl came there. For six years the four fingers of her left hand had been twisted into her palm, so that the nails were fixed into the skin and it seemed to be a fist rather than a hand. Another woman came, who was noble and of tender years, placed in a carriage; she had lost the use of half her body for almost three months. Also the force of her illness twisted the thumb of her right hand into her palm, while the bending back from above of the four fingers also pressed it down, so that the contracted hand could not serve its function. The glorious virgin came in a vision, along with the blessed Mary the mother of the Lord, and first went to the poor girl, touching her hand gently with her own and opening it, then proceeding to the noble woman and granting her healing in the same manner. And so it was that those who shared the same ailment were partners also in receiving the same grace; and this should be noted, that she visited the poor woman first and then went back to the noblewoman, for God's saints are no respecters of persons[78] when heavenly gifts are manifested.

14. Some women also came there who differed in their merit just as in their place of origin. For some, coming to the fountain on the hill, found no water, but when the others came, they filled the vessel they had brought with them. They announced that they had water. But the others were astonished and did not believe them and indignantly ordered them to show them the water. When they tilted the jar, they found it empty, although shortly before it had been full, so that those who had despised their faith should not be able to view the element. Nevertheless, they carried the vessel home and found it full, and those in that village who were sick and partook of it obtained both alleviation for the body and inspiration for the soul. So one should bring to mind that miracle of the most venerable and blessed father, archbishop John of Beverley, by whose merits wine hung unspilled on a post even when the vessel was broken.[79] It is no less a thing to find dryness in a full vessel than to turn wine into a solid.

15. A blind woman also came and, after a night of her old blindness, found a day of new healing.

16. And there was another woman, who had swelled up so much that her distended skin scarcely contained her; vomiting out a foul liquid, she obtained the gift of her former gracefulness.

17. Nor is it right to keep silent about that concerning which the tongues of many and public report do not keep silent. A knight from

silet. Miles quidam de Maltone partibus[80] sex de uxore sua liberos, quinque uidelicet filias et unum filium, sustulerat, qui, sicut successiua sibi natiuitate procedebant, ita muti natiua successione permanebant. Quod denique parentes penam esse perpendentes peccati, dolorem eorum silencii in amorem sui conuertebant supplicii. Miles namque ad cenobium Eboracensium confugit monachorum[81] et uxor eius se in Chendholm[82] ad conuersionem transtulit monialium. Liberos autem memoratos mutos post se amicorum cure relinquebant. Ex quibus una quindecim circiter annorum puella et omni iunior fuit, que ad sepedictum beate uirginis oratorium muta iam tercio uenit. Cumque longis fatigata excubiis quiesceret, uidit eandem uirginem cum beato Michaele archangelo a fenestra boreali descendentem et insuetas irrumpens in uoces exclamabat, 'Vt quid sedetis? Surgite et uenienti domine uiam parate.[83] Ecce enim uenit.' Et protinus sana errexit, nec sana protinus surrexisset nisi domina protinus aduenisset. Fatebatur nobis quod multas a cohabitatoribus suis molestias sustinuisset dum eam aliquando per pollices supsiderent, aliquando in foramine digitum cauilla constringerent; nec tanta uiolentia uocem humanam extorquerent. Gibbum quoque ostendit in capite. Factumque est ut experiencia dubitate infirmitatis probacio fieret date sanitatis.

18. Quedam de Gisburnensium territorio[84] oriunda, per insanie spiritum sex ebdomadibus extra se posita, sibi plenissime ibidem est restituta. Et alius, omnium fere membrorum sex annis destitutus officio, ad pristinam quoque uirtutem diuino reparatus est auxilio. Qui enim sicut mulier equo ueniens sedebat, sicut uir equo sedens remeabat et mutata est auersionis sessio cum sessoris mutaretur aduersio.

19. Quedam de pago Rodbirensi[85] femina, que per annos undecim cecutierat, a suis illuc est adducta. Hec per uisum astantem sibi gloriosam uirginem cum beata Margareta uidit et ex uisu spirituali uisu quoque uidere meruit corporali. Referebat etiam nobis eam dixisse et ut omnibus diceret iniunxisse, quatinus qui eius locum inuisere desiderant in memoria quoque fidelium defunctorum ueniant et eam sue sollempnitatis esse diem agnoscant, qua terrene habitacionis uestem exuit et eterne iocunditatis stolam induit.[86]

[80] Yorkshire, North Riding.
[81] St Mary's abbey, Benedictine.
[82] Yorkshire, North Riding, Cistercian.
[83] Cf. Isa. 40: 3; Matt. 3: 3; Mark 1: 3; Luke 3: 4.
[84] Yorkshire, West Riding.
[85] Northumberland.

the area of Malton[80] had had six children with his wife, namely five daughters and a son, who, just as they were born one after the other, turned out, as they were born one after the other, to be mute. Eventually the parents came to consider that this was a penalty for sin and turned their grief at their silence into love of their punishment. For the knight fled to the monastery of the monks of York[81] and his wife became a nun in Keldholme.[82] They left the mute children to the care of relatives. One of the girls, who was around fifteen years old and the youngest of them all, came mute to the oratory of the blessed virgin on three occasions. While she was resting, worn out with long vigils, she saw the virgin, with the blessed Michael the archangel, descending from the northern window and calling out loudly in unexpected tones, 'Why are you sitting? Get up and prepare the way for the lady who is coming.[83] For behold she is coming.' And straightaway she got up cured, nor would she have immediately got up cured unless the lady had immediately arrived. She confessed to us that she had borne much mistreatment from her neighbours, as sometimes they hung her from her thumbs, sometimes they afflicted her finger in the joint with a pin, but such great violence did not extort a human voice. She showed us also a lump on her head. This was done so that trial of the illness when it was doubted should provide proof that healing was given.

18. A woman from the area of Gisburn,[84] who was out of her mind for six weeks because of a spirit of insanity, was completely restored to herself there. And a man who had lost the use of virtually all limbs for six years recovered his previous strength, by divine aid. When he came he sat on the horse like a woman, when he returned he sat on the horse like a man, thus changing his seat along with his adversity.

19. A woman from the Rothbury district,[85] who had been blind for eleven years, was brought there by her relatives. She saw the glorious virgin in a vision, standing by her in the company of St Margaret and, by that spiritual vision, she earned also physical vision. She also told us that she had said and commanded her to say to all, that whoever desired to visit the place should come also in memory of the faithful departed and should recognize that that was the day of her feast, when she had put off the clothing of earthly life and put on the robe of eternal joy.[86]

[86] All Souls day is 2 November, on which a feast of Æbbe was celebrated according to the calendar of the late-13th-cent. Coldingham Breviary, BL, Harley 4664, fo. 131ʳ.

20. Adolescens quidam mutus ad tumbam eiusdem uirginis ora clausa resoluit in laudem, quatinus per hoc palam innotesceret antiquum sue quietis locum ex uacuitate membrorum non euacuari gloria uirtutum.

21. Alia apertis oculis nichil uidebat. Hec ad tumbam residens, noctem in precibus duxit insompnem. Illucescente autem diluculo, ipsa sibi illuxit quia oculos clausos aperuit, quos apertos clausos habuit, et oculorum falsa serenitas serena facta est abolite falsitatis oculositas.

22. Alia ex inflacione uentris sui in instar gerebat dolioli factaque est per quatuor annos ipsa sibi grauis et suis oneri, dum domestica fuit minus apta labori. Cumque eam ibidem assueti dolores et excubie longiores coegerant in soporem, columbam niueam conspexit, que ei mirabiliter applausit et crebro alarum uerbere uentrem perlustrauit et, sepius recedens et denuo rediens, cum idem semper opus |

fo. 172ʳ repeteret, ab oculis demum euanuit. Euigilans igitur omni illo se tumore carere sensit et ad statum pristinum reformata surrexit, abiit, ad nos uenit, gracias egit, gaudium nunciauit et gaudiorum nobis perseueranciam reliquit.

23. Alia consimili nouem annis laborabat incommodo. Cuius in sompnis pectus et uentrem beata uirgo blandis manibus attrectauit et, sicut postea claruit, curacionis officio recessit. Consurgens namque sensit se ob illum quem senserat attactum plene sanitatis sentire beneficium.

24. Puella quedam dorsum adeo habebat inflatum ut non tantum gibbosa uideretur esse, sed etiam sacculum plenum et longum in dorso portare. Hec post multas in atrio coram circumstantibus agitabatur uolutaciones, post modicum repente in oculis omnium omnem inflacionis turpitudinem exuit et prioris equalitatis formositatem reinduit.

25. Adolescens quidam, neruis in dextro poplite[a] contractis, talum retorsit in nates, qui illic ex morarum longitudine fossam sibi fecerat in cutem. Vnius pedis habebat rectitudinem, alterius uero defectum baculo iuuit. Per uisum igitur apparente beata uirgine accepit ut ad fontem suum descenderet et loca debilitatis lauaret. Descenditque, ut putabat, lauit, rediit. Venitque secundo et, quasi a manu dormientis baculum ablatura et altari oblatura, manum apposuit.

---

[a] ploplite MS

20. A youth who was dumb unloosed his closed mouth in praise at the tomb of the virgin, so that through this it might be publicly made known that the ancient place of her repose had not lost the glory of its power because her limbs were no longer there.

21. Another woman saw nothing even with her eyes open. She sat by the tomb, spending a sleepless night in prayer. As dawn came up, she was illuminated, for she opened the closed eyes, which had been closed when open, and the false clarity of her eyes was turned into clear vision and that falseness removed.

22. Another woman was like a little barrel because of the swelling of her belly and for four years she was a burden to herself and an encumbrance to her family, for she was a servant unsuited to any work. When she came there and her customary pains and long vigils had forced her to sleep, she saw a white dove, which flapped its wings at her in a wonderful way and traversed her belly with repeated beating of its wings, frequently going away and returning again and performing the same action over again, before finally disappearing from sight. As she woke, she sensed that the swelling had gone away and she arose restored to her earlier state. She left, came to us, gave thanks, announced her joy, and left to us continued joys.

23. Another woman was burdened with a similar trouble for nine years. While she slept the blessed virgin touched her breast and belly with gentle hands and, as later became clear, with the purpose of curing her, and then departed. For when she arose, she sensed a feeling of complete health on account of the touch she had felt.

24. A girl had a back so swollen that she not only appeared to be hunchbacked but also as if she were carrying a big full sack on her back. After she had rolled about many times in the churchyard in the presence of the bystanders, after a little while, in the sight of all, she was suddenly freed from that disgusting swelling and recovered the beauty of her former symmetry.

25. A youth had the muscles in his right ham contracted, so that he twisted his foot back into his buttocks, where it had remained so long that it had created a channel in the skin. He had one good foot but needed the help of a walking stick because of the deformity of the other. He was told by the blessed virgin, who appeared to him in a vision, that he should go down to her fountain and wash the afflicted place. He went down, as he thought, washed, returned. She came a second time and stretched out her hand, as if she were going to take the stick from the hand of the sleeping man and offer it on the altar.

Quo expergefactus, rectus et erectus, arrepto baculo, post abeuntem prosiliit et in salutis signum infirmitatis obtulit baculum.

26. Faber de Lanark[87] de proximo uico domum rediit et subito tenebras oculorum incurrit. Venerat autem huc semel et secundo et, sue peticionis effectu non accepto, cum fide nichil hesitans uenit et tercio. Cumque precibus pulsaret sedulo, uisum ei continuo diuina aperuit miseracio, iuxta illud, 'Pulsate et aperietur uobis',[88] et iterum, 'Qui perseuerauerit saluus erit'.[89]

27. Cecus post hec quidam, cum iam biduum in cecitate haberet, uxore sua eum ducente illuc aduenit et, illucescente in diem tercium diluculo, cum oculos de fonte, sicut in sompnis acceperat, linisset, uisum recepit. Et quibus domi post se mesticiam reliquerat, cum munere sospitatis leticie donum reportabat.

28. Mulier etiam quedam, septennio uisu priuata, de uicino uenit et beate uirginis in se uirtutem excepit. In qua curacione illud laudabile fuit, quod cum ei frontem et oculos per uisum manu attrectaret, tenebras quoque cecitatis a facie detersit.

29. Pauper quoque muliercula cum filio nuper nato ad sepulcrum uenerande uirginis biduanas excubias transegit et optatum sue peticionis effectum obtinuit. Ei namque unius oculi lumen, quod uehemens angustia partus iam pridem extorserat, reddidit et filio manum, que brachio arefacto et ad pectus extento contrahebatur in pugnum, aperuit. Commune igitur omnibus oriebatur gaudium, dum et mater de plena salute gauderet et de filio iam non superesset, de cuius inualitudine sollicita ulterius condoleret.

30. Quidam de territorio Dunelmensium adeo uentris inflacione tumuerat ut in uentro doliolum ferre uideretur, manibus quoque suis extrinsecus ad instar panis insidebat et per totum corpus eius pustule intercutanee uelut glandes se diffuderant. Voto igitur facto, ad suffragia sancte Ebbe confugit et, noctem in orationibus transigens, apparente ei beata uirgine et loca dolorum blanda manu attrectante, omnem cum sopore tumorem deposuit et petite sospitatis graciam accepit.

31. Nuper in quodam adolescente contigit noue admiracionis signum. Qui cum febribus fatigaretur in insania conuersus est. Et

---

[87] Lanarkshire.
[88] Matt. 7: 7; Luke 11: 9.
[89] Matt. 10: 22.

At this he woke up, straight and upright, and, snatching the stick, sprang after the departing figure. As a sign of his healing he offered the stick he had used in his illness.

26. A smith from Lanark[87] returning from a neighbouring village suddenly found his vision clouded. He had come here once and again and, although his petition had not been effective, he did not hesitate in his faith and came a third time. When he had struck with his prayers continually, the divine mercy suddenly restored his sight to him, according to the passage, 'Knock and it shall be opened unto you',[88] and again, 'He that endureth to the end shall be saved'.[89]

27. After this a blind man, who had been blind for two years already, came there led by his wife and, as dawn came up on the third day, when he had anointed his eyes with water from the fountain, as he had been instructed in a dream, he recovered his sight. To those whom he had left at home in sorrow he carried back the gift of joy with the health he had been granted.

28. A woman who had lost her sight for seven years came from the neighbourhood and experienced in herself the power of the blessed virgin. It was especially praiseworthy in this miracle that when she touched her forehead and eyes with her hand in a vision, she wiped away also the shadow of blindness.

29. A poor little woman with her newborn son kept vigil for two days at the tomb of the venerable virgin and obtained the fulfilment of that which she sought. For she restored to her the sight in one eye, of which the fierce anguish of labour had earlier deprived her, and opened the son's hand, which had been contracted into a fist, with the arm dried up and stretched to his chest. So all shared in the joy as the mother rejoiced in her complete health while there was no longer any ailment in her son concerning which she had to continue to grieve solicitously.

30. A man from the Durham region had a swollen belly so great that he seemed to be carrying a barrel in his belly, while it settled over his hands like bread, and intercutaneous pustules like acorns had spread throughout his body. So he made a vow, sought refuge in the help of St Æbbe, and was passing the night in prayer when the blessed virgin appeared to him and touched the painful spots with gentle hands. As he emerged from sleep the swelling disappeared and he received the grace of healing that he had sought.

31. Recently a new and wonderful miracle occurred to a youth, who was so worn out with fever that he became insane. While he slept it

obdormiens | uideret sibi eandem uirtutum operatricem assistere et ei in manus candelam imponere. Euigilans autem, nomen abeuntis uocibus prosequens, candelam acclamabat. Qua a circumstantibus accepta, eum sui ad oratorium sepedictum adduxerunt et noctem pro eo in precibus deduxerunt insompnem. Et mane facto sibi et suis sanissima mente restitutus, cum eis mansuetus rediit, a quibus antea uix teneri potuit.

32. Cuiusdam quoque patrisfamilias filia, in ortum patris uespere egressa, subito ab hoste inuaditur et, percussa in capite pila, in terram exanimis eliditur. Recurrebant ad clamores eius qui in domo erant et, cognito quia a demone uexaretur, tollentes crucem de ecclesia ori pacientis offerebant. At illa, osculum crucis declinans, suggestione hostis brachia crucifixi laniare conabatur. Inuento igitur salutis consilio, egram ad future curacionis locum deferunt et ante paui-mentum deponunt. Cumque ibi modicum pausaret, sana statim exurgens, fatebatur se suam liberatricem uidisse, que eam ad altare duxit et aqua benedicta aspersit. Tantaque erat celeritas miraculi ut idem fere fuisset illo affuisse et ilico sanam fuisse.

33. Alia omnium membrorum officio destituta ibidem diuina largicione omnibus membris suis est restituta.

34. Erat puella de Setona⁹⁰ cui dum mater sua custodiam aucarum suarum deputaret, loquelam amisit, et, neruis et utroque poplite contractis, pedes ipsius ad nates inflectebantur et, tali depressa incommodo, per quinquennium muta permansit. Cui, a parentibus suis apud Dunfermlyn⁹¹ deportate, beata regina Margareta officium membrorum restituit, ita ut baculo sustentante incederet et ad propria remearet. Cui beata regina precepit ut oratorium beate Ebbe apud Coldesburg peteret et ibidem per merita beate uirginis loquelam recuperaret. Contigit autem ut quedam femine de eadem uilla orandi gracia prefatum oratorium peterent et eandem puellam secum adducerent. Que dum inter uigilias obdormiret, beata uirgo Ebbe ei apparuit, precipiens ut surgeret et ad altare accederet. Que tamen sopore grauata rursum obdormiuit. Cum iterum beata uirgo, in specie sanctimonialis apparens, blanda manu oculos et faciem eius palpans atque per labia trahens, ait, 'Surge, quia loquelam recepisti.' Que

---

⁹⁰ East Lothian.
⁹¹ The shrine of St Margaret of Scotland in Dunfermline, Fife.

seemed to him that the miracle worker was present and placed a candle in his hands. When he woke, pursuing her as she went away by calling her name, he shouted out, 'candle'. The bystanders, hearing this, led him to her oratory and spent a sleepless night in prayer on his behalf. In the morning he was restored to himself and his family with a sound mind and he returned mildly with those who previously had scarcely been able to restrain him.

32. The daughter of a householder went out at evening into her father's garden, was suddenly assaulted by the Enemy, struck in the head by a ball, and fell senseless to the ground. Those in the house ran up when they heard her cries and, recognizing that she was vexed by a demon, they brought the cross from the church and proffered it to the sufferer's face. But she refused to kiss the cross and, at the suggestion of the Enemy, tried to break the arms of the crucified. So, following a suggestion that would bring healing, they brought the afflicted girl to the site of her future cure and placed her before the paved area. When she had stayed there a little while, she arose cured, confessing that she had seen her liberator, who had led her to the altar and sprinkled her with blessed water. The miracle occurred so quickly that to be there was almost the same as to be cured.

33. Another woman who had lost the use of all her limbs was there, by the divine goodness, restored to them all.

34. There was a girl from Seton[90] whose mother told her to look after the geese. While she was doing this, she lost the power of speech, the muscles and each of her hams became contracted, her feet were twisted back towards her buttocks, and, struck down with this disability, she remained dumb for five years. Her parents carried her to Dunfermline,[91] where the blessed queen Margaret restored the use of her limbs, so that she walked supported by a stick, and she returned to her home. The blessed queen ordered her to seek out the oratory of the blessed Æbbe at St Abb's head and there, through the merits of the blessed virgin, she would recover the power of speech. It happened that some women from the same village were travelling to the oratory in order to pray and they brought the girl with them. While she was sleeping between vigils, the blessed virgin Æbbe appeared to her, commanding her to get up and go to the altar. However, weighed down with drowsiness, the girl went back to sleep. The blessed virgin again appeared, in the form of a nun, touching her eyes and face with a gentle hand and tugging on her lips. 'Arise,' she said, 'for you have recovered your speech.' Straightaway the girl got

statim surrexit et, pristini sermonis facultate recepta, Deum benedixit et cum omnibus qui aderant Deo et beate Marie et beate Ebbe gracias egit. Volens autem presbiter qui ibi cum eis pernoctauit de uiso miraculo certiorari, prefatas feminas ad se uocauit, que tactis sacrosanctis parate erant asserere sicut prescripsimus rem se habere.

35. Quedam puella de Mersingtona[92] annorum fere duodecim, cum pomerium intraret et manum ad pomum discerpendum extenderet, subito corruit. Cui uidebatur quod eam homines nigri et deformes in arbore suspenderent et ei brachium amputarent. Quam parentes ipsius requirentes, eam ibidem male*a* uexatam inuenerunt. Que, ab eisdem in domum deportata, usum loquendi amisit. Qui cum eam ad ecclesiam beati Lawrencii ad Berwyham[93] gratia sanitatis recuperande duci disponerent, ipsa innuebat ut ad oratorium beate Ebbe duceretur; quod et factum est. Que, cum matre iter arripiens, columbam ante se uolantem quasi ducem itineris conspexit. Que*b* ad quendam fontem adueniens, quem incole fontem beate Ebbe nuncupant, lauit os et faciem. Cui statim uisum est quod beata Ebba digitum in os mitteret et statim solutum est uinculum eius lingue, acsi ei euangelice diceretur, 'Effeta',*c* quod est aperire.[94] Que statim ad oratorium beate Ebbe ueniens, ibidem in uigiliis et oracionibus pernoctabat. Et mane facto, Deo et beate Ebbe pro sui incolumitate | graciarum accione reddita, domum remeauit. Nos uero sanitatis miraculum audientes, noluimus silencio subprimere, immo cum uoce iubilo 'Te Deum laudamus' decantantes, Deo et beate Ebbe dignas laudes persoluimus. Qui gloriosus in sanctis suis, eos glorificare non cessat.

36. Erat quidam adolescens de Scocia[95] oriundus de Barrin[96] qui uili mercimonio, scilicet acuum, uictum querebat. Qui dum apud Aldekambus[97] hospitaretur, de nocturno sompno euigilans se contractum in genibus sentiebat. Nec nisi reptando*d* genibus et manibus incedere ualebat. Et per nouem ebdomadas tali incomodo premebatur. Qui cum ad oratorium beate Ebbe cum magna difficultate deueniret, Deum ac*e* beatam uirginem pro sua sospitate precabatur. Mane autem facto, omnibus ecclesiam egredientibus, ipse egressus

fo. 173ʳ

---

a mals *MS*   *b* eandem *add. MS*   *c* *corr. from* Effetha   *d* *corr. from* raptando
e hac *MS*

---

[92] In Eccles, Berwicks.
[93] St Lawrence's, Berwick, a church granted to the monks of Kelso abbey by Robert son of William during the reign of David I (1124–53): *Early Scottish Charters prior to 1153*, ed. Archibald C. Lawrie (Glasgow, 1905), no. CLXXXV, pp. 148–9; *Acts of Malcolm IV, King of Scots, 1153–65*, ed. Geoffrey Barrow (*Regesta regum Scottorum*, i, Edinburgh, 1960), no. 131, p. 194. The place-name form is unusual.

up and, receiving back her power of speech, she blessed God and, along with all who were present, gave thanks to God and the blessed Mary and the blessed Æbbe. The priest who had spent the night there along with them wished to be more certainly informed about the miracle that had been witnessed and called the women to him. They were prepared to assert on oath that everything occurred just as we have narrated.

35. A girl from Mersington,[92] almost 12 years old, entered an orchard and put out her hand to pluck an apple, when she suddenly fell to the ground. It seemed to her that hideous black men hung her in a tree and cut off her arm. Her parents sought her and found her there in great distress. They brought her into the house but she had lost the power of speech. When they determined to bring her to the church of the blessed Lawrence at Berwick[93] in order to recover her health, she gave a sign that she should be conducted to the oratory of the blessed Æbbe, which was done. As she set off on the journey with her mother, she saw a dove flying before her, as if it were a guide on their journey. Coming to the fountain which the local people call the fountain of the blessed Æbbe, she washed her mouth and face. Immediately it seemed that the blessed Æbbe placed a finger in her mouth and straightaway the bond of her tongue was loosed, as if it was said to her in the words of the gospel, 'Ephphatha', that is, 'Be opened'.[94] Coming at once to the oratory of the blessed Æbbe, she spent the night there in vigils and prayers. In the morning, giving thanks to God and the blessed Æbbe for her health, she returned home. When we heard about the miracle we were unwilling to pass it over in silence, but rather rendered worthy praises to God and the blessed Æbbe, chanting 'Te Deum laudamus' with a joyful voice. He who is glorious in His saints does not cease to glorify them.

36. There was a young man from *Scocia*,[95] born in Barry,[96] who sought his living from the humble trade of selling needles. While he was staying at Oldcambus,[97] he awoke from a nocturnal dream and felt that he was crippled in the knees. He was not able to get along except by crawling on his hands and knees. He was oppressed by this ailment for nine weeks. When, with great difficulty, he came to the oratory of the blessed Æbbe, he prayed to God and the blessed virgin for his health. Next morning, as everyone went out of the church, he went

[94] Mark 7: 34; cf. Miracle 7 above.　　　　[95] Scotland benorth Forth.
[96] Angus.　　　　[97] In Cockburnspath, Berwicks.

est et sub pariete se proiciens obdormiuit, cui dormienti astitit beata uirgo Ebba, uelata uelamine, intentibus oculis, roseo colore uultum perfusa, supra morem humanum speciosa. Apparuit*a* et ait, 'O quam miseri estis', et, inprimis premisso, 'In nomine patris et filii et spiritus sancti, Amen,'*b* ait, 'Surge et ambula';[98] qui statim euigilans eam intueri et apprehendere cupiebat, que nusquam comparuit. Ille uero pellibus solutis quas genibus ad duriciam terre cohibendam admouerat, bis uel ter eam querendo ecclesiam circuibat. Sanus autem ad Coldyngham reuersus, tam mentes quam ora hominum qui aderant in Dei laudes et beate uirginis resoluebat.

37. Parui uero temporis interuallo in eodem miraculum miraculo successit. Illius enim genu cum tybia deformis inflacio occupabat, ita ut ei uel mortem uel perpetuam debilitatem minaretur. Qui dum ad tumbam beate Ebbe in precibus pernoctaret, ei soporato beata uirgo apparuit et, blanda manu illam inflacionem confricans, eum ut surgeret precepit. Qui statim euigilans, sanum se senciens, saluatrici sue graciarum actione reddita, baculum cui innitebatur proiecit.

38. Mulier quedam de episcopatu Dunelmensi oriunda, scilicet de uilla que uocatur Akley,[99] media sui corporis parte paralisis morbo dissoluta, ad oratorium beate Ebbe peruenit. Que secunda, tercia, quarta feria absque ullius cibi percepcione in precibus perseuerauit, fixum tenens in animo quod nequaquam abcederet antequam per beatam uirginem superni beneficii gracia eam uisitasset. Tres uero fratres cenobii Coldynghamenses, ibi casu aduenientes, eam uiderunt et illius miserie quam plurimum condoluerunt. Quinta uero feria, dum ante gradus altaris obdormiret, uidebatur ei quod quedam auis pulcherrima ei super manum egram insideret, uel que auis aut cuius generis esset scire non ualebat. Sed illius decore quam plurimum delectata, manu sana eius complanabat, cui id agenti mulier incomparandi decoris assistens, ait, 'Hec auis auis est beate uirginis Marie'. Illa uero et a sompno et ab egritudine surgens, nullo sustentante ad altare accessit, cui oscula crebra impressit. Postera uero die ad Coldyngham peruenit et missam cuiusdam sacerdotis audiuit, cui factum in se miraculum enarrauit et ad patriam propriam remeauit.

39. Quidam adolescens Scoticus nacione,[100] cum esset fere sex

---

a The punctuation of the manuscript might support taking this verb with the previous sentence and regarding it as duplicating the previous 'astitit'   *b et add. MS*

[98] Matt. 9: 5; Luke 5: 23; Acts 3: 6.   [99] Co. Durham.
[100] Meaning a Gaelic-speaker.

out, threw himself down by the wall, and slept. While he was sleeping the blessed virgin Æbbe stood by him, covered with a veil, her eyes turned towards him, her face imbued with a rosy hue, more beautiful than is human wont. She appeared and said, 'How wretched you are', and, first saying, 'In the name of the Father and of the Son and of the Holy Spirit, Amen', she said, 'Arise and walk'.[98] He awoke at once and desired to see her and take hold of her, but she never appeared. Untying the hides that he had worn on his knees to protect them from the hard ground, he went around the church two or three times in search of her. Returning to Coldingham cured, he released the minds and mouths of the men who were there in praise of God and the blessed virgin.

37. After only a short time another miracle followed this miracle. An ugly swelling had affected this man's knee and leg, in such a way that it threatened him with death or permanent disability. While he was spending the night in prayer at the tomb of the blessed Æbbe, the blessed virgin appeared to him as he slept, and, rubbing the inflammation with a gentle hand, commanded him to get up. He awoke immediately, sensing that he was cured, gave thanks to his deliverer, and threw down the staff on which he had leaned.

38. A woman born in the diocese of Durham, namely in the village of Aycliffe,[99] half of whose body was disabled with paralysis, came to the oratory of the blessed Æbbe. She spent Monday, Tuesday, and Wednesday in prayer without taking any food, keeping it fixed in her mind that she would not depart before the grace of heavenly goodness had visited her through the blessed virgin. Three brethren of the monastery of Coldingham, who happened to come there, saw her and sympathized deeply with her misery. On the Thursday, while she was sleeping before the steps of the altar, it seemed to her that a very beautiful bird perched on her, on her diseased hand, though she did not know what bird it was or of what species. But, delighted very much by its attractive appearance, she stroked it with her healthy hand. While she was doing this, a woman of incomparable beauty stood before her, saying, 'This bird is the bird of the blessed virgin Mary'. The woman arose both from her sleep and from her illness, went to the altar without any assistance, and planted many kisses on it. Next day she came to Coldingham and heard the mass of a certain priest, to whom she recounted the miracle that had been performed in her, and then she returned to her own country.

39. There was a young man of the Scottish nation[100] who had been

annorum, agnos patris sui in agris pascebat, qui sopore depressus tanta sitis ariditate in dormiendo exaruit ut fere mori sibi uideretur. Et ecce quatuor mulieres accesserunt, que tantum ad potandum ei dederunt ut sitim preteritam copia superinfusa supra modum recompensaret. Ille uero post tantam potacionem uisceribus fere disruptis spiritum exalare se putabat. Tandem uero euigilans toto corpore distensus iacebat. Tumor etiam non modicus collum occupabat. Qui a patre suo quesitus et inuentus et ad domum deportatus, annis sedecim mutus permansit. Qui, ad beatam Margaretam[101] in Scociam[102] ueniens, meritis beate Margarete de uentris inflacione curacionem accepit. Tandem Coldyngham petiit | et, ad tumbam beate Ebbe pernoctans, licet non uoce tamen cordis deuocione opem beate Ebbe postulabat. Dum uero fratres in monasterio matutinis laudibus operam darent, uidebatur ei quod quedam uolucris speciosa, a fenestra australi ueniens, super tumbam descendebat et de tumba ad altare transuolabat. Que ad eum ueniens, coram eo sedebat et ecce beata uirgo nimis speciosa ei apparens, ei digitum in os posuit et discessit. Ille uero, soluto lingue uinculo, clamabat 'Gratias ago Deo et beate Ebbe! Ecce possum loqui qui mutus fueram!' et, exiens foras de ecclesia, magnam quantitatem euomuit et tumor qui in collo apparuit detumuit. Rursum uero obdormiuit et ecce beata Ebba ei apparuit et ut ad beatam Thomam martirem[103] pergeret admonuit, quam ammonicionem ille deuotus impleuit.

fo. 173ᵛ

[*Explicit sermo de uita et miraculis sancte Ebbe uirginis ex compilatione Reginaldi Dunolm' monachi.*[104]]

[101] The shrine of St Margaret of Scotland in Dunfermline, Fife.
[102] Scotland benorth Forth.
[103] The shrine of Thomas Becket at Canterbury.
[104] On this attribution, see Introduction, pp. xvii–xx.

pasturing his father's lambs in the fields when he was nearly six years old and, falling asleep, had burned with such parching thirst while he slept that he seemed to himself to be almost dying. Behold, four women approached, who gave him so much to drink that the great quantity they poured into him more than made up for his prior thirst. But, after such a great drink, his insides almost burst and he thought that he would give up the spirit. When he eventually awoke, he lay there with his whole body distended. Moreover, a large swelling filled his throat. His father sought him, found him and carried him home, where he remained for sixteen years unable to speak. Coming to the blessed Margaret[101] in *Scocia*,[102] he was cured of the swelling of his belly by the merits of the blessed Margaret. Eventually he came to Coldingham and, spending the night at the tomb of the blessed Æbbe, he begged the help of the blessed Æbbe, with a devout heart even if not with his voice. While the brethren in the monastery were engaged in matins, it seemed to him that a beautiful bird came in the south window, alighted on the tomb, and then flew from the tomb to the altar. It came to him, settled before him, and, behold, the blessed virgin appeared to him in all her beauty, placed a finger in his mouth, and departed. But he, with the bonds on his tongue released, called out, 'I give thanks to God and the blessed Æbbe! Behold, I can speak, who was dumb!' Going out of the church, he vomited a vast quantity and the swelling which appeared in his throat went down. He slept again and, behold, the blessed Æbbe appeared to him, and commanded that he should go to the blessed Thomas the martyr,[103] which command he dutifully fulfilled.

[*Here ends the sermon on the life and miracles of St Æbbe the virgin compiled by Reginald, monk of Durham.*[104]]

MIRACVLA SANCTE MARGARITE
SCOTORVM REGINE

(Madrid, Biblioteca del Palacio Real, II. 2097, fos. 26^r–41^v)

Incipit prologus in miraculis sancte Margarite^a
Scotorum regine

Quam magnus et mirabilis Deus in sanctis suis,[1] per quorum merita
ineffabilia iugiter operando prodigia, nos qui adhuc temporali uita
fruimur de sua repromissionis munificencia certificat, insinuando
uidelicet nobis quanta familiaritatis gratia et amoris priuilegio suos
extollendo beatificat in celis, quorum corpora multimodis signis
uisitando honorat in terris. Hii sunt enim bellatores incliti,
pompam mundi et omnia eius prospera uelud fenum calcantes, soli
Deo mente et opere fideliter adherentes, exemplar facti nobis uite
celestis et summe beatitudinis, ut si fuerimus eorum imitatores
accionum, proculdubio erimus coheredes mansionum. De quorum
glorioso contubernio lucidissima nostra Margarita et secundum
ewangelicum sensum pretiosa iure celorum regno assimilata,[2] ubi
manet eternaliter glorificata. Que, nostris temporibus occidentales
tenebras sue lucis splendore uelud lucifer matutinus irradiando
illustrans, quicquid tenebrarum caligine obcecatum et ignorancia
ueritatis obduratum fuerat, subtiliter et artificiose plena fide et
racione, prudens magistra agendo que docuit ad agnicionem ueri,
licet multum desudando, perduxit. Sed quia libellus de eius uita
inscriptus, qualia eius opera in presenti seculo fuerint, quanta
misericordia et pietate claruerint, sufficienter ostendit,[3] ego
quoque | licet incomposito a ueritatis tamen tramite nequaquam
uacillante modo, ea que post uite sue exitum, diuina miseracione
cooperante, ob eius merita que oculis meis partim conspexi miracula,
partim a fidelibus didici relatoribus quibus Deus per ipsam, immo
ipsa per Deum magnificata est uehementer, litterarum memorie quod
necessarium est ualde presentibus utile quidem posteris decreui
accomodare.

Explicit prologus. Incipiunt miracula.

1. De muliere a tumore brachii liberata

Fuit nacione et gente mulier paupercula Anglica apud orientales
partes huiusdem gentis manens, que multis temporibus grauissimo

---

^a Margarita *MS*

Here begins the prologue to the Miracles of Saint Margaret, queen of Scots

How great and wonderful is God in His saints.[1] He continually works ineffable marvels through their merits and thus reassures us, who are still in this earthly life, of the bounty of His promises, by making known to us with what great grace of familiarity and privilege of love He blesses His own, by raising up in heaven those whose bodies He honours on earth by visiting with many miracles. These are the noble warriors who trample the pomp and prosperity of the world like grass, cleaving faithfully to God alone in mind and deed, giving us an example of heavenly life and the highest beatitude, so that if we imitate their actions we shall without doubt be co-heirs of their mansions. One of their glorious company is our shining Margaret, 'precious' in the sense of the Gospel, rightly likened to the Kingdom of Heaven.[2] In our own days she has illuminated the western shadows with the splendour of her light like the radiant morning star. The wise mistress, full of faith and understanding, has with subtlety and skill led whoever had been blinded by the darkness of shadows and was obdurate in ignorance of the truth to recognition of the truth, doing this by acting as she taught, even though it cost much effort. But since the little book written about her life shows sufficiently well what were her deeds in the present world and how brightly they shone with mercy and kindness,[3] I have decided to commit to written memory the miracles performed with the aid of the divine mercy and on account of her merits after she departed this life, by which God through her, or rather she through God, was glorified. Some of these I have myself seen and some I learned of from trustworthy informants. I do this in a clumsy way, but never swerving from the path of truth, and it is a task very necessary for those alive now and useful indeed for posterity.

Here ends the prologue. Here begin the Miracles.

1. A woman freed from a tumour on her arm

There was a poor little woman, English by birth and race, living in the eastern regions of that people, who was afflicted for a long time

---

[1] Ps. 67: 36 (68: 35).   [2] Matt. 13: 45–6.
[3] i.e. Turgot's *Vita S. Margarite Scottorum regine.*

afflicta dolore, brachium habens, a compage humerorum usque ad extremitatem digitorum, tanto cutis et carnis tumore confectum ut nullo sui uigore hoc erigere et, nisi fune circumligato et collo eius suspenso, portare potuisset. Insuper manus adhunca neruis contractis per nouem annorum circulum nec penitus claudi potuit, nec omnino aperiri. Sed per tantum spacium, digitis ad modum fuscine a se inuicem separatis, inter utraque eius dolore manebat. Quid, rogo, illa miserrima faceret? Rerum temporalium inedia et cotidiani uictus egestate dolebat, corporis molestia, langore succrescente, sine omni consolacione manebat. Vnum solum expectabat auxilium, nichil quod mundi erat preter mortem in tanta aduersitate querebat, per quam suos iudicabat terminandos cruciatus. Sed quia Deus potens in misericordia ancille sue desolate inspirauit, ne de eius auxilio desperaret sed ore et corde ad eum qui benignus est clamaret, hec non solum mentis contricione sed corporis sui promocionem orauit ad Dominum, Galliarum partes ingrediens, ubi quoscumque martires seu confessores uel sacras uirgines in Christo magna operantes audierat, eorum intrat ecclesias, multa lacrimarum effusione exorans ut per eorum preces et merita, grates Deo queat reddere pro sue sanitatis restitutione. In hac etiam peregrinatione sua beatorum apostolorum Petri et Pauli orandi causa limina uisitauit, intrauit in ecclesiam, fideliter adorauit, sed de corporis sanitate nichil ad presens impetrauit, que ut rei exitus patuit paulisper est morata, ut Margarita per Dei dispensacionem eo mirabilius postea fuisset glorificata.

Rediit illa multum iam desolata et fere omni spe cassata remeauit ad propria, illud tamen forsan habebat in corde quod de euangelico didiscerat sermone, 'Petite et accipietis, querite et inuenietis, pulsate et aperietur uobis',[4] que prius petere pie non distulit, postmodum pulsare non cessauit. Facta igitur interdum beati Edmundi regis et martiris solennitate,[5] cum magna deuocione sacris excubando se ingessit uigiliis, ubi orans et multum se contricione affligens, sepius dominicam iterando oracionem prope galli cantum hora fere noctis media, illa tanto labore grauata iam sompno | proxima sed nec penitus sopita, in sui corporis defectu paulisper requieuit. Cui requiescenti matrona quedam, admodum uenerandi uultus, etate mediocri, integerrimo decore faciei, uidebatur astare, hiis eam

fo. 27ʳ

---

[4] Cf. Matt. 7: 7; Luke 11: 9.
[5] 20 Nov.

with a very serious ailment. Her arm, from the shoulder to the tip of her fingers, was so weakened by swelling of the skin and flesh that she had been unable to lift it by her own strength and had to support it by a sling around her neck. Moreover for nine years she was unable fully to close or fully to open her hand, which was bent like a hook because of the contraction of the muscles, but for that period of time, with her fingers splayed out like a trident, she remained a victim of both her ailments. What, I ask, should the unhappy woman do? She suffered from lack of material goods and want of daily food, her weakness grew and the affliction of her body continued without any consolation. She looked for help of only one type, seeking in such great adversity nothing in the world other than death, through which she judged her torments would be ended. But because God, who is powerful in mercy, inspired His sorrowful maidservant not to despair of His help but to call out to Him who is benevolent, she prayed to the Lord not only with contrition of heart but also by motion of her body. She went to France, and wherever she had heard that martyrs, confessors, and holy virgins were working great deeds in Christ, she entered their churches, begging them, in floods of tears, that through their prayers and merits she might be able to give thanks to God for the recovery of her health. In the course of her pilgrimage she also went to the shrine of the blessed apostles Peter and Paul to pray, entering the church and worshipping with faith, but she received nothing to help her physical health for the moment. As events showed, this was delayed for a little while so that Margaret, by God's dispensation, might later be glorified through it all the more marvellously.

She returned very downcast and came home with almost all her hopes dashed, but perhaps she still had in her heart what she had learned from the words of the Gospel: 'Seek and you shall receive, ask and you shall find, knock and it shall be opened unto you',[4] for she who had previously not delayed to seek with devotion, afterwards did not cease to knock. In the mean time the feast of St Edmund king and martyr[5] approached and she undertook to spend the night in holy vigils with great devotion, where, praying and afflicting herself with deep contrition, often repeating the Lord's Prayer, near cockcrow, around the middle hour of the night, when she was worn out with these great efforts and close to sleep but not yet completely asleep, she rested a little because of the exhaustion of her body. While she was resting, a lady of very dignified appearance, of middle age and spotless beauty, seemed to be standing there. She addressed these

allocuta sermonibus, 'Quid petis a martire quod non poteris in hoc loco optinere? Surge', inquit, 'citissime, iter tuum sine mora ad Scociam dirige, ibi ecclesiam in honore Sancti Trinitatis consecratam in loco qui ab incolis regionis Dunfermlyn nominatur inuenies; ibi sancta regina et Deo digna Margarita reconditur. Qua interueniente ecclesiam supradictam es intratura et incolumitatem quam cupis sine dilacione habitura.'

At illa quasi a sompno expergefacta in se rediens de tali uisione plurimum letificata, propter promittentis decorem et admirandam uultus reuerentiam, capiebat de repromissione fiduciam. Et quod iussum fuerat iter non segniter arripuit et quam cicius potuit ad locum desideratum peruenit. Fuit autem sacra palmarum solenni-tate,[6] die iam declinante, quando Dunfermelitanam ingressa est ecclesiam ibique ab exterioris ecclesie custode clerico quodam, Scotico quidem genere et nimis proteruo, licentiam uigilandi in eadem ecclesia postulauit. Ille quidem uim faciens et ne compos sue fieret peticionis iuramento se constringens, affirmabat illam, nisi statutis noctibus semper singula sabbata precedentibus, in quibus maxima infirmancium multitudo uigilare solet, se solam sacris edibus inesse non licere et inter hec illam ui moliebatur eicere, set illa uertens uultum cui astabat ad crucifixi altare orationem fudit ad Dominum, humiliter petens ut sua sit in hac necessitate adiutrix, que ei apparuerat domina existens sui laboris et itineris instigatrix. Res nimis mirabilis et in Deo semper laudabilis, in eadem hora omni uigore menbrorum destituta ante sacram aram uelud lapis immobilis corruit ad humum collapsa, ubi per aliquam horam a circumstantibus morti uidebatur iam proxima. Set in breui uersa est tristicia in gaudium, restituta sibi sanitate menbrorum. Cepit namque ligatura neruorum tanto rigore dissolui, ut e singulis digitis uideremus effluenciam sanguinis emanari. Confestim omnis tumor brachii deponitur et manus adhunca, acsi nullum presentiret dolorem, mobilis et ad omnem sui usum agendum habilis est inuenta. Hoc miraculum factum est .xiii. kalendas Aprilis,[7] ob meritum beatissime Margarite regine a Domino, cui honor et gloria in secula seculorum. Amen.

---

[6] The sixth Sunday in Lent.

words to her: 'What are you seeking from the martyr that you will not be able to obtain in this place? Arise', she said, 'most swiftly and make your way without delay to Scotland, and there you will find a church dedicated to the Holy Trinity in a place that the inhabitants of that region call Dunfermline; there the holy queen Margaret, who is worthy in the sight of God, is buried. You are to enter her church and by her intervention you will, without delay, obtain the health that you desire.'

The woman, awaking as if from sleep, recovered herself and rejoiced greatly at this vision. She took confidence in the promise from the beauty and marvellous dignity of appearance of the one who made the promise. Without lingering, she undertook the journey that had been commanded and came to the desired place as quickly as she could. It was late on Palm Sunday[6] when she entered the church of Dunfermline and sought permission to spend the night in the church from the guardian of the outer church, a certain clerk who was a Scot by birth and a very impudent man. He responded violently and bound himself by an oath that he would not agree to her request, insisting to her that she was not allowed to enter the holy precincts alone, but only on the ordained nights preceding each Saturday when a great crowd of sick people is accustomed to keep vigil. As he said all this he tried to eject her by force, but she, turning her face to the Rood altar where she was standing, poured out a prayer to the Lord, humbly begging that the lady who had appeared to her and was the instigator of her effort and her journey should be her helper in this necessity. A thing very marvellous and always praiseworthy in God, in that same hour she fell headlong to the ground before the holy altar like a lifeless stone, losing all strength in her limbs, and she lay there for about an hour, seeming to the bystanders to be already close to death. But soon sadness was turned to joy, the health of her limbs restored to her. For the constriction of her tendons began to relax with such force that we saw blood flow from each of her fingers. Immediately all the swelling of her arm went down and the hooked hand, as if it had felt no pain previously, was found to be mobile and adept for doing every service she required. This miracle was performed on 20 March,[7] through the merit of the blessed queen Margaret, by the Lord, to whom be honour and glory forever. Amen.

[7] During the 13th cent. Palm Sunday fell on 20 March in 1239 and 1250.

2. De curacione cuiusdam puelle a trino morbo

Alio quoque tempore puella quedam miserabili gibbo dorsi contracta, pedibus distortis et natibus talis infixis usum penitus nature in ambulando amiserat, sed contra ius naturale apcior ad gradiendum manu uidebatur quam pede. Allata est itaque ad sancte Margarite gloriosum sarcofagum ubi illud preciosum corpus tegebatur fo. 27ᵛ reconditum, | sed, decreto seniorum, signis crebrescentibus, iuxta magnum altare, ut dignum fuerat, usque in presens seruatur cum maximo honore tumulatum. Ad hoc se contulit illa miserorum commune refugium, implorans cum magna deuocione, ut quod omnibus se humilitate petentibus imperciebatur beneficium, sibi preberet sue salutis desideratum subsidium. Noctem illam lacrimis et orationibus cum magno Dei timore et corporis dolore peregit insompnem. Que dum uigili mente assidue orationi insistendo et ream se in conspectu altissimi confitendo et illud propheticum sepius iterando, 'Domine, non secundum peccata mea⁸ que feci sed secundum magnam misericordiam tuam saluam me fac', cor contritum Deo exhiberet sacrificium, illa serenissima, quam sepius reclamabat, affuit Margarita baculum gestans in manu, capite discoperto et ad modum tonsure clericorum subtus in girum quasi forficibus decenter adequato, lineo induta uestimento quod nominamus superpelicium, super quod mundissimum niuei coloris pallium totum corpus ornabat.

Adueniens in hunc modum, regina uenerabilis oculos suos omni gemma splendidiores aduersum contractam erexit et baculum quem baiulabat in manu uelud minando subleuauit et adiungens dixit, 'Surge citissime, tibi dico, surge', et admouens baculum uelud percussura tetigit eius latus sinistrum. Puella uero facta nimis de percussione eius timida et de comminacione ne amplius lederetur magis sollicita, quod per nouem annos in usu non habuit contra spem procedere temptauit. Conata est e natibus promouere sed Dei misericordia et beate Margarite suffragium suo uoto prebuerunt assensum. Iam cepit pedes a cruribus extendere et per multa tempora negatus patebat incessus. Itur ad ostium, reditur ad sepulchrum, iterum temptat incedere, iterum redire. Et quod sepius faciebat, uix se posse pre nimio gaudio confidebat. Sed

---

⁸ Cf. Ps. 102 (103): 10.

2. *A girl healed of a triple disease*

At another time there was a girl crippled by a miserable hump on her back, with feet so twisted back and ankles pressed up against her buttocks that she had completely lost the natural ability to walk, but, against the law of nature, seemed more capable of getting around on her hands than on her feet. She was carried to the glorious tomb of St Margaret, where that precious body used to lie hidden. However, according to the decision of our elders, as miracles multiplied, the body, as was proper, is kept entombed next to the high altar with great honour to the present day. The girl directed herself to the tomb, begging that common refuge of the wretched with great devotion that she should provide for her the desired relief by giving her health, that gracious gift she granted to all who entreated her in humility. She spent that night in tears and prayers with great fear of God and sorrow of the body. While she concentrated intently and constantly on her prayers, confessing herself guilty in the sight of the Almighty and repeating over and over the words of the prophet, 'Lord, not according to the sins[8] I have committed but according to your great mercy, save me', thus bringing a contrite heart as a sacrifice to God, Margaret, that most serene lady whom she had invoked so often, appeared. She held a staff in her hand, her head was uncovered and her hair was as if carefully trimmed by scissors into a circle below, in the manner of a clerk's tonsure; she was dressed in the linen garment we call the surplice, over which a spotless cloak of the colour of snow adorned her body.

The venerable queen, appearing in this way, lifted her eyes, more splendid than any jewel, towards the crippled girl and raised the staff she was carrying in her hand as if in threat. Then she said, 'Get up at once, I tell you, get up!', and, advancing the staff as if about to hit her, she touched her left side. The girl was very frightened by the blow and worried because of the threats that she might be harmed more, so she attempted, without much hope, to walk, a thing she had not been able to do for nine years. She tried to move herself on her buttocks but the mercy of God and the help of the blessed Margaret granted her wish, and as her feet began to stretch out and her knees unbend, the form of locomotion that had long been denied her was now available again. She went to the door, she returned to the tomb, again she made the attempt to go, again to return. Because of her great joy she could scarcely believe she was able to do what she did repeatedly.

malignus hostis, semper nocere paratus, eius incolumitati cepit inuidere. Qui, dum conatus suos aduersus illam exercuit, imbecilliter deambulantem in puteum, qui est sepulchro proximus fonsque sancte Margarite appellatus, nequiter impegit. Sed gloriose regine protectione inuenta est nimis immunis ab omni corporis lesione et deinceps sana effecta circumquaque deambulabat et adiutricem suam non immerito in omnibus magnificabat, cuius precibus exauditor est Deus, cui gloria et magnificencia per infinita seculorum secula. Amen.

3. De muliere a paralisi liberata et luce oculorum eidem restaurata

Nec mora postea facta in sequenti ebdomada aliud miraculum memorabile contigit ad sacratissime Margarite regine sepulchrum. Erat in eadem prouincia mulier quedam indigena, per quinquennis temporis spacium usu carens oculorum, necnon ab omni parte membrorum tam graui paralisis langore percussa, ut qualiter nisu sic tocius corporis carebat effectu. Sed quorum corda timor Domini possederat, illam misericorditer circumferebant, quia per seipsam |

fo. 28ʳ nec aliquam partem sui corporis erigere, ne quo uellet tendere, utpote cecitate dampnata nisi solo sermone potuit indicare. Hanc ipsam nostris oculis conspeximus ante ianuam monachorum ibidem Deo et sancte Margarite seruiencium, uelud recolo, per dimidium annum in nudo miserabiliterᵃ iacentem et communem elemoniamᵇ accipientem, qua ipsa cum ceteris pauperibus per singulos dies pascebatur.

Cum autem spiritui sapientie et consilii[9] placuisset, misertus eius miserie, per suam sapienciam in cor eius salutiferum inspirauit consilium, misericordiam Dei et sepe memorate regine precibus et uigiliis quantum potuisset attencius peruenire. Contulit exhinc se, quibusdam rogatu illam deferentibus, prope uenerabile sepulchrum, ubi sciebat fontem pietatis inexhaustum et multa bonitate copiosum. Hec autem prope corpore sed propior mente uelud rei euentus comprobat, pie nocturnis persistens orationibus inter spem et timorem multimoda anxietate grauata, huiusmodi preces perfudit ad dominam. 'Domina,' inquit, 'regina, Deo digna, quod mundo

---

ᵃ miseribiliter *MS*   ᵇ *This may be regarded as either a slip for 'elemosinam' or an acceptable variant of it. One original charter of the late 12th cent. for Langley priory in Leicestershire makes a point of correcting 'elemonam' to 'elemoniam': Documents Illustrative of the Social and Economic History of the Danelaw, ed. F. M. Stenton (London, 1920), no. 419, p. 311; cf. Dict. Med. Lat., i. 761, s. vv. 'elemonia', 'elemosina'*

But the wicked Enemy, who is always ready to do harm, was inspired by envy that she was so safe and sound. Exercising his wiles against her, he thrust her, as she walked so weakly, into the well which is near the tomb and is called St Margaret's fountain. But by the protection of the glorious queen, she was found completely free of any bodily harm and thereupon she walked all around, completely healthy, and glorified her helper in all things not undeservedly, whose prayers are heard by God, to whom be glory and splendour, world without end. Amen.

3. A woman freed from paralysis and whose eyesight was also restored

In no time at all, in the following week, another memorable miracle occurred at the tomb of the most holy queen Margaret. There was in that region a local woman who for the space of five years had lost the use of her eyes and was also struck by such severe paralysis in all her limbs that she could make no effort or movement in her entire body. In their mercy, those whose hearts were filled with the fear of God carried the woman around, for by herself she could not lift any part of her body nor direct herself where she wanted to go, except by indicating it by speech, condemned as she was to blindness. We saw this woman with our own eyes outside the gateway of the monks serving God and St Margaret there and, as I recall, she lay there naked and wretched for half a year, receiving the general alms by which she, along with the other poor people, was fed each day.

But when it pleased the spirit of wisdom and counsel,[9] who had mercy on her misery, through His wisdom He inspired in her heart the life-giving design of attaining the mercy of God and the queen we have mentioned so often, through prayers and vigils as intently as she was able. She therefore directed herself, carried by those she asked, to the neighbourhood of the venerable tomb, where she knew there was a spring of inexhaustible kindness and rich with all goodness. Close in body but, as events showed, even closer in spirit, she devoutly continued in her nocturnal prayers, between hope and fear, burdened with various anxieties, pouring out these prayers to the lady: 'Lady,' she said, 'queen, worthy in God's sight,

[9] Isa. 11: 2.

tacente ad tui honorem a Deo facta cotidiana proclamant miracula, aspice in me oculis pietatis et misericordie, quibus dum adhuc esses in carne pre omnibus affluebas, semper amatrix pauperum, consolatrix desolatorum, sustentatrix uiduarum et orphanorum, sis propicia afflictioni mee et da mihi corpoream sanitatem. Scis enim me omnibus temporalibus bonis immunem et quod nichil desiderem preter membrorum meorum restitucionem, quod desideratissimum munus si per te benedicta optineam, iudicabo me omni diuite diciorem.' Hec illa orante et uotum suum cum effectu sequente, quod cum magna fiducia implorauit a Deo per preces beate Margarite impetrauit. Quam magna apud Deum Margarite suffragia, per quam in una muliercula simul bina perpetrata sunt miracula. Surrexit egrota a paralitico quo tenebatur morbo liberata, luce oculorum sibi restaurata, agens grates sancte Margarite regine per quam Dominus noster Iesus Christus contulit ei suam peticionem, qui cum patre et spiritu sancto uiuit et regnat in eternum. Amen.

4. De quadam muliere que tumorem uentris habebat

Non est pede taciturnitatis conculcandum quod mulier anglicana, in Laudoniam profecta, uiro nupsit indigine.[a] Ista post conceptum metam parientibus a natura prefixam transgressa, tedioso confecta langore, annum grauida perhennauit. In modico namque uentris tumore deformata, uentrem preambulum tanquam alienum sibi usurpatum protendebat. Hec itaque cum de subsidio defideret naturali, ad diuinum se contulit et monasterium de Dunfermlyn corde contrito et spiritu adiit humiliato. Vbi, cum pernoctaret iuxta sepulchrum gloriose regine, succubuit. Apparuit autem ei quedam, niueis candidata uestibus, misericorditer inquiens, 'Euigila, mulier miserrima, euigila, mulier inconsulta, quia per me tibi celestis misericordia propiciari dignata est. Pergens ergo ad profunde uallis fo. 28ᵛ crepidinem | que cimiterio proxima est,[10] tui doloris cumulos excucies et in salutem reformaberis.' Cum hec beata prosequeretur, muliercula egrota sciscitante quenam esset, graciosa regina subintulit, 'Ego sum Margarita, cuius precibus sanitati es restituta.' Cumque hec dixisset disparuit. Post hoc illa tam preclare uisionis alloquio roborata

---

[a] 'Indigina' is common for 'indigena': Dict. Med. Lat., i. 1327, s. v. 'indigena'

[10] The churchyard was south of the church: ch. 39 below.

for, while the world is silent, daily miracles performed by God cry out aloud to your honour, look at me with eyes of kindness and mercy, virtues in which you abounded more than any other while you were still in the flesh. Always a lover of the poor, consoler of the sorrowful, supporter of widows and orphans, be favourably inclined to my affliction and give me physical health. For you know I lack any material property and that I desire nothing except the restoration of my limbs and if I obtain that most longed-for gift through you, blessed one, I will judge myself richer than any wealthy man.' As she prayed thus, she obtained her wish in reality, securing through the prayers of the blessed Margaret what she had sought with great faith from God. How great is Margaret's power of intercession with God, through whom a double miracle was performed in one poor woman. The sick woman arose, freed from the paralysis that had gripped her and with her eyesight restored. She gave thanks to St Margaret the queen, through whom our Lord Jesus Christ granted her request to her and who lives and reigns with the Father and the Holy Spirit forever. Amen.

4. A woman with a tumour on her belly

The following story should not be ground down beneath the foot of silence. An English woman came to Lothian and married a local man. After she had conceived, she went beyond the limit set by nature for those giving birth and, contracting a wearisome disease, she endured a year of pregnancy. For, somewhat deformed by a swelling of the belly, she extended a belly that went in front of her as if it belonged to someone else. Since she gave up hope of any natural remedy, she turned to divine help and came to the monastery of Dunfermline with a contrite heart and a humble spirit. While she was spending the night by the tomb of the glorious queen, she fell asleep. Then there appeared to her a woman clothed in snow-white garments, saying compassionately, 'Wake up, wretched woman, wake up, thoughtless woman, for through me the heavenly mercy has deigned to hear you favourably. Therefore proceed to the bank of the deep valley next to the churchyard[10] and you will shake off the burdens of your ailment and you will recover your health.' When the saint had said this, the sick woman asked who she was and the gracious queen added, 'I am Margaret, by whose prayers you are restored to health.' When she had said this she disappeared. Afterwards the woman, strengthened by the encouragement of such an outstanding vision, summoned

surgit, mulieres sibi deuotas ac honestas acciuit, uallem premonstra-
tam ingreditur, infirmitatis laqueo liberatur. Ossa quidem mortua
nigra sed enormia tamen ab assidentibus sibi matronis effudisse
perhibetur. Ipsi honor et gloria qui in sanctis suis semper est mirabilis
in secula.[11] Amen.

5. De quodam homine nomine Mutino ad sepulchrum eius curato

Illud quoque pretereundum non est de quodam muto factum
miraculum, qui per triginta et duos annos facultatem loquendi
amiserat. Hic quinquennis etate in pascendis uitulis paruis dum
moraretur in campis et sompno interceptus uirentibus herbis
membra sua grate preberet soporis quieti, mulieres tres siue
mulierum species ut in actibus earum comprobatur, phantastice et
nimium nephande ei appropinquantes, in hunc modum confabulan-
tur ad inuicem: 'Quid faciemus de uiro isto? Quo deferemus eum?' Ex
quibus data sentencia illum interficiendum duabus proterue procla-
mantibus, tercia quasi magis pia impiissima tamen resistendo dicebat,
'Hoc illi sufficere pomum in os eius proicere et perpetua eum
taciturnitate dampnare.' Facto ab utrisque sentencie tali consensu,
uox eius confestim maliciosum assecuta est effectum. Dormiens
namque euigilauit et quod per uisum uidit, se mutum fieri, in actu
comprobauit. Perseuerans ergo in hac sui corporis infirmitate usque
ad quadragesimum etatis sue annum, terras plurimas perambulando,
monasteria diuersorum sanctorum uisitando, sperans per eorum
merita amissam recuperare loquelam, inestimabiles perpessus est
labores, sed tandem quod diu requisiuit adinuenit.

Appropinquante enim beate regine festiuitate, que singulis annis ad
eius memoriam et ad omnium sanctorum quorum reliquie in eadem
continentur ecclesia ueneracionem recolitur,[12] in qua die sacri
corporis sui de ecclesia priori ad altare maius translacio, sicut superius
commemoratum est,[13] cum magna celebritate psalmorum et
ymnorum facta commemoratur, tertia die eandem solemnitatem
precedente in uigilando et orando ante ostium chori monachorum
excubauit. Et, mirabile dictu, ostium chori sibi soli apertum, cetere
uero multitudini ibidem simul uigilanti clausum fuisse uidebatur. Per
quod memorabilis domina egrediens et Mutino appropinquans—sic

---

[11] Ps. 67: 36 (68: 35).
[12] The Feast of the Relics, a commemoration held on different days in different

some devout and respectable women to her, entered the valley that had been indicated and was freed from the noose of illness. She is said by the ladies who were with her to have discharged some huge black bones. To Him be honour and glory who is always marvellous in His saints forever.[11] Amen.

5. A man called Mutinus cured at the saint's tomb

I should not omit to tell the story of the miracle that befell a dumb man, who had lacked the power of speech for thirty-two years. When he was five years old and out in the fields tending the young grazing stock, he became sleepy and laid his limbs down in the green grass to take a peaceful sleep. Three women—or, as their actions showed, figures in female form—approached him. These wicked apparitions spoke to each other as follows: 'What shall we do with this male? Where shall we carry him off to?' When two of them had given their opinion, proclaiming shamelessly that he should be killed, the third, as if more kindly, but in fact most evil, dissented and said, 'It will be enough for this one if we throw an apple into his mouth and condemn him to perpetual silence.' The other two agreed with this decision and immediately his voice experienced the evil result. For the sleeper awoke and confirmed in actuality what he had seen in the vision, that he had become dumb. Remaining therefore in this infirmity of body until his fortieth year of age, he wandered through many lands, visiting the monasteries of various saints, hoping through their merits to recover the power of speech he had lost. He suffered immeasurable labours, but at last found what he had long sought.

The feast of the blessed queen approached, which is celebrated each year in her memory and in veneration of all the saints whose relics are in the church,[12] on which day the translation of her holy body from the former church to the high altar, as described above,[13] is commemorated with a great celebration of psalms and hymns. On the third day before this feast the dumb man spent the night in vigils and prayers before the door of the monks' choir. Marvellous to relate, the door of the choir seemed to be open to him alone, while to the rest of the multitude keeping vigil there it appeared to be closed. The renowned lady came out through the door and approached Mutinus—for so he

churches to commemorate all the saints whose relics were located in the church. It is not known on what day this was celebrated in Dunfermline.

[13] Ch. 2; ch. 9 describes this 1180 translation at length.

enim ille uocabatur, habens nomen ex re—semel eum circueundo deambulet. Impositaque manu eius gutturi suo, pomum quo loquele fo. 29ʳ modum | antiquitus amiserat extrahendo, genas et os et que gutturi sunt proxima sanando molliter palpat. Redeunte illa, tam copiosa fulgebant in choro luminaria acsi interiora eius innumeris lampadibus fuissent referta. Parietes quoque et pauimentum et tectum splendebant ut aurum mundissimum. Ille Deo omnipotenti de hac uisione in cordis secreto agens grates et se posse loqui adhuc minime credens, timore simul et dolore interius agitatus, uelut ipse confessus est, mirum in modum exestuabat. Tandem siti compulsus a circumstantibus ex inprouiso potum querebat. At illi, audientes Mutinum loquentem et cum magna admiratione et leticia laudes omnipotenti exsoluentes Deo, gratissimam predicauerunt Margaritam, pro cuius amore promptissima usque ad uite sue exitum reddebatur Mutino loquela. Et ut omnis certam de Margarita habeat fiduciam, uidimus hunc ante quinque annis lapides ad opus ecclesie gestantem et tamen non loquentem. Erat enim fortis robore, moribus gratus et ad quodlibet opus sine murmuracione promptissimus. Vnde uisitauit eum Dominus cuius maiestas perseuerat in secula seculorum. Amen.

6. De tribus miraculis in nocte translacionis eiusdem perpetratis

Aduenit interea sue sacre translacionis dies festiuus, in quo tocius circumiacentis regionis egrotancium multitudo non modica, anime uel corporis infirmitate depressa, spe recuperande salutis festinat tantis interesse uigiliis. Vbi, ad reuelanda tam precellentis regine merita, in eadem nocte triplicata sunt miracula: muta loquitur, cecus illuminatur, puelle brachium aridum et cancri infirmitate comesum ad pristinam reformatur sanitatem. E quibus prior puella fuit indigena, que nescio quo rei euentu loquele modum amiserat et tocius corporis paciebatur defectum. Hac arbitror de causa talem sibi contigisse euentum, ut per illam opera Dei manifestarentur. Alter uero Scotus fuit genere, etate nec minus quam quadraginta annos habere uidebatur. Hic, uelud ipse confitebatur, per tres annos nec solis radios nec quicquam quod sub celo est, penitus carens luce oculorum, potuit uidere. Tercia nacione fuit anglicana, miserabilem

was called, taking his name from the fact that he was mute—and walked once around him. Placing her hand on his throat, she extracted the apple by which he had long ago lost the power of speech, and healed him by lightly touching his cheeks, his mouth, and the parts nearest to the throat. As she returned, such a great mass of lights shone in the choir as if the interior was full of innumerable lamps. The walls and the pavement and the roof gleamed like the purest gold. He gave thanks to God Almighty for this vision secretly in his heart, and, not yet believing that he could speak, he was agitated within by fear and grief, as he himself confessed, boiling over in a remarkable way. At last, driven by thirst, he unexpectedly asked the bystanders for a drink. When they heard Mutinus speak they gave praise to almighty God with great wonder and joy, declaring that Margaret was most kind, through whose love ready speech was restored to Mutinus until the end of his life. And so that everyone should have certain faith in Margaret, we saw this man five years ago bearing stones for work on the church and yet not speaking. For he was great in strength, pleasing in his ways and very ready for any task without complaining. This is why the Lord visited him, whose majesty endures forever. Amen.

6. Three miracles that occurred during the night of the saint's translation

Meanwhile, the festive day of her holy translation arrived, when from all the surrounding region a great crowd of sick people, weighed down with infirmities of mind or body, hurried to be present at such important vigils in the hope of recovering their health. On this night, in order to reveal the merits of such a distinguished queen, three miracles occurred: a deaf woman spoke, a blind man was given sight and the arm of a girl which had been dried up and consumed by a cancerous disease was restored to its original health. Of these the first was a local girl who had lost the power of speech, I do not know through what turn of events, and suffered from a weakness of the whole body. I judge that this had befallen her for the following cause, that through her God's works might be made manifest. The other was a Scot by race and appeared to be not less than forty years of age. He, as he himself said, had been completely without sight for three years, unable to see the rays of the sun or anything else under heaven. The third was an Englishwoman by birth, who had suffered for a long

diu brachii dolorem, cancro illud consumente, perpessa. Hii tres simul dissimiles quidem infirmitate, pares mente et deuocione huic sacre se conferunt solennitati.

Et dum consolatrix nostra, immo tocius regionis fidei fundamentum, per multiplicatas orationes, iterato eius nomine, non solum ab illis sed ab omni populo innumerabiliter interpellaretur, affuit illa pia compeditorum liberatrix, que semper est omnibus in qualibet iusta peticione adiutrix. Affuit quidem non corporali presencia se populo ostendendo sed iustarum peticionum facultates et corporum sanitates necnon et animarum medelas pie exorantibus exhibendo. Interea fo. 29ᵛ cepit illa quam superius | commemoraui muta balbutire et, uelud ad incipiendum locucionis modum, linguam suam mouendo et huc illucque uertendo, nil tamen adhuc loquendo, formam uerbi cum uoce non penitus intellecta subire. Nec mora prius habite murmuracionis tota ambiguitas ab auditore expellitur. Nam eius lingua per Dei graciam et potentem dominam ita ad loquendum fit habilis ut nulla penitus ueteris impedimenti in aliquo uerbo comperirentur uestigia. Nec minus qui cecus fuerat letatur, oculorum sibi luce donata. Tercia uero brachii plaga siccata et a suo languore sanata coram omnibus in eadem ecclesia orando pernoctantibus, multiplices sancte Margarite grates exsoluit cum ceteris simul cum ea a sua infirmitate curatis. Per cuius suffragia tam crebra operando miracula, suam magnificenciam et gloriam semper mirabiliter extollit. Ipsi honor et reuerencia cuius uirtus et potencia sine fine permanet in secula seculorum. Amen.

7. De uictoria sancte Margarite regine de rege Norwagie anno Domini .mcclxiii.[14]

Rex Noricorum, regnum aggressus expugnare Scotorum, copiosam nauium multitudinem congregauit et portum cuiusdam loci qui Largys dicitur[15] cum suis applicuit. Quo audito, rex Scocie exercitum tocius regni coadunauit ut regi Noricorum obuiaret. Interea quidam miles nomine Iohannes de Wemys,[16] iustus et fidelis, ui cotidianarum febrium uehementer fatigatus, dum lassa menbra infirmitate aliquantulum mitigata sompno grato exhibuit, huiuscemodi uisionem cernere

---

[14] This miracle is also recounted in almost identical words in Bower, *Scotichronicon*, x. 15 (ed. Watt, v. 336–8).
[15] Ayrshire, the site of a battle between Haakon IV of Norway and the forces of Alexander III on 2 October 1263.

time from a miserable disease of her arm, which was consumed by cancer. All three came to this holy festival together, with different afflictions but alike in spirit and devotion.

And while our consoler, or rather the foundation of faith in the whole region, was entreated again and again with many prayers and repeated utterances of her name, not only by these but by the whole people, that kind liberator of the shackled was there, she who is always a helper to all in any rightful request. She was there not showing her physical presence to the people but delivering to those who asked for them devoutly the grant of just petitions, healing for the body and cure for the soul. Meanwhile, the dumb woman whom I mentioned earlier began to babble and, by moving her tongue and turning it this way and that, like one just beginning to speak, but not actually speaking, to undertake the shape of a word, even though the sound was not completely comprehensible. Without delay all uncertainty in the hearer at the murmuring she uttered at first was driven away. For through God's grace and the powerful lady her tongue became so adept at speaking that no trace at all of the earlier impediment could be found in any word. He who was blind rejoiced no less as the sight of his eyes was given to him. The third woman, when she was cured of the drying up of her arm and of her disease in front of everyone spending the night in prayer in the church, gave repeated thanks to St Margaret, along with the others who had been cured at the same time. Through the aid she gave in working such numerous miracles He extols His magnificence and glory which are always marvellous. To Him be the honour and reverence whose strength and power abide without end forever. Amen.

7. The victory that St Margaret the queen gained over the king of Norway in 1263[14]

The king of the Norwegians set out to attack the kingdom of the Scots and, gathering a large fleet of ships, landed with his men at the port of a place called Largs.[15] When the king of Scots heard this he assembled the army of the whole kingdom to meet the king of the Norwegians. Meanwhile a knight called John of Wemyss,[16] a righteous and pious man, who was terribly wearied by the force of daily fevers, was found worthy to see the following vision when, since the illness had diminished a little, he surrendered his weary limbs to

[16] Wemyss is in Fife; the church was appropriated to Dunfermline abbey.

promeruit. Videbatur namque sibi se in ostio ecclesie Dunfermelensis consistere, dominamque omni decoratam uenustate de eadem ecclesia prodire. Que in manu dextera militem ducebat, fulgentibus armis indutum, gladio accinctum, cassidem habens impositam. Sequebantur per ordinem tres milites cum armis simili modo procedentes. Ex qua uisione miles non modice extitit perterritus, sed cum de pulcritudine domine animatus sancte regine tali loquitur affamine: 'Obsecro, domina, ut que sis michi indices et qui sunt isti armati milites.' Responditque regina, 'Ego sum Margarita, Scotorum regina. Miles uero iste quem in manu duco meus erat maritus, nomine rex Malcolmus. Tres uero sequentes tres filii mei sunt et reges mecum in hac ecclesia iacentes.'[17] 'Quo pergis', inquit miles, 'O domina?' Cui sancta regina: 'Cum istis ad Largys regnum defensura propero, uictoriam actura de tiranno qui regnum meum suo nititur subiugare dominio. Nam michi hoc regnum a Deo accepi commendatum et heredibus meis inperpetuum.' Cum autem hec regina complesset, disparuit. Milesque euigilans gaudio magno exultauit.

Mane autem facto quasi infirmitate oblita equum ascendit; quo fo. 30ʳ ascenso passio | febrium eum uexare cepit. Miles autem a proposito non destitit sed iter inceptum peregit. Cum autem ad monasterium de Dunfermlyn uenisset, priorem domus accersiuit, uisumque sompnium narrauit. Nec tale sompnium quo sepe diludimur extitit sed celitus ostensum. Hoc autem facto, loca singula circa feretrum cum lacrimis osculari cepit et continuo qui infirmus aduenerat, sanus discessit. Nec mora tempestas seua in mari exorta apparuit, nauesque Noricorum cum hominibus submerse sunt. Quidam uero Norici ferro Scotorum cedente interierunt, reliqui autem cum uite periculo et confusione magna discesserunt. Rex autem Norwagie ibidem in patria aliena obiit.[18] Sicque iusto Dei iudicio factum est ut qui aliena inuadere concupierat, uitam cum regno amitteret.

8. De miraculis factis per beatam reginam in nocte sancte Margarite uirginis

Contigit uero et aliud in eadem ecclesia non minus laudabile miraculum, ad nostre fiducie argumentum et ad Margarite, in cuius actibus Deus ubique est semper mirabilis, condigni preconii de die in diem augmentum, ut de illa illud ewangelicum manifeste completum

---

[17] Malcolm III (Canmore) (1058–93), Edgar (1097–1107), Alexander I (1107–24), and David I (1124–53), all buried in Dunfermline abbey church.

grateful sleep. He seemed to be standing in the doorway of the church of Dunfermline and a lady distinguished by every beauty was coming out of the church. She was leading by her right hand a knight dressed in shining armour, girded with a sword and with a helmet on his head. Three armoured knights followed in turn, marching out in a similar fashion. The knight was not a little frightened by this vision but was given spirit by the lady's beauty and addressed these words to the holy queen: 'I beg you, lady, to tell me who you are and who are these armoured knights.' The queen replied, 'I am Margaret, queen of Scots. This knight I am leading by the hand was my husband, king Malcolm by name. The three following are my three sons, kings who lie with me in this church.'[17] 'Where are you going, lady?' said the knight. 'I am hurrying with them to Largs,' said the holy queen, 'to bring victory over that tyrant who is attempting to subject my kingdom to his power. For I have accepted this kingdom from God, and it is entrusted to me and my heirs for ever.' When the queen had finished saying this, she disappeared. The knight woke up and exulted with great joy.

Next morning, as if he had forgotten his illness, he mounted his horse, but once he was mounted his fever began to trouble him. When he had come to the monastery of Dunfermline, he approached the prior of the house and recounted his dream-vision. It was not the type of dream by which we are often deluded but a sign from heaven. Once he had done this, he began to kiss the places around the shrine in tears and straightaway he who had arrived sick went away cured. Without delay a fierce storm arose in the sea and the ships of the Norwegians went down with their men. Some Norwegians were killed by the swords of the Scots, the rest retreated in danger of their lives and with great confusion. The king of Norway died there in a strange country.[18] And thus by the judgment of God it came about that he who had desired to invade another's land lost his life and his kingdom.

8. Miracles that the holy queen performed on the night of St Margaret the virgin

Another no less praiseworthy miracle occurred in the same church, as a support for our faith and to increase from day to day the worthy reputation of Margaret, in whose acts God is everywhere and always marvellous, so that in her this saying in the Gospels might be seen

[18] King Haakon died in December in Orkney.

uideretur: 'Omni habenti dabitur et abundabit.'[19] Quippe que super afflictos et pauperes habuit misericordiam in tempore sui, respectus abunde recepit a Deo et gratiam. Contigit tunc temporis uenerande uirginis et martiris Margarite festiuitate[20] ut singulis sabbatis fieri solet copiosam ad supradictam ecclesiam confluere multitudinem. Ille namque dies forte eo tempore sabbato aduenerat festiuus.[21] Concurrit simplicium multa turba fidelium. Et forsan propter nominis equiuocacionem quamplures assistencium preciosam martirem eodem nomine nuncupatam nostram credebant Margaritam. O quam pia fallacia, que gratia non priuatur. Et ideo qui illud pie credebant, nec a fide sunt cassati nec a sua peticione priuati. Ab illis quippe non est disiunccio, que communiter regnant in celorum palatio. Vnde utrasque Margaritas in essencia quidem dissimiles, in mente tamen et opere credimus esse consimiles. Nec mirum, cum illius multitudinis adhuc in carne uiuentis sed in Christum credentis, sicut actus apostolorum commemorant—'Erat cor unum et anima una'[22]— quanto magis que ab omni carnis liberate sunt passione et superno celorum palacio*a* locate, quas iam secum recepit diuina maiestas, cor simile ab illis et una habetur uoluntas. Ex conueniencium utique in illa nocte multitudine uidimus simul duos curatos, unum paraliticum ab omni membrorum usu a renibus deorsum ita solutum ut in eo non plus sua quam aliena menbra operi uiderentur. Alter uero a natiuitate
fo. 30ᵛ sua mutus perseuerans, circiter quinquaginta annos | habens, manifestam coram omni ecclesia recepit loquelam. Affirmant etiam laici multi simul uigilantes, in eadem nocte tredecim uiros et mulieres ex diuersis languoribus simul fuisse sanos effectos.

Nos autem in omnibus mendacii maculam fugientes, studuimus ex hiis que gesta sunt semper aliquid in relacione nostra retrahere, ne presumeremus—quod absit—modum ueritatis excedere. Hoc pro certo uolentes manifestiora tamen in nostre ordinacionis textu enodare miracula, ne si tendamus per singula prius deficiat relator quam signa. Legentibus sine omni ambiguitate innotescimus me nichil hucusque presenti cartule nostre apposuisse preter ea que oculis meis conspexi. Hec uero que sequentur a fidelissimis didici relatoribus, qui adhuc in ecclesia

---

a pallacio *MS*

---

[19] Matt. 25: 29.   [20] 20 July.
[21] There are too many occasions on which this was true for it to help in dating the miracle.

to be manifestly fulfilled: 'To everyone that hath it shall be given and it will increase.'[19] Inasmuch as she had mercy in her time for those in trouble and the poor, she receives abundant regard and grace from God. It happened at the time of the festival of the reverend virgin and martyr Margaret[20] that a great crowd gathered at the church, as happens every Saturday (for the feast day chanced to fall on a Saturday at that time).[21] A large body of ordinary faithful folk assembled and, perhaps because they had the same name, many of those present believed the precious martyr who bore the same name to be our Margaret. O what devout error, that is not denied grace! The faith of those who devoutly believed that is not made void nor are they denied their petition. There is no disunity between those who reign jointly in the heavenly palace. The two Margarets are dissimilar in essence, but we believe they are alike in mind and work. Nor is it remarkable that, just as the Acts of the Apostles record of that multitude who were still living in the flesh but believing in Christ—'there was one heart and mind in them'[22]—so all the more those who are freed from all suffering of the flesh and dwelling in the heavenly palace above, whom the divine majesty has already received to Himself, should also be alike in heart and have one will. Of the crowd who came together from everywhere on that night, we saw two cured at the same time, one a paralytic so deprived of all use of his limbs, from the kidneys down, that no longer his own but other limbs seemed to be operating in him. The other, who had remained dumb from birth and was about fifty years old, received the power of speech openly before the whole church. Many lay people keeping vigil at the same time also affirm that on the same night thirteen men and women were cured of various ailments at the same time.

In all things we have avoided the stain of falsehood and made the effort in our account to keep a certain distance from the things that occurred, lest we should presumptuously go beyond the bound of truth, which God forbid! But we certainly wish to proclaim the more manifest miracles in the course of our composition, for if we aimed at recounting them all, the teller would be exhausted before the number of miracles was. We inform the readers without any shadow of doubt that, up to this point, I have included nothing in this little account except what I have seen with my own eyes. What is to follow, however, I have learned from trustworthy informants, who are still

[22] Acts 4: 32.

nostra sunt monachi, quorum testimonio de hiis que narrabuntur omnes auditores nostri securi sint.

9. De muliere Emma nomine a dolore dencium curata

Anno ab incarnacione Domini millesimo centesimo octogesimo, consecracionis uero magistri Iohannis apud Castrum Puellarum anno primo,[23] diuinitus immittitur—ut credimus—in animo fratrum Dunfermelensis ecclesie ut mausoleum beate Margarite regine a loco in quo positum erat tollerent. Et quia minus decenter, prout eis uidebatur, locus requiecionis eius paratus fuerat, adhibito opere subtiliori locarent sublimius. Ad cuius deuocionis augmentum, pictorem quemdam Radulphum nomine, hominem magne opinionis et in operibus celature autoritatis famosissimum, iam conduxerant, qui thecam cum celatura interpositis ymaginibus, sicut res ipsa demonstrat, ad opus beate regine preparet aurifolio contectam, usque dum rerum commoditas splendidiorem representaret.[24] Determinato igitur die quo id acturi essent, et iam instante, post capitulum deputato fratre, cui cura commissa operariorum cum ministris erat, et opus propositum aggredientibus, ceteri fratres, in choro solotenus prostrati, non sine timore et tremore sed cum lacrimis, septem psalmos penitenciales cum letania incipiunt, quatinus, si forte disposicioni diuine minus gratum haberetur quod inceperant, iubilacionis hostia culpam presumpcionis dilueret. Sed quia dilectio foras mittit timorem,[25] minus ponderosum metu habebant animum, eo quod id agerent quod in eis spiritualis deuocio conceperat. Quibus finitis, amotum a loco mausoleum ad septentrionalem plagam altaris statuunt, digne ueneracionis gracia pallio decentissime coopertum.

Cementariis interim in extruendo tabulatu lapideo super quem erigeretur operam dantibus, quatinus theca desuper composita uenustius spectantibus preberet spectaculum, contigit ut quedam mulier eiusdem uille | Emma nomine, adeo intolerabili dolore dencium affligeretur, ut intumescente facie, ui grassatus tumoris totum etiam caput preoccuparet infirmitas. Cum igitur languor non minueretur sed accresceret et tederet animam suam uite sue, asciuit sibi pocius mortem quam uitam, felicius estimans morte licet immatura nature

fo. 31ʳ

---

[23] i.e. John, bishop of St Andrews, who was consecrated in Holyrood, Edinburgh, on 15 June 1180: D. E. R. Watt (ed.), *Series episcoporum ecclesiae catholicae occidentalis*, vi (1). *Ecclesia Scoticana* (Stuttgart, 1991), p. 87.

monks in our church, whose testimony about the things they relate is entirely credible to all who hear it.

9. A woman called Emma cured of toothache

In the year 1180 AD, the first year after the consecration of Master John at Edinburgh,[23] the thought was sent from above (as we believe) into the minds of the brethren of the church of Dunfermline that they should move the tomb of St Margaret the queen from the place in which it was situated. And since the place of her last repose had been prepared (as it seemed to them) in a less than suitable way, they should raise it up and employ more elegant craftsmanship. To increase devotion to her they had already employed an artist called Ralph, a man of great reputation and most renowned as a creator of carvings. He prepared a reliquary for the blessed queen, covered with gold leaf and with carved images, made more splendid by these rich objects, as can be seen from the item itself.[24] When the day appointed for the task arrived, after chapter, while the brother in charge of the workmen was beginning the proposed work, along with the servants, the other brethren lay prostrate on the ground in the choir, and began to recite the seven penitential psalms and the litany, not without fear and trembling but with tears, so that, if perchance what they had undertaken should not find grace with the divine will, the sacrifice of jubilation should wash away the fault of presumption. But since love expels fear,[25] they had a mind less weighed down with terror, because they were doing something that a spiritual devotion had conceived in them. When they were finished, they established the tomb, which they had removed from its place, at the north end of the altar, covered with an elegant cloth as a mark of the reverence that it was owed.

The masons meanwhile applied themselves in constructing a stone table on which it was to be raised up, so that the reliquary placed above might make a more beautiful sight to onlookers. It happened that a woman of the town called Emma was so badly afflicted by toothache that her face swelled up and the illness filled her whole head as it was attacked by the force of the swelling. As the illness did not decrease but increased, and made her spirit weary of life, she preferred for herself death rather than life, judging it more fortunate to pay the debt of nature by death, even if premature, than to prolong

---

[24] This translation is tentative.   [25] Cf. 1 John 4: 18.

debitum exsoluisse, quam uitam tali cruciatu circumuentam diu
protelare. Sed diuina pietas, que neminem permittit temptari super
id quod potest, subuenit misere, colluuionem turgentis faciei tali fine
consumens. Cum igitur noctem quandam sicut precedentes ex quo
tumor accidit duxisset insompnem, huc illucque se uertens in cubili
suo, ut egrotantis est pre angustia, illucescente aurora diei, pocius pre
afflictione tediose passionis quam deliberacione mentis quod multo
prius non potuit, quasi in extasim posita parumper requiescit et uidet
sibi aliquem assistere sciscitantem quanam corporis pulsaretur
incommoditate. Cui sicut res se habebat respondit. Qui astitit,
'Vade', inquit, 'cum iam tempus exegerit ad ecclesiam et, orans ad
sepulchrum beate Margarite regine cum humilitate et magna lacrimarum effusione, appone faciem lapidi et astringe, proculdubio super
afflictione tua melioracionem receptura.' Expergefacta uero ualde
mane, mulier pre gaudio uisionis spem recuperande sospitatis con-
cipiens, ut fidem adhiberet dictis commonentis, tendit ad ecclesiam
et, accepta tandem facultate intrandi ad interiora sanctuarii, flectit
genua ante sepulchrum, faciem, ut habuit in monitu, apponit lapidi,
sollicita preces effundit ut domina meritis suis et precibus, dolore
sedato, eam incolumitati restituat. Mira res, cum solicitudine adeo
necessaria precibus insisteret, sensit acsi uiuum aliquid infra dentem
quo acrius languebat, et postmodum strepitum dedisse uel quasi
crepuisse medium. Stupet itaque mulier, mouit eam et motus et
sonitus, sed, autumans ut res erat, quia uirtus Dei interuentu beate
Margarite operabatur in illa, gracias agens Deo et auxiliatrici sue,
sedato paululum tumore, domum regressa est. Nocte uero sequenti
cum se sanitati restitutam omnino putaret, sensit adhuc de intus
modicum quid pristine calamitatis serpere. Et statim in fide nil
hesitans, apposito denti puluere quem tulerat a loco quo prius
domina requieuit in ueteri ecclesia, tumor omnis cum dolore protinus
sedatus est.

10. De Reginaldo monacho eiusdem ecclesie a dolore dencium curato

Affligebatur in motu dentis unius sinistre maxille pre senectute, ut
professus est, quidam frater eiusdem ecclesie Reginaldus nomine,

a life beset with such suffering. But the divine goodness, who allows nobody to be tried beyond what is possible, came to the help of the miserable woman, eradicating the foul matter of her swollen face in the following way. For when she had spent a night without sleep, just like all those preceding it, from the time the swelling occurred, and tossed this way and that in her bed, as sick people do in their anguish, as day dawned, more from the affliction of her wearisome suffering than by a deliberate decision, she rested for a little while, a thing she had not been able to do for a long time before, and seemed to be snatched away out of herself. She saw someone by her side asking what physical affliction was troubling her. After she had explained the situation to him, the figure who was standing there said, 'Go to the church, for now the time is at hand, and, praying at the tomb of the blessed queen Margaret with humility and great outpouring of tears, place your face to the stone and press. Without a doubt you will receive relief from your affliction.' Rousing herself in the morning, from her joy at the vision the woman conceived hope of recovering her health and, trusting in the instructions of the figure who had advised her, she went to the church and received permission to go into the innermost part of the sanctuary. There she kneeled before the tomb, placed her face against the stone as she had been instructed and prayed intently that through her merits and prayers the lady would subdue the pain and restore her to health. A remarkable thing followed. While she was intent on her prayers with all the concentration that is necessary, she felt as if there were something alive within the tooth which hurt her so badly, and afterwards the middle of it gave a crack and, as it were, resounded. The woman was amazed, both the movement and the sound moved her, but believing, as was the case, that the power of God was working in her through the intervention of the blessed Margaret, she gave thanks to God and to her helper, and, with the swelling decreasing a little, she returned home. The following night when she thought she had been completely restored to health, she still felt inside some of her earlier injury spreading. Immediately, not hesitating for a moment in her faith, she applied to the tooth the dust which she had taken from the place where the lady had previously rested in the old church and the swelling and the pain completely disappeared.

10. Reginald the monk cured of toothache

A brother of the same church called Reginald was afflicted with the movement of a tooth in his left jaw, on account of age, as he said. For

adeo ut per annum integrum ex quo habitum sacre religionis suscepit, usum et facultatem comedendi ex ea parte omnino amitteret. Duas fo. 31ᵛ incommoditates pertulit: unam | quod quem natura dederat eo uti non poterat, alteram quod illum nisus est extrahere nec ualuit. Torquebatur ergo utrimque. Sed referentis hec est sentencia: quia minus incommodum patitur, cuius mola dextera sinistre suplet uicissitudinem. Pronunciato itaque precedenti miraculo in capitulo et audito quod fiebat, qualiter scilicet mulier dimissa esset ab infirmitate sua, deliberauit secum nocte subsecuta prenominatus frater ut ipse oratione premissa, eandem quam audierat in muliere factam experiretur medicaminis graciam. Nec mirum, quoniam exempla precedencium operum multociens animum ad spem meliora-cionis alliciunt. Nisi enim illa processisset et inuenisset graciam in conspectu Dei et domine, forsitan in ignauia sua torpesceret et incommodum suum prolongaret. Habebat iste prope se quo leniretur dolor eius medicamen reconditum et nesciuit. Non habebat illa, quesiuit et inuenit. Venit ergo mane ad monume⟨n⟩tum et incuruauit se et humiliatus est coram domina in precibus et tulit de puluere abraso de tumba, unde in sequentibus dicemus,²⁶ et apposuit denti interius confricans digito. Hec cum fecisset surrexit et abiit; nesciebat quod exaudita est oratio eius, sciebat autem postea cum refecturus accederet. Protestatus namque nobis est in uerbo ueritatis quod eadem die molari dente sinistro eque ut dextero usus est.

11. Miraculum de quodam nouicio

Quadam die aduesperascente cum quidam monachus nomine Rogerus super lectum suum resideret et membra sua grato sopori prebere temptaret, ecce subito per humani generis inimicum, qui quasi leo rugiens circuit querens quem deuoret,²⁷ ingens multitudo coruorum, ut sibi uidebatur, apparebat. De quorum agmine ceteris unus immanior terribili impetu ad se uolitans, quandam rotunditatem ad modum modici lapilli fluuialis in gutture suo figens, sicque cum ceteris continuo disparuit. Quo facto a planta pedis usque ad uerticem capitis inopinato languore percussus, uitali calore frigescente in terram corruens, mutus iacebat et exanimis. Irruerant enim in eum dolores subiti in tantum ut, si fas sit dicere, secundus Iob posset

---

²⁶ Ch. 21 (but already mentioned above, at the end of ch. 9).
²⁷ 1 Pet. 5: 8.

a whole year after he received the habit of holy religion he completely lost the power and ability to eat in that part. He suffered two inconveniences, first that he was unable to use what nature had given to him, second that what he tried to extract he could not. Both things tormented him. The opinion of this narrator, however, is that he suffered a lesser inconvenience, since the right jaw could make up for the problem with the left. When the previous miracle had been announced in chapter and he had heard what had happened, namely how the woman had been cured of her ailment, the brother I have named determined within himself that on the following night he would, after praying, try the same grace of healing which he had heard had taken place in the woman. It is not surprising, since the example of earlier miracles very often draws people's minds to the hope of healing. For unless she had gone forth and found grace in the sight of God and the lady, he might have remained slothful and inactive and prolonged his complaint. He had near to him a hidden medicine by which his pain could be relieved and he did not know it. She did not, but sought it and found it. So he came in the morning to the monument and bowed and humbled himself before the lady in prayer and took some of the dust scraped from the tomb, about which we shall speak later,[26] and rubbed it onto his tooth with his finger. When he had done this, he rose and went away. He did not know that his prayer had been heard but he knew it afterwards, when he went to eat. For he told us as the complete truth that on that same day he employed his left molar teeth just as well as his right.

11. The miracle that befell a novice

One evening a monk called Roger was lying on his bed and trying to secure kindly sleep for his limbs, when suddenly, through the agency of the enemy of the human race, who goes around like a roaring lion seeking whom he might devour,[27] there appeared a huge flock of crows, or so it seemed to him. One of this company, who was more monstrous than the rest, flew at the monk with a terrifying swoop, placed a round object like a small stone from a river bed in his throat and immediately disappeared, along with the rest. Once this had happened, he was struck with an unexpected weakness from the soles of his feet to the top of his head, his vital heat grew cold, and he fell to the ground, lying there dumb and unconscious. Sudden pains rushed upon him so much that, if it be right to say so, he could be thought of

meditari, excepto quod graui ulcere non cruciabatur. Fratres uero circumsedentes et hoc mirabile spectaculum intuentes—pre nimia interiori angustia contremuerunt omnia ossa sua—non sine ingente eiulatu meroreque consimili ad illum concurrentes, per caput et pedes ceteraque menbra trahentes ad domum infirmorum usque baiularunt. In qua ab hora quasi undecima diei usque ad nocturnum sensu et robore priuatus iacebat immobilis.

Hora uero noctis predicta, ut postea asserendo cum iuramento firmauit, dormientibus aliis tedio affectis, apparuit illi felix regina Margarita inedicibili claritate refulgens, sciscitans ab eo si dormiret.
fo. 32ʳ Cui cum ille responsum dare non posset, eleuauit | luculum quem manu portabat, imponensque super os infirmi dixit, 'Surge uelociter, omni postposita formidine; perge ad feretrum meum iuxta magnum altare constructum. Optinui enim a domino meo Iesu Christo, qui non uult mortem peccatoris sed ut magis conuertatur et uiuat,²⁸ ut tibi salubriorem quam hactenus habuisti recuperes sanitatem.' Languens enim erat ante per unius anni spacium. Hiis uerbis dictis, sensitᵃ eger se posse loqui, et cum eleuata uoce quendam fratrem a se non longe iacentem ut surgeret suscitauit,ᵇ dicens, 'Frater, surge, frater, surge. Nonne uides et audis que uideo et audio?' Ad hec uerba domina in celo recepta est. Euigilans alius et obstupefactus, respondit, 'Que uides uel que audis?' Cui egrotus retulit omnia efficaciter que acciderant, putans ostendere ei reginam que apparuerat. Omnes ergo qui secum fuerant conpacientes de miserabili euentu habentes zelum beati Iob dicentis, 'Flebam super eum qui afflictus erat',²⁹ cum nimia leticia et exultacione in ymnis et laudibus, ad locum quem uenerabilis regina preceperat illum statuerunt. Atᶜ ubi per spacium aliquod pernoctasset cum sanitate recepta, in domo Dei erat ingrediens et egrediens sobrie, iuste et pie uiuens, pergens ad imperium Dei omnipotentis. Cui est honor, laus et gloria nunc et per infinita secula. Amen.

12. De quadam puella in amenciam uersa magica arte per quendam clericum

Virgo quedam Hauys nomine de Northumbria originem ducens, ualde speciosa, ob quam causam plurimi, specie eius decepti, in amorem illius uehementer exarserunt. Inter quos clericus quidam in amorem

---

ᵃ sentiuit *MS*   ᵇ oscitauit *MS*   ᶜ ut *add. MS*

²⁸ Cf. Ezek. 33: 11.   ²⁹ Job 30: 25.

as a second Job, except that he was not tormented by terrible ulcers. The brethren who were round about and saw this amazing sight—all their bones shook from their great inner anguish—ran to him with great wailing and sorrow, and, taking hold of his head and feet and other limbs, they carried him off to the infirmary. He lay there immobile, deprived of all sensation and strength, from the eleventh hour of the day until nocturns.

But at that hour of night, as he afterwards asserted and confirmed on oath, while the others were asleep from exhaustion, the blessed queen Margaret appeared to him, shining with inexpressible splendour and asking if he was asleep. When he was unable to reply to her, she lifted up a light she was holding in her hand and, placing it on the sick man's face, said, 'Arise swiftly, laying aside all fear, and go to my shrine which is next to the high altar. For I have obtained from my lord Jesus Christ, who does not want the death of a sinner but rather than he should be converted and live,[28] that you will recover your health and be better than you have been hitherto' (for he had been sickly for a year before). After she had said these words, the sick man felt that he could speak, and, in a loud voice, he incited a brother who was lying not far from him to get up, saying, 'Brother, arise, brother, arise! Do you not see and hear what I see and hear?' At these words the lady was received into heaven. The other monk woke up and replied in astonishment, 'What do you see and what do you hear?' The sick monk gave him a striking account of all that had happened, thinking to show him the queen who had appeared. Therefore all those who were with him, having compassion in these miserable circumstances and possessing the zeal of Job when he said, 'I wept over him who had been afflicted',[29] placed him, with great joy and exultation in hymns and praise, in the spot which the venerable queen had commanded. He received his health in the place where he spent some of the night in vigil and he went in and out of the house of God, living soberly and righteously and devoutly, heading for the kingdom of Almighty God. To whom be honour and praise and glory now and forever. Amen.

12. A girl whom a clerk drove mad by magic

There was a maiden who came from Northumbria called Hawise. She was extremely beautiful and for this reason many people were ensnared by her appearance and burned with violent love for her. One of them was a clerk, who urged the mind of the maiden

uirginis perurgens animum, cepit plura offerre et plurima promittere ut eius concupito frueretur amore. Nichil tamen proficiebat. Tandem spiritu ductus diabolico, arte usus est magica, nec sic quidem suo potitus est desiderio. Sed in tantum predictam uirginem spiritus uexabat malignus ut, amente effecta, parentibus suis dolor incuteretur non modicus. Qui prefatam uirginem loca sancta uisitantes circumduxerunt, miserie uirginis cum lacrimis et orationibus sanitatis remedia deuote postulantes. Nec tamen exauditi sunt usque dum uenerunt ad locum ubi corpus sancte Margarite regine primo quieuit humatum. Illis siquidem ibidem aliquamdiu commorantibus, quadam nocte cum prefata uirgo, tedio et dolore affecta, membra sua sopori dedisset, cum antea ex quo talis ei accidit miseria nequaquam posset dormitare, ecce apparuit ei in sompnis quedam uenerabilis matrona, precipiens ut ad tumbam eius properaret, plenariam ibi sanitatem receptura. Puella uero gratulabunda sciscitabatur quenam esset, que sibi tam desiderabilia promeret promissa. At illa: 'Ego sum', inquit, 'Margarita, Scotorum regina.' Puella enim euigilans, que in sompnis fo. 32ᵛ uideret | parentibus exponebat. Qui uisioni sue congratulantes, uirginem cum gaudio maximo ad tumbam sancte regine adduxerunt, ubi quamtocius sanitate plenarie recepta, post paucos dies cum illis qui eam adduxerant ad patriam propriam incolumis remeauit, glorificans Deum qui per famulam suam sanctam Margaritam se sanitati restitutam non ignorabat. Cuius nomen sit benedictum in seculum seculorum. Amen.

13. De alia puella a demonio liberata

Contigit quod quedam nobilis matrona nomine Helena cum filia sua Cristina in amenitate situs sui territorii spaciando sederet, cum subito uox, acsi esset cuiusdam paruuli in quodam loco ab eis semoto, auribus illarum personuit, eiulando dicens 'Heu, heu, heu, humano destitutus solacio, hic sine auxilio morior.' Hec audientes pre nimia admiracione, timore perterrite uehementer obstupuerunt. Dixitque mater filie, 'Surge, uade uelociter et uide si forte fuerit aliquis pauper peregrinus deuians uel egenus, et induc in domum nostram ut ibi pernoctet', exemplum Abrahe et Loth imitans[30] et beati Iob dicentis 'Non mansit foris peregrinus'.[31] Respondit matri puella, 'Mater, uocem quam audiui terribilis mihi uidebatur et ideo iter arripere formido.' Cui genetrix, 'Hactenus uoluntati mee multociens contradixisti et adhuc

---

[30] Gen. 18–19.   [31] Job 31: 32.

towards love. He offered her much and promised her more if he could enjoy her love as he wished, but it was to no avail. Eventually, led astray by a diabolic spirit, he employed magic. He was still not able to fulfil his desire in that way but the evil spirit troubled the maiden so greatly that she lost her mind. Her parents, struck by this great sorrow, led the maiden around, visiting the holy places, piously entreating, with tears and prayers, that the virgin's unhappy state be remedied by healing. They were not heard until they came to the place where the body of St Margaret the queen first lay buried. One night, while they were spending a little time there, and the maiden, worn out with weariness and pain, surrendered her limbs to sleep, although since the misfortune had befallen her she had not been able to sleep, behold there appeared to her in her dreams a venerable matron commanding her to hasten to her tomb, where she would receive complete healing. The girl was overjoyed and asked her who she was, who had made her such welcome promises. She said, 'I am Margaret, queen of Scots.' The girl woke up and recounted to her parents what she had seen in her dreams. They rejoiced at her vision, and led the maiden to the tomb of the holy queen in great joy, where she recovered her health very quickly. A few days later she returned cured to her own land, along with those who had brought her, glorifying God who had not neglected to restore her to health through His handmaid St Margaret. His name be blessed forever. Amen.

13. Another girl freed from a demon

There was a noblewoman called Helen who went for a stroll with her daughter Christine and sat down in a pleasant spot on her estate. Suddenly a voice like that of a little child in a remote place came to their ears, wailing 'Alas, alas, alas, abandoned by all human aid, I am dying here with none to help me!' When they heard this, the women were struck with astonishment and fear. The mother said to the daughter, 'Jump up and go quickly and see if it is by chance a poor traveller who is lost or destitute and bring him into our house to stay the night', imitating the example of Abraham and Lot[30] and the blessed Job when he said, 'The traveller did not stay outside'.[31] The girl replied to her mother, 'Mother, the voice which I have heard seems terrible to me and therefore I am afraid to go.' Her mother said to her, 'Hitherto you have often contradicted my will and you still

contradicere non dubitas?' Hiis dictis, iubentis suscipiens imperium
confestim cucurrit ad locum in quo uox audiebatur et uidente matre
puerum quendam eleuauit habentem similitudinem fratris sui modico
tempore ante defuncti. Dixit ad illam, 'Soror mea es, da mihi
osculum.' Que renuens ait, 'Noui te fratrem meum esse, sed quia
uiam uniuerse carnis ingressus est, non licet michi te osculari.' Hiis
inter se altercantibus, guttur puelle sinistra manu apprehendit,
dextraque inter scapulas percussit, sicque prostratam recedendo
reliquit.

Cum uero mater hec omnia cerneret, super filia materne pietatis
uisceribus commota, tacta dolore intrinsecus pre nimia angustia uelud
amens effecta, flens et eiulans cucurrit ad eam, inuenitque eam
demonio arreptam, humo prostratam et morti proximam. In qua
non erat uox neque sensus. Tunc cepit contristari et mesta esse,
comam discutere, pannos lacerare et quasi leena rugiens ad familiam
suam lacrimando clamare, 'Venite, famuli mei, uenite et uidete si est
dolor sicut dolor meus.'[32] Accersitis ad dominam suam quibusdam de
domesticis, portauerunt puellam domi et in grabato locauerunt. Pater
uero puelle, audiens strepitum familie sue, de lecto surrexit et, hoc
mirabile uidens, ingemiscendo doluit. Cuius tamen dolor patris aut
matris maior erat, credi potuit, scire nequiuit.

Interea postulauit psalterium suum, nam quasi tumentes fluctus[33]
super se Deum timuit. | Et cum diu psalleret sedendo ad caput
puelle, ecce in tempeste noctis silencio,[a] eleuata uoce moribunda
clamauit dicens, 'Video domum istam uiris et mulieribus, pueris et
puellis repletam.' Addiditque, 'Ecce quam pulchra regina illa est,
quam decora facie, quam uenusto aspectu,[34] quam suauis cantus
chorum ducencium' et plurima huiusmodi similia. Quam increpauit
pater iubens dominicam dicere orationem et simbolum. Sed illa in
amencia sua perseuerans dicere recusauit. Tunc ille uirgam arripuit et
minando corripuit dicens, 'Nisi post me dixeris que iubeo, flagellis te
affligam.' Illa uero sensu alienata, uirgarum tamen asperitate perterrita patrem sequitur, utramque dicens orationem. Et cum ad finem
symboli deuenissent, dixit 'Pater mi, ecce omnes qui iam pridem hic
aderant fugerunt, tamen frater meus, qui me percussit, ad pedes meos

fo. 33ʳ

---

[a] sic, for 'intempeste noctis silencio'; exactly the same form is used again in ch. 39. Dict. Med.
Lat., i. 1424, s. v. 'intempestus', gives one example of this form from the 14th-cent. Eulogium
historiarum, marking it as a scribal or editorial error, but there are several other instances of the
usage of 'in tempestae noctis silentio' by chroniclers of the 11th and 12th cents.: e.g. Monumenta
Germaniae Historica, Scriptores, vi. 384; vii. 741, 776; viii. 48, 77. It is therefore best to
regard it as an acceptable medieval form

don't hesitate to contradict me?' When she said this, the daughter obeyed her command and she ran quickly to the place where the voice had been heard and, while her mother watched, she lifted up a boy who was just like her brother, who had died a little time before. He said to her, 'Sister, give me a kiss.' She refused, saying 'I know that you are my brother, but because you have gone the way of all flesh, I am not allowed to kiss you.' As they argued, he grabbed the girl's throat with his left hand and pushed her between the shoulders with his right, knocking her down and then leaving.

When the mother perceived all this, the bowels of maternal compassion were moved within her for her daughter, she was almost out of her mind with pain within and great anxiety, and she ran to her, weeping and wailing, and found her possessed by a demon, prostrate on the ground and close to death, lacking speech or sensation. Then she began to grieve and to sorrow, tearing her hair, ripping her clothes and like a roaring lioness she called out in tears to her servants, 'Come, my servants, come and see if there is sorrow like my sorrow.'[32] Some of the servants, summoned by their mistress, carried the girl home and placed her on a couch. The girl's father, hearing the shouting among the household, got out of bed and, seeing this amazing sight, he grieved and groaned. Whose grief was greater, the father's or the mother's, was, it can be believed, impossible to know.

Meanwhile he sent for his Psalter, for he feared God even as the proud waves[33] rose around him. When he had read the psalms for a long time, sitting at the girl's head, behold in the silence of the dead of night, the afflicted girl cried out in a high voice, 'I see this house full of men and women, boys and girls.' She added, 'Behold how beautiful that queen is, how fair of face, how lovely in appearance,[34] how sweet the song of those leading the choir' and many other things of this kind. Her father rebuked her and commanded her to say the Lord's Prayer and the Creed. But she persevered in her madness and refused to say them. Then he snatched up a rod and, reproaching and threatening her, said, 'Unless you say after me what I tell you to say, I will beat you.' Although she was out of her mind, she was frightened by the harsh rod and followed her father, saying both prayers. And when they had come to the end of the Creed, she said, 'Father mine, behold all those who were here before have fled, but my brother, who struck

---

[32] Lam. 1: 12.   [33] Job 38: 11.   [34] Gen. 29: 17.

sedet.' Surrexit ergo pater et ad pedes eius psallebat, dixitque iterum puella, 'Pater mi, ecce omnes fugerunt et frater meus cum illis, tamen cantilena eorum auribus meis confert melodiam.'

Hiis dictis, ultra cessauit loqui, sicque per totam noctem manus illius tenentes, ne corpori molestiam inferret, uigilauerunt, pro sacerdotibus et aliis uiris quam pluribus mittentes, qui omnes postea de hoc facto testimonium perhibuerunt, famulus uero qui eam intus detulerat, mox illa de manibus eius dimissa coram omnibus cecidit et usque ad gallicinium exanimis iacebat. In crastino uero, scilicet die dominica, inito consilio parentum, hora uespertina baiulata est puella ad ecclesiam sancte Trinitatis de Dunfermelyn et ante altare sancte Margarite regine collocata, ubi parentes sui uigiliis et orationibus pernoctantes, flebilibus uocibus sancte Margarite postulauerunt auxilium, ut sicut pluries multis subuenit egrotis, sic illam prospera faceret sanitate gratulari.

Tandem matrona uenerabilis, piis illorum pulsata precibus, in crastino, feria scilicet secunda, hora quasi decima, puelle dormienti apparuit dicens, 'Surge, uade ad locum ubi ossa mea requieuerunt, ibi enim receptura es sanitatem.' Statimque euigilans acsi sana effecta fuisset, sola ad locum perrexit, ibique super lapidem tumuli regine obdormiit. Rursumque domina apparuit illi, caput suum inter manus accipiens et digitum in gutture suo ponens, retractoque digito, sic allocuta est puella, 'Mater sanctissima, pro misericordia michi impensa gratias tibi refero non modicas. Sensum meum sencio me recuperasse et posse loqui. Et si locum in quo a demone percussa fui tangere uelles, scirem me sanitati penitus restitutam.' Tunc ait regina, 'Locum tangam et teipsam custodiam si de cetero in obsequio Christi, die noctuque deuota fueris, cuius misericordia precibus meis te ab fo. 33ᵛ omni lesione curauit.' Hiis dictis, puella | apparuit et domina disparuit. Euigilans autem, omnia que acciderant parentibus enarrauit. Tunc leti effecti ad feretrum sancte Margarite illam adduxerunt ibique Deo seruiendam totonderunt. Non multo post tempore puella, siciens promissa complere, in domo que uocatur Elichot[35] habitam monialis suscepit sicque felici castigata uerbere Deo et sancte Margarite seruiuit deuotissime.

---

[35] Perthshire, Cistercian; the nunnery was founded by the mother of David Lindsay on land granted by King Alexander II (1214–49): *Registrum de Dunfermlyn*, ed. Cosmo Innes (Bannatyne Club, Edinburgh, 1842), nos. 190–1, pp. 107–8; see *Pitmiddle Village and Elcho Nunnery: Research and Excavation on Tayside* (Perthshire Society of Natural Science,

me, is sitting at my feet.' The father therefore got up and recited the psalms at her feet and the girl said again, 'Father mine, they have all fled and my brother along with them, but my ears are still filled with the sound of their singing.'

When she had said this she ceased speaking and thus through the whole night they watched, holding her hand so that no harm should come to her body, sending out for priests and many other men, who all afterwards gave testimony about this. But the servant who had carried her in fell down in the sight of all as soon as he had released her from his hands and lay there senseless until cockcrow. Next day, which was a Sunday, after the parents had taken counsel, the girl was carried at the hour of vespers to the church of the Holy Trinity at Dunfermline and placed before the altar of St Margaret the queen, where her parents spent the night in vigils and prayers, seeking St Margaret's help with tearful voices, requesting that, just as she had often helped many sick people, so she should ensure that she too might rejoice in health and happiness.

Eventually next day, that is Monday, around the tenth hour, the venerable lady, struck by their devout prayers, appeared to the sleeping girl and said, 'Arise, go to the place where my bones rested, for there you will receive healing.' Straightaway, waking as if she had been cured, she went alone to the place, and there went to sleep on the stone of the queen's tomb. Again the lady appeared to her, taking her head in her hands and placing a finger in her throat, then, as she withdrew her finger, the girl said, 'Most holy mother, I give you deep thanks for the mercy you have shown me. I feel that I have recovered my senses and the power of speech. If you would be willing to touch the place where I was struck by the demon, I know that I would be completely restored to health.' Then the queen said, 'I will touch the place and I will look after you if henceforth you will devote yourself day and night to the service of Christ, whose mercy, at my prayers, has cured you from all harm.' When she had said this, the girl came to her senses and the lady disappeared. Waking, the girl told her parents everything that had happened. Then they led her joyfully to St Margaret's shrine and there had her tonsured to God's service. Not long afterwards, the girl, thirsting to fulfil her promises, received the nun's habit in the house called Elcho[35] and thus, punished by the happy rod, she served God and St Margaret most devotedly.

1988), pp. 48–84, for further details and reports of excavations at the site undertaken in 1968–73.

14. De quodam monacho habente strumam super manum dexteram

Fuit quidam monachus nomine Iohannes, super cuius manum dextram casu repentino struma crescebat immensa. Qui, consultus a fratribus ut abscideretur, dicentibus sibi hoc prouerbium, 'Vt corpus redimas' et cetera,[36] respondit se malle manum amittere quam tantam miseriam in carne sua pati et uidere. Tandem inuento salubri consilio, tumbam sancte Margarite per plures dies lacrimabiliter circuiuit orans et flagitans, ut sibi subuenire dignaretur. Erat enim gibbus tante magnitudinis ut cum manu illa manducare uel aliquid aliud facere non poterat pre pudore. Cumque talem diu frequentasset laborem, transacto dimidii anni spacio, cepit euanescere et in tantum comminui, ut nec aliquod uestigium illius tumoris ulterius appareret. Et sicut subito creuit, ita repente precibus eiusdem uenerabilis regine commutata est.

15. Item de eodem

⟨I⟩dem Iohannes prenotatus, in primitiis sue conuersacionis nouellus, sinistre manus digitorum tribus unguibus triennio carebat. Et quia doloris angustia semper de necessitate inquirit solacium, consilio seniorum sancte Margarite postulauit auxilium. Deinde, una nocte post completorium, felici furto furatus est ad feretrum, euigilans per breue spacium, sompnum suscepit salutiferum. Cumque ibi obdormisset, apparuit illi salus languencium omnium ad se confugiencium iuxta illum sedens, tante pulcritudinis circumamicta uarietate[37] ut in amenitate putaret esse positus paradisi. Dixitque illi, 'Quam a me petis sanitatem, omnipotens Dominus, precibus meis mediantibus, tibi largiri dignatus est. Et quia puro corde post Deum, meum postulasti suffragium, in breui termino ungues habebis digitorum. Surge, uade in pace, quia fides tua te saluum fecit.'[38] Qui surrexit et abiit et, in breuiori spacio quam credi potest, sanitatem recuperauit. Hic, ut dignum erat, deuocius quam antea Deo et sancte Margarite studuit sine intermissione placere.

---

[36] Ovid, *De remedio amoris*, line 229: 'Ut corpus redimas, ferrum patieris et ignes.'
[37] Cf. Ps. 44: 15 (45: 14); also, more exactly, Augustine, *De civitate Dei*, xvii. 16. 2.
[38] Matt. 9: 22; Mark 5: 34; 10: 52; Luke 7: 50; 8: 48; 17: 19; 18: 42.

14. A monk who had a swelling on his right hand

There was a monk named John. By some unexpected chance a huge swelling grew up on his right hand. He was advised by the brethren to have it cut off and they cited to him the saying, 'To redeem your body', etc.,[36] but he answered that he would rather lose the hand than feel and see such great misery inflicted on his flesh. Eventually receiving healthful advice, he went around the tomb of St Margaret for several days in tears, praying and entreating that she should deign to help him. For the swelling was of such size that he could not, from shame, either eat with that hand or do anything else with it. When he had spent a long time in such efforts over the space of half a year, the swelling began to disappear and diminished so much that no trace of the tumour was henceforth apparent. Just as it suddenly grew up, so it was quickly transformed by the prayers of the venerable queen.

15. About the same monk

In the early days of his conversion to the religious life this John whom I have just mentioned was, for three years, missing three nails on the fingers of his left hand. And since the sorrow of pain always of necessity seeks relief, at the advice of his elders he asked the help of St Margaret. Then, one night after compline, he sneaked himself away by a blessed theft to the shrine and, after keeping vigil for a little while, he was granted a healing sleep. While he was sleeping, there appeared to him the salvation of all sufferers who flee to her, sitting next to him, and of such great beauty and attired in such colours[37] that he thought he had been placed in the sweetness of paradise. She said to him, 'Almighty God has deigned to grant to you, through my prayers, the healing that you seek from me. And since you have sought my help, after God, with a pure heart, in a short while you will have nails on your fingers. Arise, go in peace, because your faith has cured you.'[38] He got up and went away and, in a shorter time that can be believed, he recovered full health. As was proper, he made continuous efforts to please God and St Margaret more devotedly than before.

16. De Wilelmo nauta subito a demone erepto

Quidam nauta Wilelmus cognomento de Aberden, de Leth[39] ueniens circa mare, quem sequebatur quidam caniculus, cum super | moram Inuyrkethyn[40] et Dunfermelyn ueloci gradu ueniret, subito arreptus demonio, ultra mensuram uexatus est, in tantum ut omnia uestimenta sua, exceptis tena et femoralibus, a se proiecerit. Canis enim quem prediximus staturam mutauerat et in forma draconis aspectu terribilis sibi apparebat, illum cupientis sine mora deglutire. Sed omnipotens Deus, qui non uenit uocare iustos sed peccatores ad penitenciam,[41] dignatus est illi apud Dunfermelyn iter dirigere, quamuis ibidem multa mala instinctu diabolico facere conaretur. Paruulos enim et uirgines, senes cum iunioribus, domos compulit intrare, et cum, bipenne quadam fortissima et acutissima quam in manibus portabat, super eos ostia infringere nitebatur. Hoc uidentes, uiri uirtutis gladio spiritus et lorica fidei accincti,[42] per plateas et uicos audacter sequebantur et infra menia sancte Margarite manus in eum iniecerunt. Quem firmiter ligauerunt et ad locum quo predicta regina per octoginta annos requieuit ligatum dimiserunt.

Ibique per tres dies et noctes, ut energuminus, clamans et uociferans, absque cibo et potu, omni destitutus auxilio, pernoctauit. Ego autem et duo fratres mecum, qui hoc miraculum uobis referimus, in tercie noctis quarta uigilia ad egrum pedetentim accessimus, ad memoriam reducentes illud euangelicum: 'Quod uni ex minimis meis fecisti michi fecisti',[43] cum ingenti labore pane modico et caseo refocillauimus, refocillatumque interrogauimus, 'Quomodo te habes?' Qui, respondens Deo et non nobis, ait, 'Iustus es, Domine, et rectum iudicium tuum,[44] tu uulneras et mederes, percutis et manus tue sanant.[45] Dico autem uobis quod, demeritis meis exigentibus, tribulaciones has et angustias perpessus sum, quia dominum meum terrenum in terra et in mari de maxima pecunia sepe defraudaui. Pro quo scelere, quoad uixero Deo et sancte Margarite, que me precibus suis pristine restituit sanitati, deuotus seruire deuoueo.' Hiis dictis, facta solennitate ut dignum erat, sanus et incolumis in propria repedauit.

---

[39] Midlothian.   [40] Fife.
[41] Luke 5: 32 ; cf. Matt. 9: 13; Mark 2: 17.
[42] Cf. Eph. 6: 14–17.   [43] Matt. 25: 40.
[44] Ps. 118 (119): 137.   [45] Job 5: 18.

16. The sailor William who was suddenly possessed by a demon

A sailor called William of Aberdeen, coming around the sea from Leith,[39] was followed by a small dog. When he came on to the moor of Inverkeithing[40] and approached Dunfermline at a speedy pace, he was suddenly possessed by a demon and troubled beyond measure, so much that he cast off all his clothes except his coif and his breeches. For the dog we have just mentioned changed its size and appeared to him in the form of a dragon, terrible to see, that wished to swallow him down without delay. But almighty God, who did not come to summon the just but to call sinners to penitence,[41] deigned to direct his journey to Dunfermline, although, at the devil's instigation, he tried to do many wicked things there. He forced indoors the little children and maidens, the old and the young, and tried to break down their doors around them with a mighty sharp axe he was carrying in his hands. Seeing this, some men, who were girded with the sword of the power of the spirit and with the breastplate of faith,[42] followed him boldly through the streets and lanes and cast hands on him within the precincts of St Margaret. They tied him up securely and brought him bound to the place where the queen had lain for eighty years.

He stayed there for three days and nights, crying out and shouting like one possessed, without food or drink, devoid of all help. I myself, who am telling you about this miracle, and two of the brethren with me, came cautiously to the sick man in the fourth vigil of the third night, bringing to mind that saying in the Gospel: 'What you have done to the least of these you have done to me',[43] and with great effort we revived him with a little bread and cheese. Once he was restored, we asked him 'How are you?' He replied to God and not to us, saying, 'You are just, Lord, and Your judgment is righteous,[44] You wound and You cure, You strike and Your hands heal.[45] I say to you that I have suffered these tribulations and troubles because of my own faults, since I have often defrauded my earthly lord of a great deal of money, both at land and at sea. For this crime, I vow to serve with devotion as long as I live God and St Margaret, who restored me to my former health by her prayers.' Once he had said this, after mass had been said, as was proper, he returned home safe and sound.

17. De quadam muliere Northumbrie plena lacertis curata

Quodam tempore erat quedam mulier in Northumbria, que quodam die tempore estiuo, calore diei feruescente, dormiebat in campestribus, in quam subito duo lacerti per os eius intrauerunt, cuius corpus acriter turbauerunt. Euigilans autem cepit egrotare, uiscera tumescere, color euanescere, et omnia membra pre doloris angustia debilitari. Et quia quod medicorum est promittunt medici, in medicis ferme totam substanciam suam largita est. Facile enim contempsit omnia, quia semper cogitabat se esse morituram. Medici uero nichil ei profuerunt. Post | hec consuluit uirum suum quid esset factura. Cui ille, 'Vade sanctorum uisitans limina, ut quod a medicis recuperare non potes, saltem a Deo per sanctorum merita impetrare merearis.' Illa, quamuis languida, tamen de responso uiri sui leta effecta est, fere omnium sanctorum Anglie loca peciit, sed a nullo sanitatem optinuit. Tandem uersus Scociam iter direxit et ad tumbam sancte Margarite in monasterio Dunfermelyn triduo uigilauit. Tercia uero nocte in sompnis apparuit illi predicta regina, dicens, 'Surge, sciens te pro certo ante horam diei nonam desideratam sanitatem recuperare.' Que euigilans postulauit uasa sibi afferri, dicens se uomendi affectum habere. Cumque allata fuissent, duo uasa plena lacertis uomendi repleuit. Sicque, cum sanitate percepta, Deo gracias agens et sancte Margarite, ad propria remeauit.

fo. 34ᵛ

18. De quodam operario auditu et loquela per quindecim dies priuato

Quidam operarius apud Gellad,[46] triturans bladum cum sociis, miserabili euentu subito corruit in terram, loquele et auditus utriusque priuatus presidio, et in eodem langore ad domum deportatus per quindecim dies morabatur. Socii uero eius et amici de miseria ipsius condolentes, scientes quod omnis salutis recuperacio est apud eum qui fines mundi intuetur[47] et pro sanctis suis mirabilia operatur, apud Dunfermelyn in quodam feretro eum adduxerunt citissime et ante locum, in quo corpus felicis Margarite longoᵃ tempore requieuit, semiuiuum reliquerunt. Transactis tribus diebus et noctibus, in quarta nocte ante diluculum coram illo astitit

---

ᵃ loco MS

---

[46] Fife.
[47] Job 28: 24.

17. The cure of a Northumbrian woman full of lizards

At one time there was a woman in Northumbria who was sleeping in the fields on a hot summer's day when suddenly two lizards entered her mouth and disturbed her body most harshly. When she awoke she began to be ill, her intestines swelled, her colour disappeared, and all her limbs became weak through the terrible pain. And because doctors promise what doctors do, she spent almost her whole wealth on doctors. For it was easy for her to despise everything since she always thought she was on the point of death. But the doctors were of no use to her. After this she consulted her husband about what was to be done. He said to her, 'Go and visit the shrines of the saints so that you might deserve to obtain from God through the merits of the saints what you are unable to get from the doctors.' Although she was weak, she nevertheless rejoiced at her husband's advice, she sought out nearly all the shrines of the saints in England, but obtained a cure from none of them. At length she turned her steps towards Scotland and kept vigil for three days at the tomb of St Margaret in the monastery of Dunfermline. On the third night the queen appeared to her in her sleep and said, 'Arise, know for certain that before the ninth hour of the day you will recover the health that you desire.' As she woke up, she asked for a container to be brought to her, saying she had the urge to vomit. When they were brought, she filled two containers by vomiting up lizards. Thus, with her health obtained, she returned to her own country, giving thanks to God and St Margaret.

18. A workman who lost the powers of hearing and speech for fifteen days

A distressing event occurred to a worker who was threshing grain at Gellad[46] along with his companions. He suddenly fell to the ground, deprived of the support of both speech and hearing, and when he had been carried home he remained in that comatose state for fifteen days. His companions and friends had compassion on his wretchedness and, knowing that any recovery of health depends upon him who looks to the ends of the earth[47] and works wonders for his saints, they carried him to Dunfermline on a litter and left him half-alive before the place where the body of the blessed Margaret rested for a long time. After three days and nights had passed, before daybreak in the fourth night,

quedam matrona uenerabilis, uirga comminando dicens, 'O hominum
stultissime, pro commissis tuis taliter flagellatus es, et nisi cicius
preces mediatricis Dei et hominum et mee coram Deo affuissent,
penis infernalibus esses addictus. An ignoras quia columpne celi
contremiscunt et pauent ad nutum eius[48] et tu miser negligenter agis?
Verumptamen tibi dico, surge et uade et amplius noli peccare,[49] ne
deterius tibi contingat.' Qui surrexit, omnia ista coram monachis
referens ordinate. Insuper et peccata pro quibus flagellatus erat, que
pede taciturnitatis pretereo,

(Versus:)   Ne super enormi si simplex conueniatur
          de quo nil sciuit, ad agendum sic moueatur.

19. De quadam muliere oculorum lumine priuata per biennium

⟨I⟩n uilla de Dunfermelyn erat quedam mulier, nomine Auicia, longo
tempore oculorum grauedine grauiter afflicta. Que, propter angustiam quam passa est, indesinenter lacrimabatur. Tandem modica luce
qua lumen celi aspicere solebat omnino priuata est, in cecitate per
biennium postea perseuerans. Transacto biennio, eius inspirante
gratia qui ubi uult et quando uult spirat,[50] audiuit de miraculis
fo. 35ʳ beate Margarite | sermocinari et quia tanto tempore segniter agens,
limina predicte regine non uisitans, cepit contristari. Que ait uiro suo,
'Fac michi conductum ad fontem domine, ut saltem illius aqua queam
refocillari; forsitan propiciabitur michi famule sue, que in omni
afflictione salus prompta est peregrinis.'

Vir autem eius eam festinanter duxit ad locum. Qua adducta ex
aqua gustauit, caput et oculos lauit, fiducialiter agens coram altari
obdormiuit. In ipso autem sopore uenerabilis regina astitit a dextris
eius, dicens, 'Quid a me postulas?' Cui mulier, 'Si te scirem sanctam
esse Margaritam, lumen oculorum, quo priuata sum, mihi restitui a te
optarem.' Ad quam illa, 'Ego sum.' Addiditque, 'Dominus omnipotens, prope omnibus inuocantibus eum in ueritate, secundum fidem
tuam tibi conferat sanitatem.' Post hec, accepta aqua de situla, sinistra
manu cece oculos apparuit et intincto digito medicinali manus dextre
aquam infudit, dataque benedictione disparuit. Ab illa autem hora
mulier euigilans surrexit, uisu recepto altare prospexit, fontem et

---

[48] Job 26: 11.   [49] John 8: 11.   [50] Cf. John 3: 8.

a venerable lady appeared before him, threatening him with a rod and saying, 'O most foolish of men, you have been beaten in this way for your sins, and unless the prayers of the mediator between God and men and my prayers come quickly before God, you are given over to infernal punishment. Do you not know that the columns of the heavens tremble and grow pale at his command[48] while you, you wretch, behave so carelessly? Nevertheless, I say to you, arise and go and sin no more,[49] lest worse befall you.' He arose and related all this in order before the monks, also his sins for which he had been punished, which I pass over with the foot of silence, lest, if a simple person come across a vice of which he knew nothing, he might be moved to do it.

19. A woman who lost her eyesight for the space of two years

In the town of Dunfermline there was a woman called Avicia who for a long time had been badly afflicted by a weakness of the eyes. She wept incessantly because of the distress she suffered. Eventually she completely lost the slight power of sight with which she used to perceive the light of the sky and remained blind for two years afterwards. At the end of those two years, inspired by that grace which blows where it will and when it will,[50] she heard talk of the miracles of St Margaret and she began to grieve that she had been so inactive for so long and had not visited the queen's shrine. She said to her husband, 'Lead me to the lady's fountain, by the water of which I may be revived; perhaps she, who is a swift deliverance for pilgrims in every affliction, will be propitious to me her handmaid.'

Her husband quickly led her to that place. When she had been brought there, she drank some of the water, washed her head and eyes, and went to sleep before the altar in great faith. While she was sleeping the venerable queen stood at her right side, saying, 'What are you requesting from me?' The woman answered, 'If I knew that you were St Margaret, I would choose to have you restore to me the sight of my eyes, which I have lost.' She said to her, 'I am she.' Then she added, 'The Lord almighty, who is near to all who invoke him in truth, confer your health on you according to your faith.' After this she took water from a bucket, opened the blind woman's eyes with her left hand and, dipping the healing finger of her right hand into the water, dripped it in. Giving a blessing, she disappeared. From that hour the woman awoke and arose and, with her sight restored, looked

omnia que infra monasterium fuerant mirabiliter intuita est, cum excelsa uoce clamare cepit, 'O beata Margarita tibi laus, tibi gloria, que uno digitorum tuorum ocellis meis lumen infudisti.' Quod scimus loquimur et quod uidimus hoc testamur. In hiis omnibus laudandus ille glorificandus est, qui facit mirabilia solus.[51] Cuius nomen benedictum in secula seculorum. Amen.

20. Qualiter quidam clericus pre nimio studio sensum amiserat

Erat quidam clericus, nomine Wilelemus de Inuyrhkethyn, qui pre nimia studendi affectione quam habebat sensu alienatus est. Super cuius euentu miserabili omnes qui eum uiderant condoluerunt. Dilectus enim erat Deo et amabilis hominibus. Interim, communi consilio amicorum, ductus est apud Lochorfrech, qui ibi ut mos est amencium cruci alligatur, nullo sequenti salutis indicio.[52] Deinde ad omnia sanctorum limina Laudonie, de quibus non aliquod sue afflictionis consequitur releuamen, sed occulto Dei iudicio magis aggrauamen. Tandem, consilio fratris sui, Walteri nomine, ante basilicam sancte Margarite regine apud Dunfermelyn assistitur eger. Cuius loci monachi quorum amicus erat, una cum amicis suis, in uigiliis et orationibus triduo deuote permanserunt, firmissime confidentes de salute eius in eo qui dicit, 'Petite et accipietis, querite et inuenietis, pulsate et aperietur uobis.'[53] In tercia uero nocte dictus clericus, nimia anxietate fatigatus, soporis sumpsit uicissitudinem, in quo apparuit ei quedam regina uultu uenerabilis et uenusto aspectu, crucis signaculo frontem eius assignans, dixitque ei placido uultu,

fo. 35ᵛ 'Compassa sum | super afflictione tua, ideo Dominus omnipotens in ista tribulacione tibi subuenit.' Addiditque, 'In nomine Domini surge sanus.' Ad hec clericus, 'Que es, domina?' Cui ait, 'Ego sum Margarita, cuius corpus in hoc requiescit habitaculo.' Et hec dicens ab oculis eius elapsa est. Euigilans uero clericus sensu recuperato, celesti uisione letificatus, in omnibus que audierat et uiderat una cum monachis et parentibus suis Deum glorificabat, omni tempore postea in laude Dei et beate Margarite peruigil perseuerans. Cuius etiam alia opera bona modernorum oculis restant manifesta.

---

[51] Ps. 71 (72): 18; cf. 85 (86): 10; 135 (136): 4.

[52] *Lochorfrech* is the original name of the parish now known as Borthwick in Lothian. Other early forms of the name include *Louchgorward*, *Lochquerwer*, and *Lochorver*: N. Dixon, 'Place-names of Midlothian', Ph.D. thesis (Edinburgh, 1947), p. 109. For the custom, cf. Jocelin of Furness, *Vita Kentigerni*, c. 41, ed. Alexander Penrose Forbes, *Lives*

at the altar, and gazed in wonder at the fountain and everything that was in the monastery. She began to call out with a loud voice, 'O blessed Margaret, to you be praise, to you be glory, who has poured sight into my eyes with one of your fingers.' We speak of what we know and bear witness to what we have seen. In all these things He is to be praised and glorified who alone performs wonders,[51] whose name be blessed forever. Amen.

20. A clerk who lost his senses through too much study

There was a cleric called William of Inverkeithing who lost his senses through studying too hard. All who saw him sympathized with his sad plight, for he was dear to God and much loved by his fellow men. His friends conferred together and took him to *Lochorfrech* and tied him to the cross there, as is the custom with the insane, but this brought no sign of improvement.[52] Then they took him to all the shrines of the saints in Lothian but he obtained no relief of his affliction at them, rather, by the secret judgment of God, a worsening of his condition. Eventually, by the counsel of his brother, who was called Walter, the sick man was placed before the church of St Margaret the queen at Dunfermline. The monks of that place, of whom he was a friend, along with his other friends, spent three days devoutly in vigils and prayers, firmly trusting that he would be healed by Him who said, 'Seek and you shall receive, ask and you will find, knock and it shall be opened unto you.'[53] During the third night the clerk, worn out with anguish, obtained the relief of sleep, during which there appeared to him a queen, venerable in her visage and beautiful in appearance, who made the sign of the cross on his forehead and said, 'I have had pity on your affliction, therefore the Lord almighty will help you in this trouble.' She added, 'In the name of the Lord, arise cured.' The clerk said to her, 'Who are you, lady?' She said to him, 'I am Margaret, whose body rests in this little dwelling.' Saying this, she disappeared from his eyes. The clerk awoke with his senses restored, rejoicing in the heavenly vision, and, along with the monks and his relatives, he glorified God for all that he had heard and seen. Always afterwards he continued intently in praise of God and the blessed Margaret. Her other good works are also plain to see in the eyes of people at present.

of St Ninian and St Kentigern (Edinburgh, 1874), pp. 233–4, where *Lothwerverd* is clearly the same place.   [53] Cf. Matt. 7: 7; Luke 11: 9.

21. De quodam puero eliphantinoso curato

Vir quidam nobilis erat in Galuethia, cui filius per septem annos et amplius miserabiliter morbo torquebatur eliphantino. Tandem disponente Deo, qui flagellat omnem filium quem recipit,[54] hospitandi gratia ad predicti uiri domum opido lassus quidam affuit peregrinus. Qui, intuens in puerum, de illius infirmitate compassionem habens, patrem suum ingemiscendo ita alloquitur: 'Numquid non audisti quibus sancta Margarita regina Scocie miraculis choruscat hiis diebus? In uera fide si filius tuus ibi fuisset cum omnia possibilia sint credenti,[55] sanitati restitueretur. Verumptamen consiliis meis adquiesce in fide nichil hesitans, ad laudem Dei et honorem beate Margarite accipe de puluere quem tuli de tumba eius et da filio tuo mixtum cum aqua ad potandum.' Quo facto, qui decem mundauit[56] per puluerem mausolei beate Margarite puerum a lepra curauit.

22. Qualiter quidam dealbator a celsitudine triginta pedum cecidit illesus

Accidit quodam die in refectorio, plenarie conuentu ad caritatem recumbente, ut quidam operarius eandem domum dealbaret et, cum gradatim ad summitatem scale mire altitudinis deuenisset, subito in duas partes confracta est scala. Cadensque operarius uoce magna clamabat, dicens, 'Sancta Margarita, succurre, sancta Margarita, succurre!' Tunc quidam de confratribus surrexerunt, estimantes illum omnino uita priuari. Quem inuenerunt infra scale fracturas stantem et reginam collaudantem, que sibi in illa hora subuenerat. Deum testati sumus qui affuimus quod nullam habuit lesionem, sed neque capillus de capite eius[57] perierat. Monachi autem, qui de tali casu erant perterriti, hoc uidentes mirabile spectaculum, glorificauerunt Deum qui facit magna et inscrutabilia, cuius nomen benedictum per infinita secula.

23. De quodam mercatore nomine Wilelmo de Dylton'[58]

Aduenit interea quidam mercennarius ad festum translacionis sancte Margarite, ut mos est mercatorum causa uenundandi. Qui, repentino

---

[54] Heb. 12: 6.   [55] Mark 9: 22.
[56] Luke 17: 11–19.   [57] Cf. Matt. 10: 30; Luke 12: 7.
[58] Possibly Dilton, Wilts., which occurs as 'Dultun' and 'Dulton' in 13th-cent. sources:

21. The cure of a boy suffering from elephantiasis

There was a nobleman in Galloway whose son was miserably tormented with elephantiasis for seven years and more. At last, by the plan of God, who punishes every son he accepts,[54] a pilgrim came, completely exhausted, to the man's house to seek lodging. He looked at the boy and, having pity on his sickness, said with sighs to the father, 'Have you not heard about the miracles with which St Margaret queen of Scotland is resplendent these days? If your son were there in true faith, since all things are possible to him who believes,[55] he would be restored to health. However, follow my advice, be confident and unhesitating and, in praise of God and in honour of the blessed Margaret, take some of the dust which I have brought from her tomb and give it to your son to drink, mixed with water.' Once this was done, He who made ten men clean[56] cured the boy from the leprosy through dust from the tomb of the blessed Margaret.

22. A painter who fell thirty feet unharmed

It happened one day in the dining hall while the whole community was sitting down to its special meal, that a workman was painting the room. When he had climbed up to the top of a very long ladder, it suddenly broke in two. As the workman fell, he cried out in a loud voice, 'St Margaret, help, St Margaret, help!' Then some of the brethren arose, thinking that he must be completely without life, but they found him standing amid the broken pieces of the ladder and praising the queen who had come to his aid in that hour. We who were present call on God as our witness that he had no injury and not a hair of his head[57] had perished. The monks who were terrified at the accident saw this wonderful sight and glorified God who performs great and inscrutable deeds, whose name be blessed world without end.

23. A merchant called William of Dilton[58]

Meanwhile a merchant came to the feast of the translation of St Margaret, as is the custom of merchants, in order to sell. It happened

Eilert Ekwall, *The Concise Oxford Dictionary of Place Names* (4th edn., Oxford, 1960), p. 144.

casu infra multitudinem ibi congregatam collisus in terram, sensum
perdidit naturalem. Tunc quidam | de populo, super illo uisceribus
moti misericordie,[59] uelud Samaritanus de semiuiuo,[60] ante altare
sancte Margarite, quod prope erat, in quodam grabato collocauerunt,
ubi multa enormia dixit et maiora fecit. Nam contra crucem et altare
saliuam proicere dedignanter non cessauit, omnium oculis intuen-
cium miserabile prebens spectaculum. Post tercium uero diem,
multitudine illius clamorem non sustinente, eicitur ab ecclesia
uagus abiens et repetens que iteranda non sunt. Iterum capitur,
trahitur, ante predictum locum sistitur et, quod mirabile est in nostris
oculis, in sequenti nocte meritis sanctissime Margarite, sicut uidimus
solennitatem facientes, sanitati restituitur.

24. De quodam carpentario a morte debita per beatam Margaritam liberato

Carpentarius quidam, nomine Vilelmus, libidinis frena non bene
retentans, ui quandam oppresserat mulierem. Pro quo facto, ut
dignum fuerat, capitur et acrius uinculis astrictus incarceratur.
Instante placiti die, coram iudicibus adducitur et, causa uentilata,
ferro iudiciali adiudicatur. Quod ferrum die statuto manu portans,
grauissimam sensit miser adustionem, manu siquidem, ut mos est,
sigillata, nocte sequenti ad sepulchrum beate Margarite eo quo potuit
affectu illius implorauit auxilium. Et ecce illi in summo diluculo
dormienti astitit regina, precipiens ut manum porrigeret. Qua
porrecta, predicta regina sufflauit in ea. Dolore itaque statim
recedente, nullam omnino sensit ille lesionem. Mane autem facto,
ad locum ubi manum iudicibus erat ostensurus adducitur, spemque
habens in dicta regina indubitatam, manum ostendit confidenter, in
qua nulla omnino adustionis uestigia apparere uidebantur. Ipse uero,
in hunc modum liber dimissus, crucem sumpsit, Deo et sancte
Margarite eius liberatrice gratias agens terram sanctam deuotus
adiuit.

25. De quadam muliere demone fugato sanato

Fuit mulier non longe a Dunfermelyn degens, peccatis exigentibus
spiritui maligno tradita, uidelicet quia decimam que Deo debetur

---

[59] Cf. Luke 1: 78; Col. 3: 12.   [60] Luke 10: 29-37.

that, in the middle of the crowd gathered there, he suddenly crashed to the ground and went out of his mind. Then some of the people, moved by the bowels of compassion[59] towards him, like the Samaritan and the man left for dead,[60] placed him on a litter before the altar of St Margaret, which was nearby. There he said many horrible things and did worse ones, for he did not cease from spitting disdainfully towards the cross and the altar, offering a most miserable spectacle to the eyes of the onlookers. On the third day the crowd was no longer able to bear his shouting and he was ejected from the church and wandered about, saying over and over things which do not bear repeating. He was seized again, dragged along and placed before the same place, and, what is wonderful in our eyes, the following night he was restored to health by the merits of the most holy Margaret, as we saw who were celebrating the service.

24. A carpenter freed by St Margaret from the death that was his due

A carpenter called William, unable to bridle his lust, raped a woman. He was seized on account of this, as was proper, bound tightly with chains and imprisoned. On the day of his hearing he was led before the judges and, after the case had been discussed, he was adjudged to trial by hot iron. The unhappy man carried the iron on the appointed day and experienced a terrible burning. His hand was then sealed, as is customary. The following night at the tomb of the blessed Margaret, he implored her help with as much feeling as he could. Behold, in the light of dawn the queen came to him as he slept, commanding him to stretch out his hand and, when he did this, the queen blew on it. The pain immediately went away and he felt no injury at all. In the morning he was led to the place where he was to show his hand to the judges and, having complete faith in the queen, he confidently showed his hand, in which there seemed to be no trace at all of burning. He was thus dismissed as a free man, took the cross and, giving thanks to God and St Margaret, his liberator, he went piously to the Holy Land.

25. A woman cured by the expulsion of a demon

There was a woman who lived not far from Dunfermline, who was possessed by a wicked spirit on account of her sins, namely that she

aut sibi retinebat aut ualde inuita reddebat. Quam ita demon uexabat immundus, ut, incessabiliter clamans, omnibus uidentibus et audientibus fastidio esset et terrori. Ad fontem siquidem sancte Margarite deducta, spectaculum cunctis miserabile prebebat cernentibus. Lapides namque et quicquid dentibus contingere potuit in frusta discerpsit. Tempore uero noctis medio, astitit ei regina a dextris sancta uidelicet Margarita, insinuans ei causam huiusmodi diabolice uexacionis, illique dicens ut redderet que Dei sunt Deo,[61] et fideliter illi per omnia seruire studeret, et si de cetero uitam suam mutare uellet in melius, sibi a Domino esse concessum miserie illius posse subuenire. Qua promissione exultans, miserrima, 'Que es tu', inquit, 'O domina mea?' Et illa, 'Ego sum', inquit, 'Margarita Scotorum |

fo. 36ᵛ regina.' Tunc illa miserrima, 'Ecce, domina, promitto me fide media uniuersa que mihi precipis fideliter quamdiu uixero obseruaturam.' Sancta Margarita ad hec uerba uirga quam manu gestabat ter illam percussit et immundum ab ea spiritum exire coegit. Euigilans autem mulier in tantum erat uexacione diabolica debilitata ut uix loqui potuisset. Tamen se senciens a demone liberatam quam plurimum iocundabatur, omnibus patefaciens assistentibus qualiter ei regina apparuerat et immundum ab ea spiritum eiecerat. Precepta enim que illi dederat quoad uixit fideliter obseruauit.

26. De quodam puero a spiritibus immundis uexato

Quidam puer, nomine Iohannes, quartum decimum agens annum, non longe a domo paterna pergens spaciatum, obuiam habuit duas nephandas mulieres, immo demones in specie mulierum, quarum una uiridi ueste erat induta, altera uero albo lintheamine cooperta. Que ueloci cursu ad puerum predictum cucurrerunt et, breue quoddam quod circa collum eius gestabat ui auferentes, in rubo qui prope erat absconderunt. Puer uero, ab eis dimissus, uersus domum paternam cucurrit, quamcicius lapides contra illas quasi se ᵃ defendendo iaciens. Mater uero pueri, a domo exiliens, uehementer mirabatur quare filius suus ita se agebat. Et apprehensa manu eius introduxit in domum suam. Qui statim ut ingressus est, omnium membrorum carens motu, similiter sensu et uoce perditis in terram corruens, per unius hore spacium quasi mortuus iacebat. Tunc meror et luctus, omnium uox

---

ᵃ si MS

⁶¹ Cf. Matt. 22: 21.

had either kept for herself the tithe that is due to God or had given it very unwillingly. An unclean demon tormented her so much that she cried out continually and was a burden and a fright to all who saw her or heard her. She was led to St Margaret's fountain, offering a wretched spectacle to all who saw her, for she ground into pieces stones and whatever else she could reach with her teeth. In the middle of the night the holy queen stood at her right side, letting her know the cause of this diabolical vexation and saying to her that she should render to God what is God's[61] and strive to serve him faithfully in all things. If henceforth she were willing to change her life for the better, then the Lord would grant that she might be helped in her wretchedness. The unfortunate woman rejoiced at this promise and said, 'Who are you, my lady?' 'I', she said, 'am Margaret, queen of Scots.' Then the unfortunate woman said, 'Behold, lady, I promise in all faith that I will conscientiously observe what you command me as long as I live.' At these words St Margaret struck her three times with the rod she was holding in her hand and forced the unclean spirit to leave her. The woman woke up so weakened by the diabolic possession that she was scarcely able to speak. Nevertheless, feeling that she was free from the demon, she rejoiced greatly and explained to all around her how the queen had appeared to her and cast out the unclean spirit from her. As long as she lived she faithfully observed the precepts that she had given her.

26. A boy troubled by unclean spirits

There was a boy called John, fourteen years of age, who was walking not far from his father's house when he met two wicked women, or rather, demons in the shape of women. One of them was dressed in green and the other in white linen. They ran quickly to the boy and snatched away a charm he carried around his neck and hid it in a nearby thorn-bush. When he was released by them, the boy ran towards his father's house, throwing stones at them as fast as he could to defend himself, as it were. The boy's mother rushed out of the house, wondering why her son was behaving in this way. She grasped him by the hand and took him into the house. As soon as he entered, he lost all movement in his limbs, likewise all feeling and power of speech, and fell to the ground and lay there for an hour like one dead. There followed sorrow and mourning, as with one voice they all

una euentum tam miserabilem plangencium. Denique parumper
melioratus, mutus tamen permanens, ad monasterium sancte Margarite a parentibus est delatus et ad sepulchrum beate regine, ob graciam
loquele recuperande et sanitatis pristine, cum suis per tres dies et
noctes iacuit, qui incessabiliter sanctissimam pro saluti pueri depre-
cabantur Margaritam. Tercia uero nocte uidebatur puero beatam sibi
assistere reginam, que plenariam illi per intercessionem suam a
Domino fuisse salutem concessam intimauit. Puer autem euigilans,
pristine sanitati restitutus, cepit loqui, cunctique qui aderant manus
ad celum tendentes, Deum collaudabant, qui per famulam suam
sanctam Margaritam talia mirabilia dignatus est operari. Mansit
autem puer ille postea in camera domini abbatis annis quamplurimis.

27. De quodam molendario lacertis pleno

Quodam molendario iuxta molendinum dormiente, introierunt lacerti
per os eius in interiora ipsius, maximo illum dolore afficientes et
angustia. Qui infra unius anni spacium in tantum sunt multiplicati
quod uentre tumescente similis uideretur mulieri puerpere et iam
fo. 37ʳ partui proxime. Bestialis erat miser ille | et fere Deum ignorans
potenciamque quam famule sue contulit sancte Margarite regine.
Tamen misertus illius Dominus, qui nichil odit eorum que fecit,[62]
dedit illi in mente ut sepulchrum uisitaret sancte regine. Qui, ad
locum deductus ubi sanctissimum corpus illius primo quieuit humatum, de aqua fontis iuxta sepulchrum existentis gustauit et obdormiuit. Dormienti illi astitit sancta Margarita, uentrem illius leniter
tangens et confestim ut sibi uidebatur in celo recepta disparuit. Miser
uero ille infra triduum incredibilem cum sanie sanguine permixta et
fetore indicibiliter lacertorum euomuit[a] multitudinem. Sicque, sanitate recepta, remeauit ad propria, Deum magnificans et sanctam
Margaritam, nichil mali de dicto infortunio unquam postea senciens.

28. De quodam monacho ad seculum disponente redire

Monachus quidam, nomine Adam, diabolo instigante propriaque
deuictus fragilitate, habebat in mente ad seculum redire. Quadam
uero nocte, illo in stratu suo quiescente aduenit, ut sibi uidebatur,

---

[a] emouuit MS

[62] Augustine, *De diuersis quaestionibus ad Simplicianum*, i. 2. 18, ed. Almut Mutzen-
becher (*CCSL*, xliv, 1970), p. 45; PL xl. 111, rephrasing Wisd. 11: 25.

lamented such an unhappy event. Eventually recovering a little, although remaining dumb, he was brought by his parents to the monastery of St Margaret and lay by the tomb of the blessed queen for three days and nights, in the hope of recovering his speech and former health. Those with him prayed to the most holy Margaret without ceasing for the boy's cure. On the third night it seemed to the boy that the blessed queen was standing beside him and she told him that, through her intercession, a complete cure had been granted to him by the Lord. The boy woke up restored to his former health and began to speak, while all who were present raised their hands to the heavens and praised God, who through his handmaid St Margaret had deigned to work such great wonders. The boy remained many years thereafter in the lord abbot's chamber.

27. A miller full of lizards

While a miller was sleeping by his mill, lizards entered his body through his mouth, giving him great pain and suffering. Within the space of a year they had multiplied to such an extent that his belly swelled up and he looked like a pregnant woman just about to give birth. This unhappy man was a primitive kind of person, almost totally ignorant of God and the power that He had bestowed on His handmaid St Margaret the queen. At last the Lord, who hates nothing that He has made,[62] had mercy on him and put into his mind the idea of visiting the tomb of the holy queen. When he was brought to the place where her most holy body first lay buried, he tasted some of the water from the well next to the tomb and went to sleep. While he was sleeping St Margaret came to him, lightly touched his belly and suddenly, as it seemed to him, disappeared into heaven. Within the next three days the wretched man vomited up an incredible number of lizards mixed with a mass of blood and stinking indescribably. So, with his health restored, he returned to his own country, praising God and St Margaret, never afterwards feeling anything from this accident.

28. A monk who intended to return to the world

A monk named Adam, at the instigation of the devil and conquered by his own weakness, had in mind to return to the secular world. One night while he lay in his bed, it seemed to him that his father, who

pater suus qui fuerat mortuus, illumque uerberauit tam acerrime quod fere exanimis factus, pre maxima sanguinis effusione uix ualebat flatum emittere, dicens illi, 'Cogitasti, miserrime, despecta tua professione quam Deo fecisti et famule sue sancte Margarite regine, ad seculum quasi canis ad uomitum redire,[63] meque et omnes amicos tuos super hoc confundere? Ecce missus sum a ipsa domina te a proposito tuo pessimo reuocare. Siquidem pro certo noueris quod si non uolueris resipiscere, multo grauiori te affligam flagellacione.' Euigilans itaque, toto corpore perfuso sanguine uniuersisque lectuli sui pannis sanguine suo madefactis, que dormiens audierat et perpessus fuerat patenter cunctis ostendit. Castigatus igitur tali uerbere destitit a sua peruersa uoluntate.

29. Qualiter quedam mulier a demonio est liberata

Quedam mulier, a demonio uexata, per totam Angliam duobus annis insana[a] ferebatur. Quam, ut sibi uidebatur, duo canes horridi et hispidi sequebantur. Cuius cutis in tantum erat denigrata, ut Ethiopissa putaretur. Tandem misertus Dominus illius, cuius misericordia super omnia opera eius,[64] salutem ipsius dedit in manu famule sue sancte Margarite Scotorum regine. Que, instinctu diuino, uersus Scociam iter arripuit. Cumque, mari transito quod Passagium Regine appellatur,[65] Dunfermelyn appropinquasset et ad hospitale quod iuxta est situm[66] uenisset, substiterunt duo predicti canes, ulterius progredi non ualentes. Intrans autem miserrima illa curiam abbacie, ita uelociter se agebat quod a nullo de curia potuit comprehendi quoadusque intrauit ecclesiam, nescientibus ecclesie custodibus. Qui, cum uiderent illam sine omni corporis tegumento, obstupuerunt | ipsamque de ecclesia expellere conati sunt. Que, semimortua effecta, in terram corruit, omni membrorum auxilio destituta. Quam predicti custodes miserie illius compacientes, ad fontem beate regine deportauerunt. Et, quamuis semimortua uideretur, tamen uinculis manus et pedes eius stringentes, lintheamine coopertam dimiserunt. Siquidem circa mediam noctem exclamauit illa iam non misera ter uoce magna, 'Sancta Margarita, sancta Margarita,

fo. 37ᵛ

---

[a] insania MS

[63] Prov. 26: 11; 2 Pet. 2: 22.   [64] Ps. 144 (145): 9.
[65] South Queensferry, West Lothian, and North Queensferry, Fife. The ferry had been instigated by St Margaret for pilgrims to St Andrews: Turgot, *Vita sanctae Margaretae Scotorum reginae*, c. 9, Symeon, ed. Hinde, p. 247.

was dead, came to him, and beat him so violently that he was almost unconscious and, because of the great loss of blood, scarcely able to breathe out. His father said to him, 'You wretch, are you thinking of disregarding the profession you made to God and his handmaid, St Margaret the queen, returning to the world like a dog to his vomit[63] and bringing disgrace on me and all your kin because of it? Behold, I have been sent by that lady to call you back from your wicked resolve, for you should know for certain that, if you are not willing to come to your senses, I will beat you much more severely.' When he awoke, he found his whole body covered in blood and all his bedclothes soaked in blood. He revealed to everyone what he had heard and what he had suffered while asleep, and, punished with such a beating, he gave up his wicked wish.

29. A woman freed from a demon

A woman who was troubled by a demon went around England for two years, out of her mind. It seemed to her that two wild and shaggy dogs were following her. Her skin was so darkened that you would think her an African. At last the Lord, whose mercies are over all His works,[64] took pity on her and gave her healing through the hand of His maidservant, St Margaret, queen of Scots. At the divine instigation, she directed her path towards Scotland and when she had come near to Dunfermline, after crossing the sea at Queensferry,[65] and had arrived at the hospital situated nearby,[66] the two dogs halted, unable to go any further. The unhappy woman entered the abbot's court and was so quick that no one from the court could catch her before she had entered the church, without the knowledge of its custodians. When they saw her, without any covering on her body, they were astonished and tried to expel her from the church. She fell to the ground half-dead, deprived of the use of her limbs, and the custodians, having compassion on her misery, carried her to the well of the blessed queen. Although she seemed half-dead, nevertheless they tied her hands and feet with fetters, then left her, covered with a linen cloth. Around the middle of the night the woman—no longer the unhappy woman—called out three times in a great voice, 'St Margaret, St Margaret, St Margaret,

[66] A hospital at Dunfermline is first recorded in 1327, though one at North Queensferry is mentioned as early as 1165: Ian B. Cowan and D. E. Easson, *Medieval Religious Houses: Scotland* (2nd edn., London, 1976), pp. 164, 167.

sancta Margarita, meritis tuis et gratia a demonio sum liberata!' Cutis
uero illius, ut prediximus, deformis et nigra, supra estimacionem
humanam quamcicius colori pristino est restituta.

30. De quodam adolescente a demone percusso

Nec hoc pretereundum quod adolescens quidam, in obsequio cuiusdam militis positus, desiderio habens uisitare parentes, licenciam a
domino suo peciit et optinuit. Veniensque ad domum patris, totam
familiam suo letificauit aduentu. Quadam uero die, sole ad occasum
tendente, dum iuxta quendam riuulum spaciandi gracia pergeret,
audiuit sonitum equorum multorum currencium. Qui, post tergum
aspiciens, uidit maximam multitudinem equitum nimis deformium
sibi ueloci cursu appropiancium. Vnde expergefactus uersus domum
paternam cucurrit quamcicius. Vnus autem ex agmine nefando, equo
insidens nigro et ingenti, illum cursu uelocissimo insequitur. Cumque
sibi apropiaret, equus ipsius equitis eleuatis pedibus anterioribus
ipsum in dorso percussit et dorsum suum, ut sibi uidebatur, fregit.
Qui, statim in terram corruens, iacebat quasi mortuus. Quesitus
undique a familia domus, inuentus est tandem omni membrorum
motu destitutus et mutus. Quem cum tristicia et merore maximo ad
domum deportauerunt. In crastino siquidem illum ad fontem beate
Margarite semimortuum et mutum detulerunt, sanctam Margaritam
pro salute ipsius deuote deprecantes. Cui summo diluculo tercie diei
soporato apparuit beata regina, dicens illi, 'Surge et quamtocius ad
tumbam meam ubi nunc corpus meum requiescit perge.' Quo
respondente, 'Domina, dorsum habeo fractum et me mouere non
possum,' dixit sancta Margarita, 'Ecce,' inquit, 'sanus factus es, surge
uelocius.' Euigilans itaque adolescens cepit loqui et erigens se,
'Eamus', inquit, 'ad tumbam sancte Margarite, que mihi loquelam
reddidit et me sanitati sua gracia restituit.' Tunc omnes qui aderant,
exultantes et pre gaudio magno lacrimantes, perrexerunt cum eo ad
tumbam, Deum laudantes qui in sanctis suis semper est mirabilis.[67]

31. Qualiter prior Gregorius a morbo pessimo est curatus

fo. 38ʳ Prior de Dunfermlyn, nomine Gregorius,[68] grauissimum | habuit
morbum sub ascella qui dicitur antrax, ad modum magne patene

---

[67] Ps. 67: 36 (68: 35).

[68] 'G., prior of Dunfermline' witnesses *Registrum de Dunfermlyn*, ed. Cosmo Innes

by your merits and grace I have been freed from the demon!' Her skin, which, as we said earlier, was ugly and black, was restored to its original colour faster then human judgment could imagine.

30. A young man struck by a demon

Nor should I pass over the story of a young man who had been placed in the service of a knight. He wished to visit his parents and sought and obtained permission to do so from his lord. Coming to his father's house, he gave joy to the whole household by his arrival. But one day as the sun went down, while he was taking a stroll by a little stream, he heard the sound of many galloping horses. Looking behind him, he saw a great multitude of hideous riders approaching him at great speed. Roused by this, he ran as quickly as he could towards his father's house. However, one of that evil company, mounted on a huge black horse, pursued him at a terrific speed and, when he got near to him, the rider's horse raised its front feet and struck him on the back, breaking his back as it seemed to him. He fell immediately to the ground and lay like one dead. The household searched for him everywhere and eventually found him, lacking movement in any limb and dumb. With sorrow and great mourning they carried him home. Next day they brought him, half-dead and dumb, to the well of the blessed Margaret, devoutly entreating St Margaret for his health. At first light on the third day the blessed queen appeared to him while he was sleeping and said to him, 'Arise and go with all speed to my tomb, where my body now rests.' He answered, 'Lady, I have a broken back and cannot move.' St Margaret said, 'Behold, you have been healed, get up quickly.' The young man awoke and began to speak. Lifting himself up, he said, 'Let us go to the tomb of St Margaret, who has given me back the power of speech and restored me to health by her grace.' Then all who were there rejoiced and wept because of their great joy, going with him to the tomb, praising God who is always wonderful in His saints.[67]

31. How Prior Gregory was cured of a serious illness

A prior of Dunfermline, Gregory by name,[68] had under his armpit a very serious affliction, which is called a carbuncle, shaped like a large

(Bannatyne Club, Edinburgh, 1842), no. 190, p. 107, but this may be prior Geoffrey who was abbot from 1238–40 (*Chronicle of Melrose*, ed. A. O. Anderson and M. O. Anderson (London, 1936), s. a.). There are no other known references to Prior Gregory.

rotundum, unde maximo dolore cruciabatur et angustia. Hic quam plures consuluit medicos, qui omnes unanimiter dixerunt illum a nullo posse curari homine. Igitur, humano destitutus auxilio, Dei omnipotentis et sancte Margarite regine implorauit adiutorium et optinuit, ueniensque ad tumbam regine, pannis ex illa parte qua morbus erat depositis, morbum lapidi reliquias beate regine continenti apposuit, et hoc tociens egit donec, fugato dolore, morboque euanescente saluti fuerat perfecte restitutus. Curatus siquidem est ita quod exinde nullum sentiret dolorem interius, nec ulla exterius predicti morbi apparuere uestigia. Vixit nempe postea annos circiter triginta, omnipotenti Deo et famule sue sancte Margarite deuotissimus.

32. De quodam monacho^a a dolore dentium curato

Monachus quidam, nomine Lambertus, dolore dencium acriter uexatus in tantum ut iuramento confirmauit quod fere amens effectus, quid faceret prorsus ignorabat; uoluebat tandem in mente quod Dominus meritis sancte Margarite huius angustiam et alias infirmitates innumerabiles perpessis subueniebat sepissime. Concurrit igitur ueluti insanus ad tumbam regine et, lapidem in quo sanctissime illius reliquie requiescunt digito tangens, digitum in ore posuit et illo dentes interius exteriusque fricans, omnem quamcicius mitigauit dolorem. Igitur, dolore fugato, nunquam postea nec minimum quidem, ut asseruit, dencium uisus est sentire dolorem.

33. De quadam muliere a tumore capitis curata

Iuuenis quidam ortus de Clacmanan[69] ancillam domus paterne quamplurimum diligebat. Pater uero ipsius iuuenis, nolens filium suum adherere ancille sue, prouidit illi uxorem. Quam etiam fecit ducere solenniter in facie ecclesie. Mortuo tandem patre, iuuenis ille, despecta propria uxore, predicte ancille furtiue adherebat. Quadam uero die dum hora meridiana ipsa dormiret sola, uenit pater, ut sibi uidebatur, ipsius iuuenis qui mortuus fuerat, illamque manu sinistra iniecta per guttur arcius stringendo cepit, dexteraque caput ipsius circumquaque durissime uerberauit, dicens, 'Impudica meretricula, filius meus instinctu tuo iacet in anime sue periculo.' Sicque recessit. Vespere uero facto, aduenit familia domus miseramque illam surdam

---

^a monocho *MS*

---

[69] Clackmannanshire.

round dish, and this tormented him with great pain and suffering. He consulted very many doctors, who all said unanimously that no man could cure him. So, deprived of human assistance, he begged for and received the help of God almighty and St Margaret the queen, coming to the queen's tomb, removing the clothes from the diseased area and pressing the diseased part against the stone that contained the relics of the blessed queen. He did this repeatedly until the pain disappeared, the disease went away, and he was restored to perfect health. He was so thoroughly cured that henceforth he felt no pain within nor was there any external trace of the disease. He lived afterwards for around thirty years, devoted with all his heart to God and his handmaid, St Margaret.

32. A monk cured of toothache

A monk called Lambert was so severely troubled with toothache that he swore on oath that he was almost out of his mind. He really did not know what to do, but he reflected that, through the merits of St Margaret, the Lord had very often cured sufferers from this ailment and countless other illnesses. Therefore he ran like a madman to the queen's tomb and touched with his finger the stone in which her most holy relics rest, then put the finger in his mouth and rubbed both the front and the back of his teeth with it. At once he soothed the pain and, once it had gone, never afterwards, as he asserted, did he seem to suffer the slightest trace of toothache.

33. A woman cured of a tumour on her head

A young man from Clackmannan[69] was deeply in love with a servant from his father's house. The young man's father, unwilling that his son should be involved with a servant, provided a wife for him, whom he married solemnly before the church. Eventually his father died and the young man, disdaining his own wife, became involved with the servant in secret. One day, at midday, when she was sleeping alone, it seemed to her that the young man's father, who had died, came and grabbed her around the throat with his left hand, squeezing it tightly, while he beat her fiercely about the head with his right hand, saying, 'You shameless little whore, it is your fault that my son lies in peril of his soul!' And thus he went away. When it was evening, the household came home and found the unhappy woman deaf and

et mutam penitusque uisu carentem inueniens, uehementer mirabatur quidnam esset quod illi acciderat. Caput namque informe et deforme, ad modum glomeris habebat rotundum, in quo nec aures nec oculi nec nasus nec mentum apparere uidebantur. Sicque iacebat miserrima | illa usque ad quartam noctis uigiliam, sepius in corde suo ut poterat sancte Margarite regine implorans adiutorium. Circa horam uero quam prediximus, uenit beata regina illique dixit, 'O misera, peccatis tuis exigentibus talia pateris infortunia. Verumptamen quia tociens me inuocasti, misertus tui Dominus concessit mihi tibi posse conferre salutem.' Tunc sancta regina, manu ori illius miselle apposita, extraxit pomum pronuncians illud euangelicum, 'Ecce sana facta es, uade et noli amplius peccare'.[70] Statimque omni capitis deformitate remota, uisu, auditu loquelaque redditis, magna uoce sanctam cepit collaudare Margaritam. Sicque, sanitate recepta, quamcicius potuit tumbam sancte regine adiuit deuota.

fo. 38ᵛ (margin)

34. De quodam monacho[a] a graui infirmitate curato

Quidam monachus, nomine Adam, dum esset nouicius grauissimam infirmitatem per tres annos est perpessus. Sepius namque in terram corruens, uoce et omni membrorum motu carens, a cunctis cernentibus morbum caducum pati putabatur. Cuius infirmitati fratres multum compaciebantur, quia eum ualde diligebat. Quidam uero monachus beneficia sancte Margarite sepissime expertus, admonuit eundem ut ad tumbam illius pergeret, deuote supplicans pro sua salute. Qui respondit se hoc facere ausum non esse, quia si suus magister hoc scire posset, illum etiam coram omnibus quod illud per ypocrisim fecisset irridendo proclamaret. Cui predictus monachus, uir ualde religiosus, qui prior tunc temporis eiusdem erat monasterii, 'Ego', inquit, 'do tibi licenciam ut si non palam hoc uelis facere, saltem ceteris dormientibus ad tumbam pergas, pro certo sciens si dominam reginam recto quesieris corde, sanitati restitueris perfecte.' Nocte uero sequenti spem habens in domina iuit ad eius tumbam, ubi tantam sensit suauissimi odoris fragranciam, acsi in deliciis paradysiace amenitatis esset positus. Ipse uero uehementer odoris suauitatem admirans, eleuatis ad celum manibus, deuote deprecebatur ut Dominus meritis sancte Margarite illius dignaretur subuenire miserie.

---

[a] monocho MS

---

[70] John 8: 11.

dumb and completely unable to see. They wondered very greatly what had happened to her, for her head was shapeless and distorted, round like a ball in form, in which there appeared to be neither ears, eyes, nose, or chin. The wretched woman lay there until the fourth watch of the night, frequently begging in her heart the help of St Margaret the queen, as far as she was able. Around the time we have mentioned the blessed queen came and said to her, 'Wretched woman, you are suffering this misfortune on account of your sins. But since you have invoked me so often, the Lord has had mercy on you and has allowed me to grant you your health.' Then the holy queen placed her hand on that unhappy woman's mouth and drew out an apple, saying these words from the Gospel: 'Behold you are healed, go and sin no more.'[70] Immediately the deformity of her head disappeared and the powers of sight, hearing and speech returned. With a great voice she began to praise St Margaret and thus, with her health restored, she came devoutly to the tomb of the holy queen as fast as she could.

34. A monk cured of a serious illness

A monk called Adam endured a very serious illness for three years while he was a novice. For he often fell to the ground, lacking the power of speech and any movement in his limbs, and was thought by all who saw him to have suffered from the falling sickness. The brethren had great compassion for his ailment, for they loved him dearly. A monk who had often experienced the favours of St Margaret advised him to go to her tomb and pray devoutly for his recovery. He replied that he dare not do this, since if his master knew, he would denounce him derisively before them all as moved by hypocrisy. The monk, who was a truly devout man and prior of the monastery at that time, said to him, 'If you do not wish to do this in public, I give you permission to go to the tomb at least while the others are sleeping. Know for sure that, if you beseech the lady queen with a righteous heart, you will be restored to perfect health.' The following night, with his hopes placed in the lady, he went to her tomb, where he experienced such a sweetly smelling fragrance that it was as if he had been placed among the delightful pleasures of paradise. He wondered greatly at the sweetness of the smell, raised his hands to heaven, and prayed devoutly that the Lord would deign to help him in his misery through the merits of St Margaret. He lay

Ibique prostratus iacuit et usquequo matutinis percantatis ibidem
dormiens requieuit. Quidam autem frater, multum sanctam diligens
reginam, qui qualibet nocte post matutinos eius circuibat tumbam,
illum ibidem inueniens soporatum, a suo sompno excitauit, precipiens ut ad lectum suum rediret. Qui, pudore perfusus, ad lectum
est reuersus, nullum huiusmodi infirmitatis postea senciens incommodum.

35. Quomodo mulier quedam tactu sacre manus regine a tumore uentris sit curata

fo. 39ʳ Mulier quedam de Aberden cuius uenter | ita intumuerat ut uix cutis
interiora ne erumperent ualeret retinere. Hanc uisitauit Dominus ex
alto,[71] dans illi in animo ut ad sepulchrum beate Margarite pro-
peraret. Quod illa misera cum maximo dolore et angustia duxit ad
effectum. Veniens itaque ad sepulchrum beate regine, aliquamdiu
ibidem morabatur. Tandem domum est reuersa. Tercia siquidem
nocte aduentus sui ad domum propriam, apparuit illi regina, dicens se
salutem ipsius a Domino optinuisse uentremque eius leniter tangens
abscessit. Mulier autem, a sompno surgens, saniem permaximam cum
fetore putrido euomuit.ᵃ Itaque, salute recepta, forcior et ad quelibet
expedicior quam unquam prius fuerat effecta, gracias omnipotenti
Deo et sancte Margarite, per quam sibi cognouit salutem esse
concessam, quolibet anno ad tumbam ipsius deuota persoluit. Bene-
dictus Deus qui per famulam suam sanctam Margaritam cernentibus
nobis quod plurima operari dignatur miracula!

36. De uisione cuiusdam monachi

Erat quidam monachus in lecto suo nocte quadam quiescens, cui
talis apparuit uisio. Vidit ipse duos canes, ingentes, horridos et
hispidos, dormitorium intrare, quorum unus erat ruffus, alter uero
nigerrimus. Ruffus autem, exiliens ipsumque stragulare cupiens, per
guttur cepit et, ecce, adiutrix suorum propicia, sancta Margarita,
uirgam manu tenens, ambos canes eadem uirga uerberando a
dormitorio fugauit. Qua recedente, intrauerunt secundo predicti
canes. Quibus iterum a sancta regina fugatis, recessit ipsa. Tertio
siquidem eisdem canibus dormitorium intrantibus, sanctissima

ᵃ emouuit MS

there prostrate and slept in that place until matins had been sung. A certain brother, who loved the holy queen very much and went round her tomb every night after matins, found him there slumbering and raised him from his sleep, commanding him to return to his bed. Covered in shame, he went back to his bed, never afterwards being troubled by this illness.

35. How a woman was cured of a tumour on her belly by the touch of the queen's holy hand

There was a woman from Aberdeen whose belly was so swollen that her skin was scarcely able to prevent her insides from bursting out. The Lord visited her from on high,[71] putting it into her mind that she should hasten to the tomb of the blessed Margaret, which the unhappy woman achieved with great pain and anguish. She came to the tomb of the blessed queen and stayed there a while. Eventually she returned home. On the third night after her arrival at her own house, the queen appeared to her, saying that she had obtained her cure from the Lord and departing after touching her belly lightly. The woman arose from sleep and vomited a huge loathsome body of matter that stank foully. And so, having recovered her health, made stronger and more capable at anything than she had ever been before, every year at her tomb she paid thanks devotedly to God almighty and St Margaret, through whom, as she knew, she had been granted health. Blessed be God who deigns to perform many miracles in our sight through His handmaid St Margaret!

36. A monk's vision

There was a monk, resting one night in his bed, who witnessed the following vision. He saw two huge wild and shaggy dogs enter the dormitory, one red, the other jet-black. The red one sprang up and seized him by the throat, desiring to strangle him, and behold, the gracious helper of her own, saint Margaret, carrying a staff in her hands, drove both dogs from the dormitory by beating them with that staff. When she went away, the dogs entered for a second time. They were again driven off by the holy queen, who then departed. When those dogs entered the dormitory for a third time, the most holy

---

[71] Cf. Luke 1: 78.

Margarita, ut sibi uidebatur irata, minata est ut, si aliqui alicui suorum monachorum inquietudinem aliquam inferre presumerent, sic illos uinculis strictos castigaret, ne alicui nocere ualerent de cetero. Monachus uero euigilans, que uiderat fratribus enarrauit.

37. De quodam monacho deuiare uolenti uoti sui

Cuidam monacho a proposito deuiare uolenti, sub tali forma subuenit sancta Margarita. Videbatur namque eius nutrici, que eum lactauerat et iccirco eum arcius amauerat, mulieri siquidem honestissimam uitam ducenti, se uidere quamdam matronam decentissime ornatam, cum qua etiam erat puella perpulchra, in manu per frenum tenens equum album pergrandem decenter stratum; uidit et alterum equum nigrum non longe ab illo distantem eiusdem magnitudinis. Cui, magnitudinem equorum admiranti, dixit uenerabilis predicta matrona, 'Scisne cuius est equus ille nigerrimus?' Cui illa ait, | 'Minime, domina.' 'Equus iste', inquit, 'est filii tui, habitum monachilem in domo mea de Dunfermelyn gerentis, quem sibi preparauit cui ille seruire disposuit. Verumptamen, si a praua uoluntate sua conuersus resipiscere uoluerit, istum album equum illi tribuam et in mea protectione ipsum recipiam.' Quo audito, euigilans mulier, de dilecti filii sui salute ualde sollicita, quamcicius potuit ea que in sompnis uiderat predicto monacho uoce lacrimabili enarrauit. Qui, tali uisione castigatus, in fide firmior et in perferendis aduersis, carnis uidelicet et aduersarii, fortissimus effectus, Deo omnipotenti et sancte Margarite sue infirmitatis consultrici deuotus perseuerat. Benedictus Deus qui nouit etiam cum temptacione facere prouentum!

fo. 39^v

38. De quodam clerico a dolore uentris curato

Erat quidam clericus, militis cuiusdam filius, nomine Robertus, cuius uenter ad modum maris fluctuantis, modo plenus, modo uidebatur inanis et uacuus. Siquidem quotquot eum uiderunt, estimauerunt mirum aliquod, cuius pulsu et mocione ita tumesceret illius inesse utero. Hic dominam Margaritam sedulus interpellabat precibus, ut illum a tali dignaretur curare miseria. Cui in lectulo suo quadam nocte dormienti astitit regina, in manu sua cyphum argenteum oblatis et uino plenum deferens, sibique porrigens precepit ut oblata

Margaret, who seemed to him to be angry, threatened that if anyone dared to cause any distress to any of her monks, she would punish them with such tight bonds that they would not be able to harm anyone ever again. The monk woke up and told the brethren what he had seen.

37. A monk who wished to abandon his vows

It was in the following way that St Margaret came to the assistance of a monk who wished to turn aside from his profession. For it seemed to his nurse, who had suckled him and thus loved him more deeply, and was a woman who led a most respectable life, that she saw a lady, gracefully adorned, with whom there was also a most beautiful girl, who held by the reins a huge white horse with a lovely saddle. And she also saw a black horse of the same size not far distant from them. While she was wondering at the size of the horses, the venerable lady said to her, 'Do you know who that jet-black horse belongs to?' and she answered her, 'No, lady.' 'That horse', she said, 'belongs to your son, who wears the monk's habit in my house of Dunfermline, and it has been made ready for him by the one he has decided to serve. But if he is willing to come to his senses and turn from his wicked decision, I will give him this white horse and receive him under my protection.' As she heard this, the woman woke up, very worried about the salvation of her beloved son, and as soon as she could she related to the monk, in a tearful voice, what she had seen in her dream. He was chastised by such a vision and became firmer in faith and very strong in sustaining the attacks of the flesh and the Enemy, and he persevered in his devotion to God and St Margaret, his counsellor in his weakness. Blessed be God who knows how to make even temptation turn out to the good!

38. A cleric cured from stomach ache

There was a clerk called Robert, the son of a knight, whose belly, like an undulating sea, appeared now to be full, now to be empty and vacant. When people saw him, they deemed that there must be something remarkable by whose pulse and movement the contents of his belly swelled in this way. He diligently begged the lady Margaret with his prayers that she would deign to cure him from this misery. One night the queen stood by him as he slept in his bed, carrying in her hand a silver dish full of wafers and wine, and, stretching it out to

comederet et uinum potaret. Quo fere exhausto, illud modicum quod
in uase remansit, effudit ipsa domina super caput egrotantis dicens,
'Hoc tibi signum quod sanus sis effectus, et in domo mea sancte
conuersacionis habitum es suscepturum.' Euigilans itaque predictus
clericus ualde letabundus, que sibi predicta regina, ut sibi uidebatur,
fecerat*a* et dixerat, abbati de Dunfermlyn omnibusque amicis suis
congaudentibus intimauit. Non post multum uero temporis monachus effectus, quoad uixit Deo et sancte Margarite deuotissime
seruiuit.

39. De quadam muliere ydropica

Ydropica quedam totam Angliam, loca sanctorum uisitando, per
septem annos circuiuit, querens sibi requiem et non inuenit.
Tandem uersus Scociam iter arripiens, audierat enim Deum per
famulam suam sanctam Margaritam ibidem multa operari mirabilia.
Veniens itaque ad sepulchrum beate regine, ultra modum tumefacta,
uentrem uidebatur habere preambulum, facies uero illius et cetera
corporis membra in tantum erant macillenta, quod nichil habere
uideretur preter cutem et ossa. Illa siquidem ad fontem beate regine
in tempeste noctis silentio*b* dormiente, uidebatur sibi quod quedam
uenerabilis matrona et puella ualde decora, de choro uenientes, sibi
fo. 40*r* appropinquerent. Cumque uenissent ad locum ubi illa | iacebat,
pretereuntes perrexerunt ad altare quod ibidem in honore sancte
Margarite est edificatum. Deinde reuertentes, substitit predicta
matrona, intendens in ipsam infirmam, illique dixit, 'Surge, ueni
mecum.' Qua respondente, 'Domina, ne indigneris si te interrogem
quo appelleris nomine.' Cui domina, 'Ego sum', inquit, 'Margarita
Scotorum regina.' Apprehensaque manu eius dextra, duxit illam per
chorum ad tumbam suam, de tumba ad claustrum, de claustro ad
refectorium, et sic per omnes abbacie officinas. Tandem duxit illam in
cimiterium ex parte australi ecclesie. Tunc sancta regina dixit puelle
que secum erat, 'Apprehende manum ipsius sinistram.' Quo facto,
ascendentes ipsam infirmam inter se in summitate ecclesie deportauerunt. Illaque ibidem dimissa, ascendit in celum regina cum sua
puella. Mulier uero ualde perterrita, cum non haberet unde se tenere
posset, ut sibi uidetur retrorsum*c* cecidit. Vnde expergefacta euigilans, tantum euomuit putredinis quantitatem, quod incredibile
uideretur humano corpori posse tantam inesse putredinem. Ipsa

---

a facerat MS   *b* see critical note to ch. 13 above   *c* retrosum MS

him, she commanded that he should eat the wafers and drink the wine. When this was almost all gone, the lady poured the little that remained in the container over the sick man's head, saying, 'This is a sign for you that you have been healed and you will receive the habit of the holy way of life in my house.' When he woke up the clerk was full of joy and he informed the abbot of Dunfermline and all his overjoyed friends what the queen, as it seemed to him, had done and said to him. It was not a long time afterwards that he became a monk and served God and St Margaret devoutly as long as he lived.

39. A woman with dropsy

A woman with dropsy travelled around the whole of England for seven years visiting the shrines of the saints, seeking relief but not finding it. At length she directed her journey towards Scotland, for she had heard that God worked many miracles there through his handmaid St Margaret. So she came to the tomb of the blessed queen. She was enormously swollen and appeared to have a belly that went ahead of her, but her face and other limbs were so wasted that she appeared to be nothing but skin and bone. While she was sleeping at the blessed queen's spring in the silence of the dead of night, it seemed to her that a venerable lady and a very beautiful girl came from the choir and approached her. When they had come to the place where she lay, they passed by and proceeded to the altar built there in honour of St Margaret. Then, as they returned, the lady stopped and turned towards the sick woman, saying to her, 'Arise, come with me.' She answered, 'Lady, do not become angry if I ask what is your name.' The lady said to her, 'I am Margaret, queen of Scots.' She took her by the right hand and led her through the choir to her tomb, from the tomb to the cloister, from the cloister to the dining hall, and so through all the domestic buildings of the abbey. Eventually she led her into the churchyard south of the church. Then the holy queen said to the girl who was with her, 'Take her left hand.' Once she had done this, they lifted her up between them and carried her to the very top of the church. Releasing her there, the queen and the girl with her ascended into heaven. The woman was terrified for she had nothing to support her and, as it seemed to her, she fell backwards. Aroused by this, she woke up and vomited such a great quantity of foul matter that it seemed incredible for a human body to have so much foul

autem post paucos dies, uiribus receptis, ad propria remeauit, benedicens Deum et famulam suam beatam Margaritam.

40. Qualiter beata Margarita regina nauem suam et nautas in mari periclitantes liberauit

Non reor esse silendum quod quedam nauis apud Berwych frumento fuit onerata, quod ad opus monachorum de Dunfermelyn erat emptum et ad caritatem tam penes pauperes quam diuites ibidem aduentantes sustentandam. Conscendunt itaque nauem qui eam erant recturi et ad altum maris aura suaui et cursu prospero deuenerunt. Et ecce subito tonitruorum et uentorum tempestate mirabili et miserabili exorta, spes nulla salutis, nullum fuit uite presidium quin omnes a minimo usque ad maximum contremendo mortem formidarent imminentem. Malus namque nauis in partes confringitur et uelum rapido turbine asportatur. Consilio ergo inito, communiter consenciebant quod tota illa massa frumenti que in naui erat in mare proiceretur. Rector uero nauis, qui erat uir prouidus et discretus, respondit hoc nequaquam debere fieri, sed, inuocata Trinitate indiuidua et beate Margarite adiutorio, cuius erant ea que in naui continebantur, animam suam et omnium qui secum inerant ipsi commendauit, cuius potestas in celo et in terra, in mari et in omnibus abissis.⁷² Cumque omnes, genibus flexis, ipsum deprecarentur qui uentis imperat et mari⁷³ et sanctam Margaritam in auxilium inuocarent, ob metum mortis trepidantes, subito apparuit eis quasi in nube illa felix et misericors regina | Scotorum, eleuataque manu sancte crucis signaculo ipsos consignauit et in hora momentanea tempus illud tediosum et tenebrosum et omni formidine plenum, ipse temporum dispositor precibus eiusdem beate regine luce et tranquillitate misericordie sue serenauit. Nauis uero, saluis omnibus, celeri cursu ad portum applicuit preoptatum.

fo. 40ᵛ

41. De quodam sacerdote languescente insperate curato

Sacerdos quidam, nomine Douenaldus, in lecto egritudinis per quatuor menses et septem dies decubans, grauissimam perpessus est corporis inualitudinem. Consultis igitur circumquaque medicis, ab uniuersis unanimiter dicebatur quod fuit incurabilis. Egritudine

---

⁷² Ps. 134 (135): 6.

matter in it. After a few days she recovered her strength and returned to her own country, blessing God and His handmaid the blessed Margaret.

40. How St Margaret the queen saved her ship and its sailors when they were in peril on the sea

I do not think I should pass over in silence the following story. A ship was loaded at Berwick with grain, that had been purchased for the needs of the monks of Dunfermline, to support charitable giving to their guests, both rich and poor. The crew boarded the vessel and set off onto the high seas with a calm breeze and fair voyage in prospect, but suddenly a remarkable and lamentable tempest of thunder and wind arose. There seemed no hope of survival, no way of preserving their lives, so all from the least to the greatest trembled in fear of imminent death. The ship's mast shattered into pieces and the sail was carried off by the hurricane's grasp. They debated together what to do and decided that the cargo of grain should be thrown into the sea. The ship's captain, however, who was a careful and thoughtful fellow, said that they should not do this, and, invoking the Holy Trinity and the help of St Margaret, to whom the cargo belonged, he commended his soul and the souls of the other passengers and crew to Him whose power is in heaven and earth, in the sea and the deeps.[72] When they had all knelt and were praying to Him who commands the wind and sea[73] and calling on the aid of St Margaret, trembling in fear of death, suddenly the blessed and merciful queen of Scots appeared to them, as it were in a cloud. She raised her hand and made the sign of the cross over them and in that very hour He who disposes the weather calmed that worrying and dark weather, full of fears, at the prayers of the blessed queen and through the light and tranquillity of her mercy. The ship made swift passage and came to its destined port with all on board safe.

41. The unexpected cure of a priest who was languishing from disease

A priest called Donald lay sick in bed for four months and seven days, suffering a very severe physical infirmity. He had consulted doctors far and wide but they all said unanimously that he was incurable. As

---

[73] Luke 8: 25; cf. Matt. 8: 26.

namque ingrauescente, in tantum erat debilitatus quod nisi manibus seruiencium adiutus ad ea que natura poposcit pergere non posset. Itaque, de uita desperans, testamentum condidit, sacramentisque sancte ecclesie, scilicet confessione, iniunctione peractis, communioneque sancta percepta, diuinam prestolabatur uoluntatem. Nocte siquidem cene dominice,[74] dum aliquantulum soporaret, audiuit uocem dicentem sibi, 'Surge et ad tumbam meam perge.' Quo audito, cogitabat eger intra se quod uox esset sancte Margarite, cuius meritis et precibus sibi sanitatem posse conferri credebat. In crastino siquidem precepit suis ut ipsum ad tumbam beate ferrent Margarite. Quibus iussioni illius obtemperantibus, delatus est ad tumbam, illamque deuote ex omni parte deosculans, reportatus est ad fontem, ubi usque ad diem pasche semimortuus iacebat, non ualens pedes suos uel extendere uel retrahere pre maxima debilitate. Mira res: die pasche, sine alicuius iuuamine, sanus effectus perrexit ad domum suam, glorificans Deum et sanctam Margaritam, cuius intercessione gloriosa, insperata obtinuerat sanitatis remedia. Ipsi Deo honor et gloria qui per famulam suam talia operatur mirabilia, cuius numen et imperium permanet in secula seculorum. Amen.

42. De puella a neruorum contractione curata

Inter alia eciam miranda manifestauit Dominus Iesus iterum famulam suam beatam Margaritam Scotorum reginam: manifestauit autem sic. Fuit quedam puella, nomine Maria, in Laudoniam in uilla que dicitur Klenchors in obsequio cuiusdam patris familias, que in uigilia sancti Laurencii[75] pectinibus ferreis lanam hospite sue carpebat. Hora uero transacta qua uigilia, sicut mos est, festiue deberet obseruari, cogitabat illa intra se dicens, 'Non dimittam opus meum cum parum lane habeam iam ad carpendum, donec tantilla particula que superest omnino preparetur.' Dum ergo intra se talia cogitaret, | pectinibus a manibus suis subito elapsis, infelix illa de sedili quo sedebat in terram corruit, totis uiribus corporeis destituta, et fere per spacium unius hore diei ibidem quasi mortua iacebat. Accurrerunt ergo hospes et hospita totaque familia domus, admirantes quid circa illam tam subito accidisset.

Tandem cum misella illa aliquantulum ad memoriam reuerteretur, inuenta est manus eius dextra miserabiliter contracta, ita quod pollex uole manus iungeretur, digitis desuper fixis firmiterque contractis,

fo. 41ʳ

[74] The Thursday before Easter.   [75] St Lawrence's day is 10 Aug.

his illness became worse, he was so weakened that he could only go to meet the demands of nature supported by the hands of his servants. He thus despaired of life, made his will, and, after the sacraments of confession and extreme unction, received holy communion and awaited the divine will. On the night of Maundy Thursday,[74] while he was sleeping a little, he heard a voice saying to him, 'Arise and go to my tomb.' When he heard this the sick man thought within himself that the voice was that of St Margaret, by whose merits and prayers he believed he could obtain his health. Next day he ordered his men to carry him to the tomb of the blessed Margaret. They obeyed his command and he was brought to the tomb, kissed every part of it with devotion, and was then carried to the well, where he lay half-dead until Easter day, unable to stretch out or withdraw his feet because of his great weakness. An amazing thing happened: on Easter day, without anybody's help, he went to his home restored to health, glorifying God and St Margaret by whose glorious intercession he had obtained this unexpected cure. To God be honour and glory, who worked such wonders through His handmaid, whose spirit and power endure forever and ever. Amen.

42. A girl cured from contracted muscles

Among other wonders, the lord Jesus again made known His hand-maid the blessed Margaret, queen of Scots, in the following way. There was a girl called Mary, in Lothian in the village called Glencorse, in the service of a householder, and on the eve of St Lawrence's day[75] she was carding wool with iron combs for her master. As the time came when the vigils are accustomed to be solemnly observed, she thought to herself, 'Since I have so little wool to card, I will not stop my work until I have finished the little bit that remains.' While she thought such things to herself, suddenly the combs fell from her hands, and the unhappy woman slipped from the seat in which she was sitting onto the floor, deprived of all physical powers, and lay there for almost an hour like one dead. The master and mistress and the whole household came running, amazed at what had happened to her so suddenly.

Eventually, when the wretched woman had recovered her memory to some degree, her right hand was found to be miserably contracted, so that the thumb was joined to the hollow of the hand, with the fingers fixed above it and contracted so tightly that it

puncti uero pocius formam pretendebat quam manus. In pede similiter sinistro uis morbi maxime preualuerat, que pedem contractione neruorum, talo scilicet ante et digitis retro retortis, fere penitus priuauit incessu. Illius uero pedis officium baculo redimebat atque sine baculi adminiculo nullam gradiendi habuit facultatem. Stupebat ergo ad tactum membrorum contractorum, si illa manu propria uel leuiter contigisset. Excitata tandem miraculorum fama que per sanctos Dei fiebant, causa salutis recuperande pluribus sanctis per Scociam et Angliam exiit supplicatura. In eadem uero infirmitate per quinque annos et amplius perseuerans, sanctorum limina pro infirmitatis sue relaxacione querere non cessabat. A nullo autem sanitatis graciam potuit optinere. Venit tandem ad capellam sancte Katerine in loco qui dicitur Pentland[76] et ibi per dies aliquos moram faciens, beate uirginis et martiris suffragium implorabat.

Quadam autem nocte, cum membra sua sopori dedisset, apparuerunt illi tres matrone, uestibus decentissimis perornate, promittentes ei quod, si locum ubi corpus beate Margarite Scotorum regine quiescit translatum deuote quereret, proculdubio sanitatis graciam recuperaret. Tali autem uisione expergefacta et uehementer recreata, in diem crastinum iter suum uersus monasterium felicis regine prout potuit arripere non omisit. Dum uero taliter per longum temporis spacium uersus dictum monasterium itinerasset et quadam die loco illi qui dicitur Morhale[77] appropinquasset, apparuit ei uigilanti et ambulanti quedam matrona, uestibus sanctimonialis induta, que illam uerbis consolatoribus ita alloquitur, dicens, 'O nimis afflicta mulier, quo uadis?' At illa, 'Quero', inquit, 'monasterium regine sed michi uires desunt.' Et domina, 'Mea tu uestigia quere, en te precedam mulier, quoniam uocor illa quam petis; accedas ad me, quia si bene credas, leta reuerteris tu sospes et egredieris.' Hiis itaque dictis, disparuit domina et dicta puella quamcicius potuit, licet cum magno fo. 41ᵛ tedio | et dolore, multum ex manifesta uisione confortata, eius uestigia sequebatur. Postquam uero mare transfretasset, iterum apparuit illi dicta domina in loco qui dicitur Portus Sancte Margarite Regine,[78]

[76] St Katherine's chapel, Pentland, later known as St Katherine's 'in the Hopes'. It belonged to Holyrood abbey from at least 1236: Liber cartarum Sancte Crucis, ed. Cosmo Innes (Bannatyne Club, Edinburgh, 1840), nos. 57–9, pp. 45–6. See Ian B. Cowan, The Parishes of Medieval Scotland (Scottish Record Society, xciii, 1967), p. 177. It was submerged beneath the Loganlea reservoir when Edinburgh's modern water supply was established in the first half of the 19th cent. The six-inch Ordnance Survey map of 1852 marks the 'Ruins of St Catherine's Chapel Submerged' in the centre of the reservoir (there called 'Glencross Resevoir'). Judith George of the Open University gave generous advice on this subject.

presented the appearance of a point rather than a hand. Likewise, the force of the illness seriously affected her left foot, so that because of the contraction of the muscles, bending the heel forward and the toes backward, the foot was completely useless for walking. She used a walking stick instead of that foot and had no ability to go anywhere without the aid of the stick. She was discomfited when the contracted limbs were touched, if she happened to contact them with her own hand even lightly. At length stirred up by talk of the miracles which were being performed through God's saints, she traversed Scotland and England beseeching many saints for the recovery of her health. Enduring her affliction for five years and more, she did not stop seeking out saints' shrines for the relief of her affliction, but was able to obtain the grace of healing from none of them. She came at last to the chapel of St Katherine in the place called Pentland[76] and stayed there for some days, imploring the aid of the blessed virgin and martyr.

One night, when she had given her limbs up to sleep, three matrons, dressed in magnificent clothes, appeared to her and promised that if she devoutly sought out the place where the body of St Margaret, queen of the Scots, lies translated, without a doubt she would recover the blessing of health. Awakened by this vision and much revived, next day she did not fail to direct her journey towards the monastery of the blessed queen as best she could. When she had travelled for a long period of time towards the monastery and one day was nearing the place called *Morhale*,[77] there appeared to her, while she was awake and walking along, a matron dressed in nun's clothing, who spoke to her consolingly, saying, 'O sorely afflicted woman, where are you going?' She replied, 'I am seeking the queen's monastery but my powers are failing me.' The lady said, 'Follow my footsteps, woman, for I shall go before you. I bear the name of the one you seek. Come to me in firm belief and you will return again happy and sound.' Once she had said this, the lady disappeared and the girl, as quickly as she could although with great trouble and pain, followed her footsteps, much comforted by this manifest vision. After she had crossed the sea, the lady appeared to her again in the place called the Port of St Margaret the Queen,[78] commanding her to

---

[77] Possibly in modern Colinton, whose earlier name was 'Hala' or 'Hale' (as preserved in East Hailes and Wester Hailes): N. Dixon, 'Place-names of Midlothian', Ph.D., thesis (Edinburgh, 1947), p. 146.

[78] North Queensferry, Fife.

iterum precipiendo ei, ut eam confidenter sequeretur. Et infirma respondit, 'Ignosce mihi, domina mea, quia angustiis intolerabilibus oppressa, ire cicius non possum.'

Talibus ergo admonicionibus edocta, in diem crastinum, scilicet dominicam, festiuitatem sancti Luce precedentem,[79] anno gracie .mcclvii., ad tumbam beate Margarite regine, ubi corpus eiusdem sancte ante translacionem suam primo quieuit humatum in monasterio suo de Dunfermlyn peruenit ibique se per tres dies et noctes in oratione prostrauit, feria uero quarta circa horam diei terciam post dominicam dictam, capite suo ante altare in honore sepe dicte sancte ibidem constructum reclinato, pre infirmitatis tedio obdormienti astitit beata Margarita regina, et prius manum infirmam puelle et postea pedem eius contractum manibus suis apprehendens, ita fortiter digitos utrorumque manus et pedis contractos retraxit, et in rectitudinem status pristini extendit, quod in ipsa extensione factus est quidam sonus, ac si quedam cordule rumperentur, qui de loco quo iacebat a sacerdotibus ecclesie audiebatur. Hiis peractis, puella super salute optenta inopinanter letificata et continuo surgens erecta, tam coram abbate de Corsraguel[80] et priore de Pasleto[81] et duobus fratribus Iacobinis[82] tunc temporis ibidem presentibus, quam coram priore et monachis eiusdem loci et omni clero et populo ad illud spectaculum confluentibus, non absque summa cordis contricione et lacrimarum magna effusione, beneficia que ei domina fecerat enarrauit. Omnes igitur tam clerus quam populus in huius delectabilis miraculi aspectu multipliciter letificati, abbate 'Te Deum laudamus' incipiente, et ceteris eundem ymnum angelicum prosequentibus, accensis cereis et pulsatis campanis, Deum qui in sanctis suis semper est mirabilis[83] et beatam Margaritam reginam uoce melliflua laudauerunt. In hiis igitur omnibus ille glorificandus est, qui facit mirabilia solus.[84] Cui laus et preconium, honor, uirtus et imperium, potestas et gloria per seculorum secula. Amen.

Expliciunt miracula glorisissime Margarite Scotorum regine

[79] 14 Oct.
[80] Ayrshire, Cluniac.
[81] Renfrewshire, Cluniac.

follow her with faith. The sick girl replied, 'Forgive me, my lady, for I am suffering terrible anguish and can go no faster.'

On the next day, which was the Sunday before the feast of St Luke[79] in the year of grace 1257, the girl, instructed by these admonitions, came to the tomb of the blessed Margaret the queen where, before her translation, the body of the saint first lay buried, in her monastery of Dunfermline. There for three days and nights she lay prostrate in prayer, but around the third hour on the Wednesday after the Sunday just mentioned, while out of weariness she was bowing her head in sleep before the altar built there in honour of the saint, blessed Margaret the queen stood by her. Grasping in her hands first the girl's infirm hand and then her contracted foot, she pulled back the fingers of the hand and the toes of the foot so powerfully and stretched them out into their correct original state, that the stretching produced a sound like strings being broken, which was heard from the place where she lay by the priests of the church. When all this had been done, the girl, rejoicing at the cure she had unexpectedly received and immediately getting up, recounted the good deeds the lady had performed for her, with great contrition of heart and floods of tears, not only before the abbot of Crossraguel[80] and the prior of Paisley[81] and two Dominicans[82] who were present at the time but also before the prior and monks of that place and all the clergy and people who had rushed to the sight. So all the clergy and people rejoiced much, seeing this delectable miracle, the abbot began the 'Te Deum laudamus' and the others continued that angelic hymn, candles were lit and bells rung, and they praised God who is always wonderful in His saints[83] and St Margaret the queen with sweet voices. In all this He is to be glorified who alone performs wonders.[84] To Him be praise, honour, power and command, power and glory forever. Amen.

Here end the miracles of the most glorious Margaret, queen of Scots

---

[82] There were at least nine Dominican houses in Scotland by this date, including some close to Dunfermline (Edinburgh, Stirling, Perth).

[83] Ps. 67: 36 (68: 35).

[84] Ps. 71 (72): 18; cf. 85 (86): 10; 135 (136): 4.

INDEX OF BIBLICAL CITATIONS
AND ALLUSIONS

INDEX OF NAMES

Places are identified by their historic counties. King is abbreviated kg., bishop bp.